Feeling White

CULTURAL PLURALISM DEMOCRACY, SOCIO-ENVIRONMENTAL JUSTICE
& EDUCATION

Volume 2

This book series aims to develop a field of overlapping research that crosses and integrates the domains, disciplines, subjects and themes of cultural pluralism, democracy and social justice. Each theme is taken up individually in many debates but our focus is to bring together advanced and critical analyses that transcend boundaries, languages, disciplines and theoretical and conceptual approaches. We are interested in books that can problematize cultural pluralism in relation to, with and around democracy and socio-environmental justice, especially in relation to education. Our focus on cultural pluralism is intentional, and we aim to move the debate on identity, difference and lived experience forward within a critical lens, seeking to create new, varied and meaningful discussions that go beyond the normative labels of multiculturalism and interculturalism. The literature around education for democracy that underscores political literacy, critical engagement and transformative education is also highly relevant here as is the field of social justice, which examines power relations, laws and policies, structures and experiences at myriad levels. The guiding principles for books in this series include: critical analysis; interdisciplinary; nuanced and complexified thinking; epistemological interrogation; varied research approaches; innovation; openness to international and comparative studies. The books in this series will include case studies, comparative analyses, and collaborations across linguistic, social, ethnic, racial, national, religious and gender boundaries, which may include empirical, conceptual and theoretical frameworks and analysis.

While not an exhaustive or exclusive list, some of the areas that will be of interest for this book series include: *Migration, immigration and displacement; Identity and power; Globalization, neoliberalism and cultural pluralism; Critical epistemology; Democracy and diversity; Social justice and environmental justice; Media analyses and studies; Macro-sociological studies; Political ecology; Cultural diversity; Educational change*

Feeling White

Whiteness, Emotionality, and Education

Foreword by Zeus Leonardo

Cheryl E. Matias
University of Colorado, Denver, USA

SENSE PUBLISHERS
ROTTERDAM/BOSTON/TAIPEI

A C.I.P. record for this book is available from the Library of Congress.

ISBN: 978-94-6300-448-0 (paperback)
ISBN: 978-94-6300-449-7 (hardback)
ISBN: 978-94-6300-450-3 (e-book)

Published by: Sense Publishers,
P.O. Box 21858,
3001 AW Rotterdam,
The Netherlands
https://www.sensepublishers.com/

All chapters in this book have undergone peer review.

The following book chapters are reprinted here with permission from the publishers:

Chapter 2: Matias, C. E. (2013). On the "Flip" side: A teacher educator of color unveiling the dangerous minds of white teacher candidates. *Teacher Education Quarterly*, *40*(2), 53–73.

Chapter 3: Matias, C. E., & Zembylas, M. (2014). 'When saying you care is not really caring': Emotions of disgust, whiteness ideology, and teacher education. *Critical Studies in Education*, *55*(3), 319–337.

Chapter 4: Matias, C. E., & Allen, R. L. (2013). Loving whiteness to death: Sadomasochism, emotionality, and the possibility of humanizing love. *Berkeley Review of Education*, *4*(2), 285–309.

Chapter 6: Matias, C. E. (2014). White Skin, Black Friend: A Fanonian application to theorize racial fetish in teacher education. *Educational Philosophy and Theory*, *48*(3), 221–236.

Chapter 9: Matias, C. E. (2013). Tears worth telling: Urban teaching and the possibilities of racial justice. *Multicultural Perspectives*, *15*(4), 187–193.

Chapter 10: Matias, C. E. (2013). Who you callin' white?! A critical counter-story on colouring white identity. *Race Ethnicity and Education*, *16*(3), 291–315.

Cover design by Tin Hoang

Photograph cover by David McNew/Getty Images, reproduced with permission

Printed on acid-free paper

PRAISE FOR
FEELING WHITE

"In *Feeling White*, Cheryl E. Matias blends astute observations, analyses and insights about the emotions embedded in white identity and their impact on the racialized politics of affect in teacher education. Drawing deftly on her own classroom experiences as well as her mastery of the methodologies and theories of critical whiteness studies, Matias challenges us to develop what Dr. King called "the strength to love" by confronting and conquering the affective structures that promote white innocence and preclude white accountability."
– George Lipsitz, Ph.D., Professor, University of California, Santa Barbara, and author of *The Possessive Investment in Whiteness*

"A searingly honest account of the continued traumatization of students of color in our educational system. A must read for those who wish to lift the white veil of pretense and racism that imprisons and diminishes the spirit and dynamism of our students of color."
– Lee Mun Wah, Director of *The Color of Fear*

"Drawing on her deep wisdom about how race works, Cheryl E. Matias directly interrogates the emotional arsenal White people use as shields from the pain of confronting racism, peeling back its layers to unearth a core of love that can open us up. In *Feeling White: Whiteness, Emotionality, and Education*, Matias deftly names and deconstructs distancing emotions, prodding us to stay in the conversation in order to become teachers who can reach children marginalized by racism."
– Christine Sleeter, Ph.D., Professor Emeritus, California State University Monterey Bay

"A frank and fascinating analysis of the mechanisms that connect whiteness and emotion to a sense of innocence and the preservation of ignorance regarding race in and far beyond teacher training programs. Deft use of theory and unflinching autoethnography mark this as a searching contribution to the discussion of liberalism and how schools fail."
– David Roediger, Ph.D., Foundation Distinguished Professor, University of Kansas

"The racialized state of white emotionalities has been largely invisible to the intellectual prism of teacher education literature and practice. Delivered with passionate and provocative writing, this book addresses this gap and truly opens our eyes to 'see' the racist power structures that divides us, and how we submit to them via our words, actions and emotions. Cheryl Matias has written a compelling intellectual and personal account of how white emotionalities never get fully understood. She offers a bold and impressive analysis of the how white emotionalities operate in teacher education and perpetuate racist power structures."
– Michalinos Zembylas, Ph.D., Associate Professor, Open University of Cyprus

"So many of our racial analyses are focused on what people think about issues of race. In this groundbreaking, and extremely creative work, Cheryl Matias inverts this paradigm and offers a fresh way of examining the intersection of Whiteness and education. Ultimately, Matias challenges us to more critically examine our own racialized emotions if we are to ever move toward the elusive goal of dismantling systemic racism."
– Nolan L. Cabrera, Ph.D., Assistant Professor, University of Arizona

This book is dedicated to my husband and children. Your presence, patience, and support give me the hope and inspiration to do the work of racial justice every day. I do this for you all.

Mahal kita

TABLE OF CONTENTS

ZEUS LEONARDO

FOREWORD

Whiteness and Emo-Social Justice

When it comes to race, it is a well-researched phenomenon that Whites abandon the cherished tenets they've passed down from the Enlightenment. Ostensively valuing detachment, Whites now dive headlong into the abyss of racial attachment. From classroom to boardroom, they "suddenly" become attached to a racialized orientation, something which they otherwise and usually insist is contiguous with people of Color. When confronted by challenges to their unearned advantages, Whites become possessively invested in identity politics based on race, and cling on to the idea of meritocracy, even as they claim that Whites have deserved their disproportionate share of advantages in social life (Lipsitz, 1998). Formerly elevating reason to the highest achievement a human being could attain since Kant (see Biesta, 2010), Whites now exhibit flights from reason, support illogical statements, and betray discombobulated mental states when asked to engage racialized patterns (Bonilla-Silva, 2003). Before such reactions become associated with the uneducated white mind, or the usual alibis of the White working class or White Southerners (see Leonardo & Zembylas, 2013), Mills (1997) reminds us that some of the most erudite White philosophers suffer from such ignorance in classical and neoclassical senses. Whether they display lack of racial knowledge as a form of classic neglect, or assert their ignorance *as* knowledge, Whites as a group seem unable to grasp the significance of race. They ultimately misunderstand the world they have created, shocked by the lines on the palm of their own hands.

All this leads us to the subject matter of Cheryl Matias's book *Feeling White*. She captures the panoply of white strategies to deflect their assumption of responsibility, under the analytic of "emotionality." Her central theme recalls Lee Mun Wah's (1994) film, The *Color of Fear*, and the White character's emotional appeal to minimize his co-participants' experiences with racism. Matias offers educators – White or otherwise – a way into racial understanding that does not underestimate the affective content or stakes when we teach about or research race in general, whiteness in particular. In fact, white emotionality is perhaps the most egregious violation of Enlightenment principles because it represents the gateway practice leading to denial, failure to weigh social science evidence, and, ultimately, violence. Moreover, emo-social white strategies are not emotional practices in general, which critical theories of education do not necessarily reject (see Grumet, 1988; hooks, 1994).

White emo-sociality is precisely what prevents emotional praxis from developing as an educational force to lead to a more accurate understanding of our predicament (Zembylas, 2008). A philosophy of emotional praxis, to borrow a bit from Gramsci (1971), represents an embodied education that does not remove the subject from his or her own subject-making. As a counter-hegemony to the terror of Cartesian mentalism, Matias reclaims the body as part of the feeling, sentient agent within emotional praxis. With the horror associated with Deleuze and Guattari's (1983) phrase, "bodies without organs," interpreted by Kellner (1989) as bodies without regimes of organization imposed on them, we may add that the Cartesian reign in education gave birth to *humans without bodies*. With Matias's text, we wrestle with the implications of reinventing education with bodies in mind (pun intended).

With Roediger (1994), we take seriously the idea that whiteness as one of the most formidable obstacles to a clear and concrete understanding of why social life – and education in particular – takes the shape it does today. Because the ideology of whiteness subverts even (or especially) Whites' apprehension of social relations, structures appear inverted (as if people of Color, even admitting to their fallibilities, were responsible for their lot [Leonardo, 2004]), accumulation seems natural (as if white wealth has little to do with centuries of enslavement, colonization, and dispossession [Oliver & Shapiro, 1997]), and social institutions take on a phantasmagoric form (as if the law, from inheritance to criminal, does not stem from white politics of recognition [Haney López, 2006]). Matias lends credence to Roediger's (1994) claim that it is not just that whiteness is false and oppressive; it is *nothing but* false and oppressive. This particular status makes anything associated with whiteness immediately suspect, white emotions included. Seen this way, emotions are not just expressions of feeling, but of politics. Or, to imitate that useful Radical Feminist saying, "the personal is political," we may argue that "the emotional is political." On their part, white emotions reflect a selective process of attaching affective reactions to social situations which protect white racial advantage such as crying during difficult conversations about race in classroom settings, and changing the dynamics in those settings by redirecting sympathy away from people of Color (see Leonardo, 2002). Such emotional outbursts as these may be interpreted in several ways including assuaging guilt, admitting wrongdoing, or having certain surprise that people of Color were paying attention to racism all along. That said, white uptake of discussions around racism is never innocent, even if it is at times naïve. Emo-social relations are part of race relations, and whiteness distorts their imbrication by encouraging the absolution – rather than abolition – of whiteness. Matias does not accept this predicament; she insists that educators can do better.

Ultimately, Matias projects hope onto Whites in cases where they have not earned it, or yet, do not deserve it. This gesture represents one of the ironic sacrifices scholars and educators of Color make in order to avoid the vortex of whiteness: resentment, distance, and cynicism (see Leonardo, 2013). And, it is not ironic that Whites may end up resenting and distancing themselves from this gift, thus reconfirming their political cynicism. In other words, Matias's project more accurately falls within the category of an "act of love" in the sense that Freire (1993) once described the oppressed's attempt to speak back to – indeed dialogue with – the oppressor (see Allen, 2004). In a radical moment of engagement (see also Fanon, 2008), people of Color avoid the despair that is the hallmark of whiteness. In our insistence on a radical critique of whiteness, we affirm our commitment to engagement and connection despite that Whites may use it as evidence of everything wrong with race analysis. Radical educators of whiteness do not speak heresy as much as they speak truth to power. They do not look for "safe spaces" for race conversations, i.e., holy grails of safety like protective understanding, and "it's okay" reactions to white resistance; instead they put everyone at risk because something greater is threatened: the perpetuation of whiteness itself. Safe dialogue around race is misguided because its centerpiece is an unsafe topic. Radical race educators do not seek to reduce the emotions that typically accompany racetalk, but redirect them toward social justice and greater understanding. They do not add fuel to the fire as much as they light a fire under whiteness.

Race emotionality is not the problem – the emotionality of Whites and the whiteness of sanctioned emotions are. On the road to the abolition of whiteness, Whites reclaim their ability to express true emotion borne of uncertainty and ambiguity, even if the goal is clarity. It takes a reconstructive understanding of personal and collective complicity at the level of white family history (in the sense of one's immediate family as well as the White race [see Sleeter, 2011]). This is diametrically opposed to feigning emotion as a way to mask domination and accountability. Liberatory emotion is yet to be understood fully in a context that downplays the role of emotion in schooling, specifically race education. Although Whites' emotional strategies are not the lynchpin of racism but play a part in its overall architecture, white emotions are often enough to block progress in racial understanding. They frequently lead to a process of disenlightenment. In Freire's (1993) sense, they comprise a "limit situation" that must be transcended. Although they are arguably the target of this transformation, it is difficult to imagine Whites leading the movement. However, they are the potential concrete partners of people of Color toward a new regime of emotionality that, while certainly not inevitable, is preferable to the current arrangement. Whites will share in the burden of emotional labor that is partly the undoing of racism, which in turn en/lightens the weight of race relations on people of Color. In this task, Cheryl Matias's work becomes invaluable, not as a manual of sorts, but as an example of the risks educators should consider taking.

REFERENCES

Allen, R. (2004). Whiteness and critical pedagogy. *Educational Philosophy and Theory*, *36*(2), 121–136.
Biesta, G. (2010). Education after the death of the subject: Levinas and the pedagogy of interruption. In Z. Leonardo (Ed.), *Handbook of cultural politics and education* (pp. 289–300). Rotterdam, The Netherlands: Sense Publishers.
Bonilla-Silva, E. (2003). *Racism without racists: Color-blind racism and the persistence of racial inequality in the United States*. Lanham, MD: Rowman & Littlefield.

Deleuze, G., & Guattari, F. (1983). *Anti-oedipus: Capitalism and schizophrenia* (R. Hurley, M. Seem, & H. Lane, Trans.). Minneapolis, MN: University of Minnesota Press.

Fanon, F. (2008). *Black skin, White masks* (R. Philcox, Trans.). New York, NY: Grove Press. (Originally published in 1952)

Freire, P. (1993). *Pedagogy of the oppressed* (M. Ramos, Trans.). New York, NY: Continuum. (Originally published in 1970)

Gramsci, A. (1971). *Selections from prison notebooks* (Q. Hoare & G. Smith, Eds. & Trans.). New York, NY: International Publishers.

Grumet, M. (1988). *Bitter milk: Women and teaching*. Amherst, MA: University of Massachusetts Press.

Haney López, I. (2006). *White by law*. New York, NY: New York University Press.

hooks, b. (1994). *Teaching to transgress*. New York, NY: Routledge.

Kellner, D. (1989). *Jean Baudrillard*. Stanford, CA: Stanford University Press.

Leonardo, Z. (2002). The souls of White folk: Critical pedagogy, whiteness studies, and globalization discourse. *Race, Ethnicity & Education, 5*(1), 29–50.

Leonardo, Z. (2004). The color of supremacy: Beyond the discourse of "white privilege." *Educational Philosophy and Theory, 36*(2), 137–152.

Leonardo, Z. (2013). *Race frameworks: A multidimensional theory of racism and education*. New York, NY: Teachers College Press.

Leonardo, Z., & Zembylas, M. (2013). Whiteness as technology of affect: Implications for educational praxis. *Equity & Excellence in Education, 46*(1), 150–165.

Lipsitz, G. (1998). *The possessive investment in whiteness*. Philadelphia, PA: Temple University Press.

Mills, C. (1997). *The racial contract*. Ithaca, NY: Cornell University Press.

Oliver, M., & Shapiro, T. (1997). *Black wealth, White wealth: A new perspective on racial inequality*. New York, NY: Routledge.

Roediger, D. (1994). *Toward the abolition of whiteness*. New York, NY: Verso.

Sleeter, C. (2011). Becoming White: Reinterpreting a family story by putting race back into the picture. *Race, Ethnicity & Education, 14*(4), 421–433.

Wah, L. M. (Producer/Director). (1994). *The color of fear* [Video]. Oakland, CA: Stir-Fry Productions.

Zembylas, M. (2008). *The politics of trauma in education*. New York, NY: Palgrave MacMillan.

AUTHOR'S NOTE

For purposes of an in-depth discussion about race and the historical inequality between Whites and people of Color, I capitalize the words "Black," "White," and "people of Color" to represent races, much like one would capitalize "Latin American" or "Filipina," for example. However, since "whiteness" is a state of being that goes beyond an individual's racial identity – Blacks can express gestures of whiteness – I choose not to capitalize this word or its adjectival form "white." However, I do capitalize "Blackness" as it indeed represents a particular race-specific state. This sense is also applied in the capitalization of "the Other."

Further, for purposes of remaining gender-neutral, I utilize the more common first-person structure of "s/he" and "her/him" (and other incarnations) with no intended disrespect to those who identify as transgender or queergender; this is simply a construct in absence of a universal term for the non-gendered.

The English language is an evolving and powerful tool to express myriad points of view. Here, in this book, I seek to explicate the importance of using accurate words to describe specific ideas because doing so is, in itself, an act of humanly love.

– C.E.M.

ACKNOWLEDGEMENTS

I wrote this book to provide a deeper understanding of how whiteness operates emotionally, especially in the context of recent increased racial tensions in the U.S., not to mention the world. By providing a deeper and different analysis of how race – specifically whiteness – operates, I hope my readers come away with the understanding that we must first do the individual work on ourselves before we can whole-heartedly advocate for systemic change. Race is still a topic that burns in our heart, and thus it causes great emotions to surface. As such, this book is a labor of love, in that as I wrote it, I, like the entire nation, was under the emotional trauma of racial protests, racial profiling, and racial discontent.

Having been influenced by critical race theory, critical whiteness studies, feminist theories, and critical emotion studies, I chose the title *Feeling White* to indicate both a racialized state of emotions and the white racial identity that state attaches to. Although I am not racially White myself, the emotions so felt in whiteness are those I have to deal with in teaching teacher education. These are the strong emotions that make the possibility of racially-just education so hard achieve. Despite increasingly diverse faculty, culturally-infused teaching approaches, and proclaimed commitment to social justice, the topic of racism – let alone whiteness – is blocked simply because it becomes too emotional to bear. This book is an attempt to dig deeply into those emotions that stonewall the hope for racial justice.

Because the topics of whiteness and emotionality are difficult to even mention, I found solace, guidance, and intellectual stimulation from many mentors. To my mentors Zeus Leonardo, Ricky Lee Allen, Christine Sleeter, Dave Stovall, Allyson Tintiangco-Cubales, Don Nakanishi, and Michalinos Zembylas: my intellectual prowess is cultivated by your scholarship, mentorship, and our on-going, in-depth discussions on race. I appreciate all you all do to support my scholarly development. To scholars and racially-just educators like David Roediger, George Lipsitz, Sonia Nieto, Beverly Tatum, Albert Memmi, Franz Fanon, Derrick Bell, Lee Mun Wah, Thandeka, Eduardo Bonilla-Silva, bell hooks, David Gillborn, and many more: it is through your work that I thrive and flourish. Thank you for your contributions to humanity. I hope that my work pays homage to that you have already laid before me.

None of this would be possible without the honest and supportive critiques of my scholarly homies. To Kip Austin Hinton, Nolan M. Cabrera, Christine Malsbary, Korina Jocson, Brian Johnstone, Felisha Hererra, Maria Salazar, Jaime Del Razo, Robin DiAngelo, Michael Dumas and the entire Bruin Ph.D. family: your friendship provides me the space to rethink what I think I know and explore what I do not know. Thank you for pushing me to think beyond what has already been defined.

To my colleagues in the School of Education and Human Development at UC Denver, especially, Sheila Shannon and Dorothy Garrison-Wade, and my colleagues all over UC Denver, especially, Brenda Allen, Omar Swartz, and Marty Otanez: thank you for sharing your critical intellectualism. It makes me feel at home despite being a thousand miles away.

My doctoral students are fierce scholars who encourage me to risk it all while reminding me that we will forever face the hate behind bigotry, racism, and white supremacist thinking. Roberto Montoya, Naomi Nishi, Geneva Sarcedo, Pete Newlove, Sherry Hunter and Lisa Silverstein: thank you for collegiality, trust, and honesty.

A special thanks goes out to a few people who made this book possible. To Tin Hoang, thank you so much for your artistic design. It both scares and entices readers – two emotions so intrinsic to talking about race. To Jennie Cook: your commitment to my work is greatly appreciated. Without you I could not have done this. To my "sista-from-another-mista" Kiechelle Russell: you are a fierce educator in Los Angeles and inspire me to continue to fight the good fight despite the haters; you give me strength to keep on going.

Finally, this book is for my husband, my twins, and my new baby girl, whose presence, support, and love are what make my heart beat every day. I do this for you and for all the families who want a better world for their children.

CHAPTER 1

"BUT *I* NEVER OWNED SLAVES!"

Intersections of Whiteness, Emotionality, and Education

*"Racism isn't my fault! **I** never owned slaves!" cried Hayley, tears streaming down her flushed cheeks, smearing the blue eyeliner that matched her eyes. Wiping her eyes dry, she lifted her face so that her college classmates could see her tears, seemingly trying to mask the deep-rooted fear of being labelled a racist by those of Color. She looked frantically at the other White faces in the classroom, hoping they would bail her out of the ideological trap of claiming race is not an issue but crying about it. Some White students in the class shook their heads to display clear opposition to Hayley's attempt to justify her position, one that was nonetheless entrenched as it was in whiteness, the subject we were discussing in class. Almost in unison, these students took a slow a deep breath, as if choking back words that opposed both Hayley's exasperated comment and her behavior. Yet, they did not dare utter a word.*

A few other White students nodded their heads in agreement with Hayley, noticeably clenching their fists and shifting both nervously and angrily in their seats. True to the dynamics of masculinity, some White males came to Hayley's rescue. "You always make this about race!" barked Thurston, a 21-year-old straight, middle-class White male who once revealed that the "good community" he had grown up in included only a few people of Color. Directing his comment to Malina, an African American female who often and vehemently averred that African Americans continue to face racism daily, Thurston continued, his face red and veins bulging, "Race is not an issue. You all are being racist for bringing it up!" His outburst stirred him physically, so much so that he loudly thumped his chair to the floor in emphasis. He then turned his face away from the group, crossed his arms, and defiantly checked out of the conversation.

Sitting next to Thurston was Becky, a self-identified "liberal-minded White female," who announced in class that she planned to teach in an urban school predominate with African American and Latino students. Although she passionately addressed social injustice and educational inequities in previous class discussions – specifically the disparate academic achievement of students of Color – she often found herself at a loss when the topic of white privilege or whiteness was broached. In the moment following her classmates' outbursts, Becky sat motionless and speechless to Hayley's tears, as if emotionally frozen.

Too afraid that taking a deep, noisy breath would redirect the attention from Hayley to her, she took shallow breaths. She didn't even turn away when Hayley lifted her face, displaying – for all to see – how hurt she was that anyone would insinuate that she was racist – an insinuation that was never stated or implied in the discussion beforehand, yet was one Hayley emotionally responded to.

Amidst the tension, some students of Color and allied White students chose to silently roll their eyes and shift uncomfortably in their chairs. Although they seemed as if they wanted to say something, some chose to bite their lips as if they were physically trapping choice words behind them. Others closed their eyes and, in between their deep breaths, rolled their necks as if trying to self-soothe their way out of the discomfort in the room.

***

As evidenced by Hayley's tears, Thurston's fist pounding and Becky's emotionally frozen "expressionless expression," a seemingly invisible state of emotionality intoxicates us all when we talk about race. Needless to say, emotions are forever present in the work of race. To not deny or further repress those emotions, and the state of discomfort they create, makes us nothing more than somnambuliacs, walking through life asleep. Imagine, if you will, the hypocrisy in how one is living a life, proclaiming life, protecting life yet refusing to *feel* life itself. Is that truly life?

Despite this emotional reality, there are those who still claim we must not "get emotional" when discussing race, claiming that to do so would be counterproductive to any racially-just project. They assert that emotions are nothing but mere distractions, uninformative to the project at hand. Some individuals will tell Whites to "get over it" when it comes to the guilt they feel when learning about race, or "don't get too emotional" about the hurt people of Color feel when they share their painful personal experiences with race. Either way, this kind of sentiment renders tears as useless, anger as non-instructive, and fear as irrelevant. The supposed uselessness of these often "unwanted" emotionalities then inadvertently renders the "wanted" emotionalities of love, hope, and human connection worthless too. That is the tragedy.

Suffice it to say that, we, as a collective humanity, cannot pick and choose which emotions we consider important and which we consider unwanted, precisely because emotions can never be divorced from one another. Love feels hurt. Sadness feels hope. Anger feels unwelcomed. And these emotions don't materialize from thin air; indeed, they stem from somewhere deep within us. This plea for apathy persists from naysayers who, in their zeal to repress that which they truly feel, eventually form apathetic identities. These identities have developed a false sense of callousness – one that pretends to be tough but instead is a weakness because it merely avoids the topic rather than face it head on – in order to survive racism by denying racism altogether; in so doing, they cannot be strong, brave, or fierce enough to feel the emotional process vital to achieving antiracism. The emotional openness so needed to proudly simultaneously resist and endure racism – and find love within a racist state of life – must still be felt in its entirety lest we succumb to an anaesthetic life, forever numb to feel. For that matter, how can these individuals expect to be committed to antiracism – moreover, racial justice in any form – if they cannot: (1) feel their emotions, (2) recognize their emotions, (3) understand from where these emotions stem, nor (4) develop the emotionally ovaries to withstand the ups and downs of discussing race? In this lack of understanding and disregard of our own emotionalities – moreover, our inability to even identify these emotionalities – misconceptions of them arise, tightening the shackles of racism even more. As erroneous as it is to assume that something as terrifying as death does not involve the human emotionalities of survival, despair, and a desire to live, it is equally erroneous to assume that those same emotions are not also present when facing the historical realities of racially-biased lynching, rapes, and the neo-institutionalized extermination of Black men.

This is a state of fear. But, alongside fear is the state of love. Take, for instance, the recent police shootings of unarmed Black men across the U.S. Responding with fear, the national community recognized a state of racial policing. Fearing the safety of their babies, mothers cried for their sons of Color to stay indoors and acquiesce to any officer's demands, even in the face of police wrongdoing (Matias & Montoya, 2015). These Black boys were once societally deemed "cute" by White society when they were younger, like puppies in a Louis Vuitton shoulder bag; but when these puppies grew up, they were subjected to racial bias and erroneously labelled "thugs" or "dangerous suspects" simply by wearing hoodies.[1] That is, from Trayvon Martin, the African American teenage boy who was stalked, shot, and killed by a security officer claiming that he "looked suspicious," to Tamir Rice, a twelve-year-old African American boy who was shot and killed for holding a toy gun, the moniker of black skin renders a different lived reality for darker-skinned boys in a racist society. Parents responded to this. Some developed strict dress codes for their Black boys,[2] others were forced to become vigilant in protecting them.[3] Regardless of the action, parents who had darker-skinned boys had to take additional precautions to protect their sons from racism.

As a motherscholar[4] of Color, I too faced the inhumane task of telling my own brown-skinned son about the racial realities of dark-skinned men in the U.S. Despite my decades of training in pedagogy and curriculum, and my international research and lectures on race, racism, and white supremacy, I found myself without words, unable to articulate how fearful I was for my son's life. I was helpless, like any other mother staring at her seven-year-old child's eyes, not knowing what to do about an overwhelming threat. Nothing was more unbearable than telling my son he was more likely to get shot by police because he is darker-skinned than his *chinita*[5] twin sister.

As my son saw my fear, he feared too and cried out, "Mama? Mama?" He wanted me to hug him, to feel safe again. It was then that I lost all composure. How could I protect my son from a racist world? My voice quivering, I begged him to never

3

make any sudden movements with the police once he got older. At this his tiny frame shook uncontrollably and with frightened eyes he cried, "But Mama, what if I need my inhaler?" Here was my baby, who just learned how to ride a bike, rationalizing whether he should choose death by asphyxiation or death by police. I sank at both his comprehension and his conflict. I was terrified, too scared to move, too frightened to hold my composure. Wasn't I supposed to be the strong one? Mothers are supposed to protect and reassure their babies and here was an instance that I could not because the world would not treat him in a way from which I could shield him. I felt angry at this predicament – angry that a racist reality stole my child's innocence, my right to protect my children, and the belief that all humans are worthy of life.

Yet, fear was not the only response to the institutional extermination of Black youth. Responding with love, the national community banded together to protest such atrocities as the spate of recent police fatalities by insisting that "Black Lives Matter."[6] In particular, since the death of Trayvon Martin in 2012, demonstrations occurred across the U.S. with citizens of all Colors linking arms in front of gun-drawn police officers, illustrating how we, humanity, come together in solidarity to peacefully protest the unjust murders of unarmed Black men. Little African American boys began wearing homemade T-shirts with slogans like, "Let me live," Don't shoot me!," Isn't my life important too?," and "I'm not a thug." Acts of love responded to racism.

My own family recently participated in Denver's Martin Luther King Parade with close to 30,000 other participants. During the middle of the walk, a large group "took a knee" and put up their fists à la the Black power movement gestures of the 1970s. These protesters were not all Black civilians; they were White, Asian American, Middle Eastern, and Latino. The group included police officers, the police chief, council representatives, and many other government and community organizers. During this momentary pause, they sang "We Shall Overcome." Some were crying. Some were vigilant. Yet, regardless of the personal sentiments each used to express his/herself, there was one feeling that united them all: love. That is, they – *we* – so love humanity that we will forever be vigilant, militant, disobedient, and resistant to anything that attempts to destroy it.

Naysayers may assume that such "hard-headedness" is a display of hate, but that ignorantly overlooks the deeper meaning of *why* hateful things, qua racism, diminish the quality of life for all. Take for instance how cancer patients can vehemently hate cancer in vigilantly fighting against it to live: they love life too much. Hate is undergirded by love; when others affected by cancer – be they family members or friends of patients, those who participate in fundraising events to combat the disease, etc. – a love for humanity emerges from that hate. This can likewise occur in fighting racism.

All these vignettes expose the many misconceptions about emotions. For one, although seemingly ontological, the emotionalities of fear and love are not. Instead of viewing sentiments as separate entities isolated from one another, or as entities located on a linear continuum, emotions should be pictorially described as intricate three-dimensional circles that overlay each other on a myriad of axes, depending on the situation. Too often emotionalities are depicted like plots on a linear progression;

take the Kübler-Ross model of the five stages of grief[7] for example: denial → anger → bargaining → depression → acceptance. In the same vein, emotions are also depicted as typologies like Plato's Eros, Philia, and Agape, personae that describe specific and different types of love,[8] or something that can be capitalistically acquired through a mechanic processes like the "five love languages" (Chapman, 2010). Though I depart from these views of emotions greatly, I still commend humanity's continued romance with emotions and its eternal quest to understand them. We are always trying to make sense of emotions – in their broad and specific forms, bad to good, personal to universal – and that, in and of itself, is an act of love.

Rarely considered, however, is how emotions can be a state of being; that is, emotions are embedded in humanity inasmuch as life. How we experience them are part-and-parcel both nurture and nature, working simultaneously with our environment and the essence of our humanity. Fortuitous is this perspective in that we need not search for love, for love is already within us. Yet, because of how our environment interacts with us, love becomes redefined, re-felt, and re-interpreted in finite ways. Take for example the desire and need to provide flowers, chocolates, and diamond rings to express a romantic love for another: this is a love redefined under the social spread of capitalism, neoliberal globalization, and strategic marketing practices. Did we not express, feel, and engage with the emotion of love before the advent of the diamond ring? Therefore, love pre-existed the newly socialized world of capitalism, yet has been redefined for the purposes of a changing environment. Love is both nature and nurture.

Positing emotions as both innate *and* social leads us to ask, what are other social institutions that structure our emotions? If we have a society built around the supremacy of whiteness, patriarchy, capitalism, and heterosexism, then are these the very institutions that structure how our emotions are felt, expressed, and understood about racism, women, poverty, and same-sex love? In fact, Boler (1999) argues that emotions are about "feeling power" because they are framed within the context of power relations. Using the example described above, if love is redefined by the capitalistic accumulation of materials such as flowers and diamonds, then rhetorically speaking, the one who does *not* receive or give such material gains actually lacks the ability to love. This socialization adheres to the power structure of capitalism and therefore attempts to structure how we feel our emotions.

With respects to race then, if white supremacy, upheld by the ideological beliefs in whiteness, continues to maintain a racial power structure, then the emotions subjected to such a structure will also be impacted by it. Hayley's tears "outpower" those of Malina's racial reality because the racial processes that purport whiteness to an elevated social echelon render Whites' behaviors, emotionalities, discourse, and ideologies as supreme, while socially denigrating the emotionalities of people of Color. This is evidenced when Thurston turns angrily to Malina, blames his feelings on her, and then belittles her feelings by saying, "You always make this about race!" Such a comment places the burden of race back on Malina's shoulders. The implication – as purposed by the institution of whiteness – is that Malina should not

5

only continue to survive in a racist society, but she also has no right to talk about it. This is how the social environment of whiteness impacts emotions, whether fear or love. To succumb to whiteness solely on the nurture argument is to deny the nature of our humanity; the innate sense of our emotionalities still lurks beneath our skins.

Take for example how one may respond to seeing a White women cry as compared to a Black woman: the socialization of whiteness becomes a racialized process when we consider that a person of one race has more of a right to cry than the other. This is the underlying premise in many "White savior" films (Vera & Gordon, 2003) like *Dangerous Minds, Freedom Writers,* and *The Blind Side*: the White female protagonist is depicted as the savior in the midst of the savagery of people of Color, whether the environment is an urban school or a college football field. Through her trials and tribulations, wrought with tears and well-intentioned behavior, the White woman's tears are deemed worthy of sympathy because of her strength to endure people of Color. However, in the same films, the people of Color are portrayed in ways where their emotionalities – their tears – are pitied for their weakness thus are in need of white saviority. Let me be clear, the tears of White ladies are depicted as a symptom of innate goodness which is not mutually recognized in the tears of people of Color. People of Color in these films are rendered as nothing more than products of an environment created by their own innate volitions. The emotionalities of whiteness are given innate humanly status, whereas the emotionalities of people of Color are rendered both a symptom of social construction and innately *un*worthy of humanity; White women are Pavlov, people of Color are his dog. Understanding racialized emotions is a vital source of what makes us human, and that in itself makes it noteworthy for examination.

This book is a project to reaffirm our humanity by recognizing the racialized state of our emotionalities, its association with the permanence of whiteness, and how education can be one avenue that can lead us down a path that liberates our communal heart. Understandably, this is perhaps an insurmountable task; however, it is still an initial therapeutic necessity if humanity is to really understand why we feel the way we feel. Knowing that social institutions of power continue to influence our emotions, it is imperative that we excavate the remnants of our emotionalities lest we succumb to a strictly socialized state of emotion.

Although this book is purposely designed for White educators because they make up close to 90% of the U.S. teacher force, it is also designed for any educator who wants to deeply understand the underlying sentimentalities and emotionalities that resist socially-just concepts. That is, in order to truly promote the ideals of racial justice, educators and advocates will need to understand what they are up against when teaching and learning about race. However, beyond the U.S., this book is also intended for White teachers (the colonizers) who teach in colonized countries where their student populations are predominately people of Color (the colonized). As argued in the proceeding chapters, though the context may be different than what exists in the U.S., the elements of whiteness nonetheless manifest themselves elsewhere. So, in order to create a global movement towards racial justice, the dynamics of the emotionality of whiteness – what it is, what it feels like, how it operates, why it is there, what to do about it – is a vital step. Though this book focuses on a U.S. racial context for its unique racial makeup and historical racial violence amidst proclamations of being the "Land of the Free," I invite the international reader to apply these theories to other countries' unique racial histories. Furthermore, this book is also intended for White teachers who teach in predominately White communities, those who claim to "not see race" in their pedagogy because, like the films mentioned above, regardless of good intentions, these teachers-in-denial are either unknowingly or knowingly (through passive aggressive racial repression) disseminating the dominance of whiteness ideology and emotionality. That is, similar to Gramsci's (2012) concept of "hidden curriculum of capitalism" that maintains capitalism by structurally producing the haves and have-nots, there is a hidden curriculum of whiteness being taught to students, of Color and White alike. This practice of teaching structurally reinforces white supremacy and denies humanity to people of Color. Finally, this book is for racially-just individuals who fight tirelessly to provide a more racially-just society. May this book help you navigate the intoxications of whiteness that attempt to hinder racially-equitable progress.

This book is different in that it mixes theoretical scholarly research with creative narrative writing so that one comes away with a deeper understanding of whiteness while experiencing the feelings of whiteness: one cannot truly understand the emotionalities of whiteness until one actually experiences them first. Therefore, this book will make the reader feel guilt, shame, anger, defensiveness, dissonance, sadness, and/or discomfort, not to persecute the readers, but rather to show them the manifestations of these feelings and invite them to delve deep into why these emotions so manifest. Essentially, readers will know – and better yet, begin to understand – what happens and why it happens when one is "feeling white."

The following chapters move from identifying emotionalities of whiteness to deconstructing their psychoanalytical roots, with the final chapters exploring what can be done about these emotionalities for both people of Color and for Whites. Chapter 2 illustrates how whiteness is felt and expressed in everyday university teaching experiences. Chapter 3 theorizes and illustrates how the emotionality of whiteness is sentimentalized and thus masks a deeper disgust for people of Color, as well as how such a sentiment can impact one's commitment to racially-just education. Chapter 4 deepens the theorization of the emotionality of whiteness by detailing how it connects to sadomasochistic tendencies, and how adopting such sentiments leads one down a dehumanizing path. Chapter 5 explores the role of narcissism in whiteness, and delves into the psychoanalytical roots of this sentiment and how it impacts education. Chapter 6 explores the emotionality of whiteness as racial fetish and how antiracist approaches can be disingenuous if one does not consider why Whites feel the need to befriend (or proclaim false friendships with) people of Color. Chapter 7 landscapes the emotions of grief, melancholia, and loss when dealing with the emotionalities of whiteness; it provides a glimpse into what one will emotionally experience when attempting to let go of whiteness, and why such an emotional process is necessary. Chapter 8 describes how whiteness can act as a surveillance mechanism which institutionally watches over society à la Big Brother in order to enforce elements of whiteness. Chapter 9 diverges from the previous ideas in that initiates a focus on strategies, i.e., what can be done to resist the emotionality of whiteness as it impacts K-12 classrooms and how to in acts of racial justice amidst standardized curriculum. Chapter 10 follows suit by showing what an antiracist educator will experience when s/he engages in prolonged projects of racial justice; it also reveals pedagogical strategies to use in the classroom, and better prepare educators with what to expect both emotionally and ideologically. Chapter 11 is written specifically for White teachers and examines the emotional steps needed to try to decolonize the mind and heart of a racial colonizer; but, also provides strategies for people of Color who may have internalized the emotionalities of whiteness for survival. Chapter 12 concludes the preceding chapters and provides an urgent call for racial justice.

In all its theorizations, postulations, and considerations, this book can be an emotional roller coaster. Although discomforting at times, I ask the reader to stay committed, for this is just the beginning of an enduring emotional journey toward a fuller, more racially-just humanity; as such, you the reader will never be alone once your heart and mind open to all.

NOTES

[1] In reference to the murder of Trayvon Martin whose killer was not indicted due to racial bias: Trayvon was presumed violent, dangerous, and a criminal simply because he was a Black boy in a hoodie.

[2] See http://abcnews.go.com/Nightline/video/black-parents-strict-dress-code-rules-kids-27544055

[3] See http://www.cnn.com/2015/04/28/us/baltimore-riot-mom-smacks-son/

[4] One word, no hyphen; meaning both mother and scholar simultaneously: each term better informs the other identity, and both terms are inextricably intertwined similar to Zeus Leonardo's concept of "raceclass."

[5] Tagalog and Spanish for "Asian looking."

[6] See http://blacklivesmatter.com; https://en.wikipedia.org/wiki/Black_Lives_Matter; and https://www.facebook.com/BlackLivesMatter/

[7] See https://en.wikipedia.org/wiki/K%C3%BCbler-Ross_model

[8] See http://www.iep.utm.edu/love/#H1

REFERENCES

Boler, M. (1999). *Feeling power: Emotions and education.* East Sussex, UK: Psychology Press.

Chapman, G. D. (2010). *The 5 love languages/Things I wish i'd known before we got married set.* Chicago, IL: Moody Publishers.

Gramsci, A. (2012). *Selections from the prison notebooks.* New York, NY: International Publishers.

Matias, C. E., & Montoya, R. (2015). When Michael's death means our own children's death: Critical race parenting in a time of racial extermination. In K. Fashing-Varner & N. Hartlep (Eds.), *The assault on communities of color: Exploring the realities of race-based violence.* New York, NY: Rowman & Littfield.

Vera, H., & Gordon, A. M. (2003). *Screen saviors: Hollywood fictions of whiteness.* New York, NY: Rowman & Littlefield.

ON THE "FLIP" SIDE

Unveiling the Dangerous Minds of White Teacher Candidates

A dominant narrative in many films and within mass media is a fear of the urban student of Color (Kellner, 1995; Leonardo & Hunter, 2007). These narratives indicate that when innocent, well-intentioned White women enter urban schools, ridden with gangs, promiscuity, and drugs, they themselves become victims of the urban illness that plagues people of Color. In doing so, they become White martyr-messiahs for having taken on the risk of contaminating their inherent purity (Vera & Gordan, 2003a). According to this structure, the fears are real for White teachers willing to sacrifice themselves in the battle to humanize savage students who cuss at them, disrespect their presence, and cannot even read.

As this narrative of benevolent white "saviority" persists in the recountings of countless films, newscasts, and textbooks, society cries and empathizes with the heroic action of weeping White teachers. As society watches tears of anguish roll down the clean white cheek of this harmless teacher, it can barely survive witnessing how these White knights painfully tolerate the daily aggressive attacks of urban students of Color. Plainly stated, society falls to its knees when White women cry because their pain is felt by society at large in the way we all grieve with the Virgin Mary in Michelangelo's *Pietà*. Their pain becomes real through society's engagement of sympathy.

This White savior narrative is indoctrinated in the minds of countless White teacher candidates. Each semester my White teacher candidates – students who are in teacher preparation programs – enroll in our urban-focused teacher preparation program ready to sacrifice and give back to disadvantaged students of Color with the intention to change the injustices that pervade urban schools. They are prepared to roll up their sleeves and help close the achievement gaps for urban students of Color, knowing that it is not fair that suburban schools have more resources, better buildings, and more qualified teachers. This is similar to how Ricky Lee Allen (2002) relates Neo, the White protagonist in the movie *The Matrix*, to the Chosen One who will "fight the racist Whites" (p. 120). Essentially, my White teacher candidates become the heroic liberal warriors who will save students of Color from failing (Vera & Gordan, 2003b).

Imagine, if you will, then, the cognitive resistant reaction of my White heroines when I walk into the lecture hall with my obvious brown skin and urban mannerisms and introduce myself as "Doctor Matias." How will they help me, the embodiment of who they perceive needs saving, if I am the professor for the course?

ANATOMY OF COLORED PAIN: DEVELOPING A PEDAGOGY OF TRAUMA

Contrary to popularized notions of the painful lives of Whites who *serve, help, or save* people of Color, this paper cries for the need to counter this one-sided account of what constitutes humanizing pain; for, in adhering to that litmus of pain, Whites then elevate their pain above that endured by people of Color. Essentially, our tears become only three-fifths of the pain of a White person's.[1] And as a brown-skinned[2] Pinay[3] teacher educator from urban Los Angeles, I painfully attest that teaching in a white institution with White colleagues and White students is "traumatic," an experience that relentlessly terrorizes my heart, soul, and psyche on a daily basis. In order for me to heal my torn soul and shadowbox the racism (see James, 1999), I developed my *pedagogy of trauma.*

This chapter focuses on the conceptualization and operationalization of this pedagogy of trauma as a survival mechanism and model for other teacher educators of Color who undertake the grave task of training self-affirmed "colorblind" White teacher candidates at the expense of our pain. In doing so, we can finally counter the dominant narrative that impacts the learning receptivity of our White teacher candidates (see Matias, 2012a). Just as how people of Color experience racial microaggressions, my experiences with my White teacher candidates became a counterstory of my semester-long racial microaggression that subjected me to pain, a pain I must voice in order to counter White narratives of pain (Delgado & Stefancic, 2001; Solórzano, Ceja & Yosso, 2000; Sue, Capodilupo, Torino, Bucceri, Holder, Nadal, & Esquilin, 2007). I feel it is essential that White teacher candidates know of this pain because, in order to foster a mutually-respectful learning environment for their soon-to-be urban students of Color, White teacher candidates must first accept their teacher educators of Color.

My pedagogy of trauma first developed after realizing that, in order to survive the numerous racial microaggressions maintained by institutional racism and white supremacy, I needed a process to heal myself (see Gillborn, 2010; Lewis & Manno, 2011; Matias, 2012b; Nieto & Bode, 2008; Tatum, 2003). With respect to critical race theory, I needed a *transformational resistance,* a concept which not only articulates how I overcame the microaggression, but how I endured it (Solórzano & Delgado Bernal, 2001) and, in some ways, still do. Paul Willis (1977) describes how the "lads in England" endured and resisted school hegemony by creating an in-school counter-culture, albeit it was never accepted into dominant culture and ultimately led to self-defeating purposes. Giroux (2001) describes the necessity for resistance as an oppositional behavior, for such a behavior "becomes the object of theoretical clarification" (p. 110). Therefore, my pedagogy of trauma is the cultivation of an oppositional behavior that emotionally prepares me for the unceasing flogging of my heart that I am subjected to each time my students see me, respond to me, interact with me, and unknowingly resist learning from me. These are the real fears I am subjected to each time my White teacher candidates scream at me about how "race is not important!" and thus should not be discussed. When I do not relent, these student aggressively circulate emails to strategize ways of getting me fired, an action which causes me to name this a "trauma" and locate within it my inflicted suffering from their persistent racial microaggressions. However, I do not locate my suffering to relish in a state of victimization (Freire, 1993); rather, I do so to demonstrate how I transformationally resist by engaging with my pain in order to carry out the socially-just ideals of racial equity.

A FEMINIST LOOK INTO IDENTITY AND EMOTIONS

bell hooks (1995) corroborates the need to "locate one's suffering" when she claims that in order to heal, people of Color must "begin to collectively name and confront this suffering in ways that are constructively healing" (p. 144). As such, my pedagogy of trauma constructively confronts my pain by emotionally anticipating the level of severity within the racial microaggression. Again, I do not let the pain languish in some reservoir of self-pity; rather, I let this recurring trauma transform *how* I understand my pain. Essentially, feeling this pain is a process of humanization.

Before I delve deeper, there are many humanists who so love humanity that they empathetically acknowledge and see, in a Freirean (1993) sense, beyond my brownness and almond-shaped eyes to recognize that I am a human being complete with rightful emotions in response to coping in a racialized society. Just as Black feminist scholar Patricia Collins (1986) acknowledges how Black women having insightful sensitivity to mechanisms of patriarchy and sexism, humanists acknowledge that my emotional response to racism as a brown-skinned female is an insightful depiction of how humans subjected to racism survive. In this humanizing revelation, they cry out to me and say, "Sista! This is unhealthy, almost sadomasochistic. Just forget them and move out of teacher education." But that is not who I am. After years of growing up as a student of Color in an urban public school system and teaching in both South Los Angeles and Brooklyn, I admit that I am a teacher at heart who is dedicated to racially-just education despite taking the agonizing racelessness route needed to get there (see Fordham, 1988). Further, I argue that is not who *we* are.[4]

White feminist scholar Sandra Harding (1998) asserts that in multicultural science, women are medical heroes because their nuanced knowledges of the body "prove more reliable" (p. 106) than medical diagnosis, precisely because of our societal subjugation, under patriarchy, to perform roles as nurturers and caregivers. Reflexively, scholars of Color are also constantly challenged heroes who, because of our nuanced knowledge of race and racism, and intimate understanding, know that hegemonic whiteness blinds White folks to us. We are the warriors that shoulder this agonizing racial burden despite being chastised as being non-collaborative, often wrongfully accused of being personally mistrustful – or worse, mislabeled as a "real" racist – when we bravely engage how the ugly reigns of race manifests itself. These accusers, whether intentionally or not, have repressed issues to a colored face that symbolically reminds them of their white guilt.

11

WHY THE "I" AND "WE"?

I also strategically use the word "I" to remind my readers that I always account for my positionality, my individuality, and how I personally engage in this pedagogy of trauma. Despite the various mechanisms we employ to survive, we must remember that we do not do this kind of work without truly believing that change can happen. We understand that our increasing presence in the academy in itself does not mean that change has been wholly achieved. We do this precisely because we can no longer bear the inhuman condition of racism that subjugates our pain to white narratives of pain, and will be damned to sit by and let another generation grow up without hearing and truly humanizing our pain. However, in order to teach White teachers in higher education, we must first emerge from the safety of our prideful urban communities of Color that protected us against White aggression to pursue our degrees and teaching credentials. We bravely did – and do – so despite knowing that the journey through the ivory towers of the academy that trains us is wrought with institutional racism. Eerily like my White teacher candidates, we want to make a change, though one that does not center on the pain of White folks.

However, what is missing from the narrative of popularized urban education is the painful process that we people of Color underwent to get here. Embedded in that painful process is a schooling experience wherein White public school teacher after White public school teacher outweighed and ultimately ignored our pains as students of Color. These were the White public school teachers who were not trained to deal with their whiteness in response to our rich, beautiful colorfulness (McIntyre, 2003). So, after years of experiencing racism as people of Color – moreover, experiencing racism *and* sexism as women of Color – we are forced to develop a seemingly healthy callousness for survival. According to Audre Lorde (2001), a Black lesbian feminist, we develop this callousness for an "illusion of protection" (p. 177) because the hardening of our souls and hearts protects us from the trauma incurred by the endless barrage of racial and gender microaggressions (see Sue et al., 2007).

Sadly, there was a moment in my early career where I too became so hardened that I lost my feelings. I lost my pain. Yet by losing my ability to feel pain, I inadvertently repressed the painful counterstories needed to offset the dominant narrative of white pain. Notwithstanding, within the numbing effect that detracted from a beautiful, emotional, human quality, I realized that my pain counted as a *whole* human experience, one that my White teacher candidates must hear in order to re-examine their defaulted need to superiorize their pain, a process learned by the unquestioned recycling of dominant narratives. This is say that I invoke my pain in order to offer and remind us all that our continually silenced tears[5] are genuinely raw and intimately reflect how painful racism can be, particularly to blind exertions of whiteness. However, in doing so, I recognize that by relocating my lost and repressed pain, I also relive the painful experience of the trauma of race and gender all over again.

This chapter provides a look into a day in my life as a Filipina teacher educator teaching White teacher candidates in a white institution for the purpose of illustrating the "flip" side of how colored pain provides a counter to the grand narrative of white pain. Instead of coding my pain and trauma with masculine concepts such as *notions of exile* (Said, 2002), *dehumanization* (Freire, 1993), or *responsibility for neo-abolitionism* (Allen, 2012; Leonardo, 2009), I center my discourse on pain to remind us that it is ever-present in the work we do and the mission we strive to fulfill. Unfortunately, only when society rightfully redistributes the burden of race off of the shoulders of people of Color to those who benefit from our subjugation, can pain be alleviated. As for now, I critically theorize my own pain and bravely express my tears because, as LatCrit[6] scholars inform me, my *testimonio*[7] of colored pain is a powerful emotion that undergirds the heart. This is my pedagogy of trauma.

CHRONOLOGY OF COLORED PAIN EVEN BEFORE THE FIRST DAY OF CLASS: A THEORETICAL PRECURSOR

As each semester begins, the surge of fear engulfs, consumes, and almost suffocates me. I feel this way because I know that teaching in a white institution with White students and White colleagues, unknowingly and knowingly indoctrinated with their repressed emotional, social, and psychological investment in whiteness, will produce a first day that resembles a recurring trauma, like Bill Murray in *Groundhog Day*. Yet, almost sadomasochistically, I do it over and over again because beyond my pain of this recurring trauma are the never-hushed cries of my former Black and Brown public school students.

bell hooks (1995) calls this pain a "psychic trauma" inflicted on people of Color by racial aggressors. Although relevant, I posit that such a trauma is also an *emotional* trauma that so stabs my heart, I find myself waking up periodically throughout the night before class, hoping to cry myself back to sleep. Denying me sleep is a recurring lived nightmare of White teacher candidates resorting to their whiteness by feigning colorblindness upon my obvious almond-eyed, brown-skinned face with a Spanish surname (see Bonilla-Silva & Embrick, 2006). True to nature, after my four years in the academy and the piles of literature to support my work in critical race theory and critical whiteness studies, my White teacher candidates sadly and predictably claim that "race is not an issue" because they do not "see" race. I remember one of my White male students exemplified this when he employed a white "diss-course"[8] to adamantly argue that he does not see race or gender. While gripping his table and fervently pointing his finger at me, he strongly and loudly asserted, "The fact is YOU telling me to see race and gender IS racist and sexist! I mean, when you first walked into the classroom all I saw was a beautiful Asian lady."

He was correct. According to white diss-course, he had not seen race and sex at all. All he saw was a "beautiful" "Asian" "lady" so dehumanized by the phenotypes that socially construct her presence that they outshined the human essence of who she is/I am. This young man's white diss-course masked the saliency of race and racism behind a seemingly innocent ocular of colorblindness, while casting a false verdict of what constitutes true racism. This diss-course is dangerous because Whites

13

then position themselves as the knowledge bearers of race, despite their claims of never seeing it. When they engage it, it hurts people of Color.

At times, "beautiful Asian lady" still echoes in my ears. Feminist scholar Yen Lee Espiritu (2001) describes this process of Asian racialization and sexualization as never divorced from the Western representation of Asian women being dubbed either the "Dragon Lady" or "China Doll." She describes that Asian women are bound to racialized and sexualized ideological representations of being both erotized as hypersexual objects of pleasure and inferiorized as docile submissive servants. These are the "ideological assaults" I am also subjected to, which Espiritu (2001) claims must be challenged in order to "transform the existing hierarchical structure" (p. 199). However, in the center of this process to challenge patriarchy and racism is my heart and the fact that robbing me of blissful ignorance is the painful reality of it all. I stay awake, almost petrified of the fear of knowing that I will, without a doubt, again experience how the accusing white finger will point to my brownness and the blind white eye will deny my humanness.

In her examination of the false love of our Mexican American students, Angela Valenzuela (1999) demands an "authentic" love. Tormenting me is the question of how I will continue to give authentic care to Valenzuela's authentic love that I demand my White teacher candidates feel for their future students of Color. Further, how do I continue to give up my authentic love without receiving that same love in return from blinded White teacher candidates? Although I agree that teachers should be ever-present to serve the needs of their students, there is a different power dynamic when teaching a course on race when the teacher is the only person of Color inside the classroom. Schick (2010) outlines the white resistance she experienced from White college students while teaching antiracist pedagogies and admits "as a White woman, it would also be disingenuous on my part to separate myself from my White students" (p. 97). By doing so, she includes herself with the group identification of her White participants and parallels her trauma with her participants' trauma by virtue of being White. Yet, I am not a White researcher so I cannot parallel my trauma with my White students' trauma and dissonance precisely because my trauma is an effect of their refusal to both feel their trauma and recognize mine.

In race dynamics, colored trauma is not only different from a person of Color's perspective, it is also more substantiated. Di Angelo and Sensoy (2012) write about fears of Whites and people of Color when doing interracial race dialogues. They uncover that, in interracial race dialogues, White students fear being called racist, feeling guilt, being blamed, and/or beco,ing uncomfortable. Essentially, their fears are based on their white sensibilities or sentiments of discomfort. On the other hand, people of Color fear tangible repercussions (e.g., losing their jobs or houses, physical threats, and ostracism). In their analysis, DiAngelo and Sensoy (2012) argue that the fears held by Whites are not equivalent to the real fears of people of Color because the latter's fear is produced by the historical surveillance of people of Color under a system of racism. In fact, the authors point out how Whites believe that racism against Whites is *more prevalent* than racism against Blacks, a mal-informed response to their unsubstantiated fear. So, when I ask how I can authentically love my White students, invested in their whiteness, when they unknowingly or knowingly refuse to return love, I realize that this race dynamic produces a sadomasochistic relationship wherein I must submit to the difficult relationship in love despite the racialized resistance. These painful acts of resistance torment me because I simply want to be seen as a human being who deserves humanly love.

Amidst the late-night bellows of stray dogs, I lament over whether my heart will no longer beat loving thumps because of my commitment to supporting humanity by dismantling hegemonic whiteness. For what is not understood in popularized notions of pain is that teacher educators of Color who continue to day-in and day-out commit to teaching their White students about race incur a great loss too. The emotional toll we pay for our commitment is a restless mind and a heart that is constantly bombarded with how we will respond to the eerily predictive and resistive performance of our White teacher candidates.

UNVEILING THE PAIN BEHIND WHITE DISS-COURSE: A COUNTER ANALYSIS

Example 1

Although there may not be any malintent in the verbal or written responses of White teacher candidates when learning about race, racism, and whiteness from a teacher educator of Color, pain in what is said and/or written by White teacher candidates entrenched in whiteness exists. To clarify, this chapter is not about excavating white sensibilities of White teacher candidates; rather, it is about unearthing a professor of Color's emotional pain behind the verbal, written, and behavioral expressions made by White teacher candidates regardless of their intent. Below are selected answers from an IRB[9]-approved study on the pre-course student surveys I administered to gauge resistance. I employ them to help teacher educators, at large, understand how such answers invoke a pedagogy of trauma for me as a teacher educator of Color. In order to gauge their familiarity with interactions with people of Color, I asked the following question:

Q: Have you had experiences with people of Color who are in authority? How about one who was not in authority? Please describe the circumstances. (Student Survey Question #5)

A: I have not had experiences with people of color in authority. I do not think my view on not having people of color in authority will change or anything. Respect is key no matter what my view. (Student Survey Entry, 1/12)

To better contextualize, just like pain, there is a social construction of what constitutes "respect" such that it becomes a contested knowledge set. Michel Foucault (1980) documents this in his discussion of how and why certain

15

knowledges are superiorized above other knowledges in a process of power. Applicably, my White students come into class with a white fund of knowledge that, through racial hegemony, has superiorized itself above people of Color's funds of knowledges[10] (Moll, Amanti, Neff, & Gonzalez, 1992). Specific to my emotions, such a hegemonically-powerful white fund of knowledge will continue to resituate itself above my colored knowledge, despite the qualifying degrees that substantiate it. So, when my student says "respect is key," what I fear most is what definition of respect is referred to – the one that merely caters to her needs, or the one that rightfully distributes the power embedded in respect? As a teacher educator of Color coping with daily racism that colorblind Whites will not even give credence to, how respectful is it to state "I do not think my view on not having people of color in authority will change or anything." In saying "it won't change or anything," I fear I am witnessing one of those racializing moments wherein Whites refuse to hear because they do not *want* to hear. Yet, if asked if this is true, I fear they will become violent, aggressive, accusatory, and/or relish the guilt. So, as a teacher educator who teaches about race for the hope of antiracism, what is the point of all my expertise (twelve years of higher education, three degrees, seven years teaching in the urban classroom, and a lifetime of racialized experiences) if all that work "won't change anything"? Although critics may argue that this disrespect is more pervasive due to modern times, I continue to question whether its ubiquity negates the relevance of racial positionings. That is, the normative mantra to claim that this type of disrespect happens to all professors totally ignores the specificity of racialized issues so described in countless literature (Cleveland, 2004; de Jesús, 2004; Matias, 2012b; Stanley, 2006; Williams & Evans-Winter, 2005). Hence, as critical race theory so asserts, the dynamics of race did not just disappear with changing, modern times.

I agree that respect is "key," but respectfully speaking, a comment like this only respects the White writer's own viewpoint and emotions on what constitutes *respect*. To better illustrate, would it be respectful of me as a professor, with power over my students, to say, "I am the professor and although I never really worked with students, I know that learning about your needs as students won't change my views on anything. *Ipso facto*, respect to me is "key"? Simply put, by not acknowledging the processes of power, we cannot respect each other.

However, when I do accept this perverted version of respect, I deny myself respect from my White students because their need to feel respected goes beyond my need for respect as their professor. As such, I end up getting emails from my White teacher candidates that say things like "Hey, print this out for me, yeah?" without an ending signature; "It's been a week and you haven't graded my paper" (sent from an iPhone); or, "I don't mean to be disrespectful, but did you really read my paper? I don't deserve a B." Is this what my White teacher candidates mean when they say "respect is key"?

Hence, dangerously accepting my White teacher candidates' definition of respect denies my human right to a respect that is not self-serving or self-catering to one group over another. Although the survey prepares me with knowledge of how my students will engage in a white diss-course of what constitutes respect, I am left feeling embarrassingly disrespected and hurt. Shamefully, I ponder whether I will have them understand that respect is not, *ipso facto*, my submission to their need to feel respected. Cheating me of sleep the night before class is an overwhelming feeling of shame and humiliation because I know I will have to convince my White students of the simple human fact that I deserve respect too.

I know the diss-course must be "flipped" onto them; so, amidst my agony and self-shame, I evolve to find a rudimentary source of healing in knowing what I must do. Instead of denying the reality of my pain, I learn that it is because of my pain that I must forcibly engage it – moreover, *feel* it. Therefore, I assert that they call me "Dr. Matias" because there's a different power dynamic when all my students are White and I am the only person of Color in a course on race. I also show them how to email me in a respectful way. Finally, I realize I have to be actively ready to call out their aggressive offensive attacks each time they resort to whiteness and feel it is okay to disrespect me. I relocate my pain to empower and remind myself that it is *not* okay that my White students see me as another subordinate person of Color who is expected to submit to their masterly needs.

Example 2

> Q: Have you talked about race and racism before? With whom do you feel most comfortable in talking about this topic? Please describe. (Question #7)
>
> A: In my Sociology of Race and Ethnicity class, that's all we talked about. I feel most comfortable talking with like-minded thinkers. I am uncomfortable around people who are racists or people who accuse people of racism when it's not there. So I guess I'm uncomfortable around people who don't actually know what racism is. (Student Survey Entry, 1/12)

When I read this response, fear builds in my heart because it sounds like an exasperated comment in the context of this White female candidate preferring *not* to discuss race in a sociology of race and ethnicity course! Let me restate that. Indulge me if you will on my feelings. How do you think I feel, as a scholar of Color who does race-related research, when a White female student claims that "all they talk about is race" in a sociology of race and ethnicity course? If this student is exasperated by discussing a topic that the entire course is about, a course she enrolled in, and by her own admission only feels comfortable with "like-minded thinkers," then certainly she will be uncomfortable with me: I am the only person of Color in my courses, courses that explicitly employ a critical race and critical whiteness lens to interrogate social foundations of urban education.

Again, draining me from strength is my pondering over whether this student will think, as many White folks do, that I am "pulling out the race card" when simply analyzing operations of race. Further, when modeling how to dialogue about race and racism in an academic manner, what is scary for teacher educators of Color is that our White teacher candidates will either: (a) cry, which is symbolic of the normative story of how people of Color are the ones who cause Whites pain, which both stifles conversation and elevates white emotionality above the pain that people of Color face daily; or, (b) act aggressively, symbolic of the repressed pain of lying about a colorblind stance (Matias, 2012b). Emotionally terrifying is deciphering which response will I be subjected to the next day and how will I emotionally prepare in response to these disturbing performances of whiteness. These mere routine performances constitute "ripping off the Band-Aid" from my heart, a Band-Aid that I carefully placed a semester ago to heal from the last trauma of regularly performed whiteness. Although I understand that white racial identity (Helms, 1990) can take some time, I, on the other hand, have no time to grieve because I must engage in this trauma every semester.

My pedagogy of trauma relates to Gloria Ladson-Billings's (1998) documentation of how the colonized education of urban African American males is like an ongoing psycho-cultural assault. However, unlike daily racial microaggressions experienced in interpersonal encounters, Ladson-Billings's psycho-cultural assaults are like an ongoing systemic racial slap in the face. The onslaught of Eurocentric curriculum, deplorable schooling conditions, and the refusal to interrogate one's own culpability in recycling dominant ideologies, force our African American students to experience a colonized education no different than one in, say, apartheid Soweto. In applying this notion of psycho-cultural assaults, the tables are no different when the context is flipped, for race and its disparaging corollary (racism) is not only a numbers game, it is also about power. Despite the fact that I am the professor of the course, I am still outnumbered by White folks; more detrimental is that I am outpowered by whiteness. My White students' whiteness is shown through their interactions with me, which thus produces a tangible fear to be careful not enrage a white mob. As defined by the litany of critical race research, and my own experiences as a brown-skinned racialized being, I cannot help but mull over whether I will be one of the people my student is uncomfortable with because I will accuse her/him of racism despite her blindness to understand when it's really there.

This White female teacher candidate leaves me with the haunting disclosure of "So I guess I'm uncomfortable around people who don't actually know what racism is." She has already predetermined that she is the bearer of knowledge when it comes to race and racism, a discussion that exhausts her so. If her exasperation in studying race in a course about race is indicative of her self-proclaimed knowledge of race and racism, then I have something to fear, precisely because she right out threatens to be uncomfortable with me. Within our normative experiences of white discomfort in discussions of race and racism, her discomfort is tantamount to the uncomfortable exasperations of, "Do you know how much it hurts to be called a racist?" or "*I* never owned slaves, so why are you blaming me? I didn't do anything to deserve feeling bad for being White." By adhering to this mentality, White folks are then so invested in their whiteness that they superiorize their discomfort above the daily discomfort people of Color experience. What leaves me so baffled is, don't my White teacher candidates understand that, by elevating their discomfort above mine, they hurt me? Just as they cry out, "Why are you blaming me? I didn't do anything to deserve this," I cry out the same words. In professing their victimhood they are fervently pointing their finger at me. They stare at me as the sole embodiment of their own emotional racial angst and thus misappropriate their projection of guilt onto a false mistrust of me. All this happens while I sit silently while they continue to scrutinize and tally my every word.

Example 3

> Q: How many teachers/professors of Color have you had while growing up (elem, middle, HS, college)? What courses? How did the prevalence (or lack thereof) of educators of Color impact you? Please describe. (Question #4)

> A: I have had no professors of color... During my first semester, I noticed a few professors of color and it struck up a certain emotion in me. Not that I didn't think they were capable of being professors; rather, I simply found it odd. (Student Survey Entry, 1/12)

Odd? As a professor of Color, I never found myself "odd." I admit to feeling odd not by my self-infliction; rather, I feel "oddened" by White teacher candidates like this who unintentionally (or intentionally) misplace a racialized label on me as if I am "a commodity as spectacle," as critical theorist Guy Debord (2006) claims, a bewilderment of some sort that abnormally manifests itself within the normative realms of whiteness or, as Debord further describes, the embodiment of a spectacle "which has become objectified" (p. 118). This is no different than when Filipinos were placed in cages during the St. Louis World's Fair in 1904,[11] or falsely heralding the accomplishments of a few people of Color[12] as representative of *all* people of Color. Although it is absolutely *odd* in and of itself that this White female admits to never having had a professor of Color, feels compelled to say that encountering one (like an object) will produce "a certain emotion" in her; the oddity is placed on the professor of Color rather than on herself.

As the cold rocky mountain breeze passed over our little city in the early morning hours, I couldn't help but contemplate why these White students see me as the odd one in this relationship. bell hooks (1995) describes this odd relationship quite clearly when she reflects on why Black and White feminists had difficulty building coalitions in the early stages of radical feminism. She states that one of the major barriers was "the servant/served paradigm" (p. 218) since Black women occupied lower echelons within a workspace, whereas White women were positioned higher. hooks expands on this by stating that White feminists had a hard time letting go of their "mummification" of Black women, wherein the purpose of Black women's presence in the workspace was to serve the needs of White women. Pondering this notion, I cannot help but feel trapped by how my White teacher candidates expect me to be a mammy (or more appropriately, a Filipina nurse) to their needs, while my needs are not even considered.

This sentiment was confirmed when one of my White teacher candidates claimed that she had never met any person of Color in authority, but regularly meets with people of Color who serve her:

Example 4

Q: Have you had experiences with people of Color who are in authority? How about one who was not in authority? Please describe the circumstances. (Question #5)

A: I have not had experiences with people of color in authority as I don't have a boss who is of color and haven't had to deal the law enforcement. However, I have had experiences with people of color who were not in authority. This includes people where I get my hair done, my doctor's office, and shopping in many stores. The circumstances were normal and nothing unusual. They were just like the people of non-color and, in some places, they were nicer to me. (Student Survey Entry, 1/12)

Predictively, this student (like my many other students who come from White, middle class suburbia) admits to not having had experiences with people of Color who are in authority. Even more telling is her pairing of law enforcement with people of Color. What causes me pain is knowing that, given that her *only* experiences with people of Color have been within the service industry, she believes thinking and saying that "they were nicer to me" than White folks is a positive statement. This "just-serve-me-and-we're-all-good" attitude scares me because I know she will expect me to serve her needs despite my position of authority. This turned out to be quite true because later in the semester she barraged me with emails about how each reading brought her discomfort because "focusing on whiteness was not right."

What I need my White teacher candidates to understand is that, for people of Color, our funds of knowledge are *not* a spectacle, not a metaphoric salsa that one can add to Latinize whiteness at whim. Rather, they are formed by the daily lives we live as human begins. Metaphorically speaking, we cannot add the salsa when we want to it is the context in which we must survive.

In the end, I am not the odd one, for in teaching White teacher candidates who sadly and characteristically perform their whiteness to a point where they regularly and sometimes apologetically cry or shout at me, I am the loving one who continues to stand there and take it for the end goal that they can learn, even at the price of my racialized humiliation. Until a White person truly sees the dehumanization process of investing in their whiteness, standing before them will always be a person of Color who is demoralized by it.

HUMANIZING COLORED PAIN: HONORING MY FLIP SIDE OF TRAUMA

Eight night hours go by and the midnight moon fades behind the early morning sunlight. I get up, get my twins to their urban public school, put on my suit, and look at the mirror to make sure I am "presentable" – meaning, appearing suitable under the white scrutinizing gaze– for my first day of class. Buried within my petite five-foot frame and hundred-pound stature is the heart of a woman – moreover, a motherscholar – who relentlessly engages in a pedagogy of trauma, not because I need it to survive nor necessarily want it, but because it is my duty to humanity to provide this knowledge for my children and the generations thereafter.

In the end, this is my story of pain and the pedagogy of trauma I use to heal myself. This pedagogy stems from the deep humanizing love that I – and I recognize that others do as well – self-enlist in order to simply "pay it forward."

NOTES

[1] A reference to the "Three Fifths Compromise of 1787" in which slaves were counted as 3/5's of a person in order to establish population for legislative representation. See https://en.wikipedia.org/wiki/Three-Fifths_Compromise

[2] Colorism in the U.S. context is significant in that the pigment of one's skin color leads to societal consequences from racial categorization to one's legal right to citizenship. Being darker-skinned thus has a noteworthy social and racial significance. Additionally, Filipinos range from light-skinned *chinitos* (Asian-looking) to *meztizas* (Spanish mix). The U.S. racialization process responds to the racial phenotypes of Filipinos in vastly different ways.

[3] *Pinay* is a slang term for a Filipina. After hundreds of years of Spanish colonization, the Philippines underwent U.S. colonization after the 1898 Spanish-American War. Having had U.S. national status, many Filipinos enlisted in the U.S. armed forces, attended U.S. colonial schools, spoke English, and traveled freely to and from the U.S. for migrant labor work. Therefore, the U.S. has had a long colonial history with the Philippines. American-born Filipinos, like myself, are remnants of that colonial history.

[4] By using the pronoun "we," I speak directly to teacher educators/scholars of Color who proudly endure this cyclic trauma to ensure that humanity wins over the dehumanizing social constructions of racial separatism despite being subjected to racial dehumanization themselves (see Berry & Mizelle, 2006; Stanley, 2006). I also speak to true antiracist White allies who work through their own pain on a daily basis without erroneously misplacing their feelings of white guilt and shame on people of Color, and self-invest in shouldering the emotional, political, and spiritual burden of race precisely because it is the human thing to do (see Sleeter 2001). I specifically engage the word "we" because I want to remind us that we are not alone in this painful work, a work tied to a higher duty to humanity.

[5] And although tears are socially-constructed as signs of weakness (an unfortunate popularized connotation that stems from a sexist depiction of a woman's weakness instead of her strength to survive painful trauma), I attest that my tears are my brave engagement.

[6] *LatCrit* refers to Latino Critical Theory. See http://www.latcrit.org/

[7] *Testimonio* is adapted from LatCrit scholars Delores Delgado-Bernal, Rebecca Burciaga, and Tara Yosso, to name a few. It refers to the intimate testimony of Latinos that counters the dominant narrative under a system of race and racism.

[8] I use the term "diss-course" because this type of communication "disses" or insults people of Color behind a façade of innocence and/or normalized speech (Rodriguez, 2009).

[9] IRB: Institutional Review Board.

[10] This phenomenon connects to Yosso and Garcia's (2007) articulations of "culture of wealth" found in communities of Color. Namely, since knowledges (or what constitutes cultures or capitals of

wealth) subjugate through a process of power, communities of Color in a racist society are then forced to combat dominant narratives that depict them through a deficit lens by asserting their funds of knowledge or capital. To simply argue that a culture holds beauty is to also recognize that a dominant culture has denied that characterization in the first place.

[11] See http://www.npr.org/templates/story/story.php?storyId=1909651

[12] Such as President Obama (first African American U.S. president), Kobe Bryant (famous African American U.S. basketball player), Sonia Sotomayor (first Latina U.S. Supreme Court Justice), J Lo (Latina pop singer and actress), Jeremy Lin (famous Asian American U.S. basketball player), and Oprah (famous African American actress, entrepreneur, and talk show host).

REFERENCES

Allen, R. L. (2011, April). *From sadomasochism to humanization: An abolitionist theory of white guilt.* Paper presented at the 2011 meeting of the American Educational Research Association, New Orleans, Louisiana.

Allen, R. L. (2002). Wake up Neo: White identity, hegemony, and consciousness in *The Matrix.* In J. J. Slater, S. M. Fain, & C. A. Rossatto (Eds.), *The Freirean legacy* (pp. 104–125). New York, NY: Peter Lang Publishing.

Berry, T., & Mizelle, N. (Eds.). (2006). *From oppression to grace: Women of color and their dilemmas in the academy.* Sterling, VA: Stylus Publishing.

Bonilla-Silva, E., & Embrick, D. (2006). Racism without racists: "Killing me Softly" with colorblindness. In C. Rossotto, R. L. Allen, & M. Pruyn (Eds.), *Reinventing critical pedagogy.* Lanham, MD: Rowman & Littlefield.

Cleveland, D. (Ed.). (2004). *A long way to go: Conversations about race by African American faculty and graduate students* (Higher Education, Vol. 14). New York, NY: Peter Lang.

Collins, P. (1986). Learning from the outsider within: The sociological significance of Black feminist thought. *Social Problems, 33*(6), S14–S31.

Collins, P. (2000). *Black feminist thought* (2nd ed.). New York, NY: Routledge.

Debord, D. (2006). The commodity as spectacle. In M. Durham & D. Kellner (Eds.), *Media and cultural studies: Key works* (pp. 117–121). Oxford, UK: Blackwell Publishing.

de Jesús, M., & Ma, S. (2004). RAW: "Raunchy Asian women" and resistance to queer studies in the Asian Pacific American studies classroom. *The Radical Teacher, 70,* 26–31.

Delgado, R., & Stefancic, J. (2001). *Critical race theory.* New York, NY: New York University Press.

Di Angelo, R., & Sensoy, O. (2012). Getting slammed: White depictions of interracial dialogues as arenas of violence. *Race, Ethnicity, and Education, 17*(1), 103–128. doi:10.1080/13613324.2012.674023

Espiritu, Y. (2001). Ideological racism and cultural resistance: Constructing our own image. In M. Andersen & P. Collins (Eds.), *Race, class and gender: An anthology.* Belmont, CA: Wadsworth/ Thomas Learning.

Freire, P. (1970, 1993). *Pedagogy of the oppressed.* New York, NY: Continuum.

Fordham, S. (1988). Racelessness as a factor in Black students' school success: Pragmatic strategy or pyrrhic victory? *Harvard Educational Review, 58*(1), 54–84.

Foucault, M. (1980). *Power/Knowledge.* New York, NY: Vintage Books.

Gillborn, D. (2010). The colour of numbers: Surveys, statistics and deficit-thinking about race and class. *Journal of Education Policy, 25*(2), 253–276.

Giroux, H. (2001). *Theory and resistance in education.* Westport, CT: Bergin & Garvey.

Haley, A. (1965). *The autobiography of Malcolm X.* New York, NY: Ballantine Books.

Harding, S. (1998). *Is science multicultural?* Bloomington, IN: Indiana University Press.

Helms, J. (1990). *Black and White racial identity: Theory, research, and practice.* Westport, CT: Praeger.

hooks, b. (1995). *Killing rage: Ending racism.* New York, NY: Henry Holt & Company.

Huber, L., Malagon, M., Velez, V., & Solórzano, D. (2008). Getting beyond the 'symptom,' acknowledging the "disease": Theorizing racist nativism. *Contemporary Justice Review: Issues in Criminal, Social, and Restorative Justice, 11*(1), 39–51.

James, J. (1999). *Shadowboxing: Representations of Black feminist politics*. New York, NY: St. Martin's Press.

Kellner, D. (1995). *Media culture*. New York, NY: Routledge.

Ladson-Billings, G. (1998). From Soweto to the South Bronx: African Americans and colonial education in the United States. In C. Torres & T. Mitchell (Eds.), *Sociology of education: Emerging perspectives* (pp. 247–264). New York, NY: SUNY Press.

Ladson-Billings, G., & Tate, W. (1995). Toward a critical race theory of education. *Teachers College Record, 97*, 47–68.

Leonardo, Z. (2009). *Race, whiteness, and education*. New York, NY: Routledge.

Leonardo, Z., & Hunter, M. (2007). Imaging the urban: The politics of race, class, and schooling. In W. T. Pink & G. W. Noblit (Eds.), *International handbook of urban education* (pp. 779–802). Medford, MA: Springer Science & Business Media.

Lewis, A., & Manno, M. (2011). The best education for some: Race and schooling in the United States today. In M. Jung, J. Vargas, & E. Bonilla-Silva (Eds.), *State of White supremacy: Racism, governance and the United States*. California, CA: Stanford University Press.

Lorde, A. (2001). Age, race, class and sex: Women redefining difference. In M. Andersen & P. Collins (Eds.), *Race, class and gender: An anthology*. Belmont, CA: Wadsworth/Thomas Learning.

Matias, C. E. (2012a). Who you callin' White?!: A critical counterstory on colouring White identity. *Race, Ethnicity, and Education, 16*(3), 291–315. doi:10.1080/13613324.2012.674027

Matias, C. E. (2012b). Beginning with me: Accounting for a researcher of color's counterstories to inform socially just research design. *Journal of Critical Thought and Praxis*. Retrieved from http://elps.hs.iastate.edu/jctp-current.php

McIntyre, A. (2003). Participatory action research and urban education: Reshaping the teacher preparation process. *Equity & Excellence in Education, 36*(1), 28–39.

Moll, L., Amanti, C., Neff, D., & Gonzalez, N. (1992). Funds of knowledge for teaching: Using a qualitative approach to connect homes and classrooms. *Theory into Practice, 31*(2), 132–141.

Munoz, Jr., C. (1989). *Youth, identity, and power: The Chicano Movement*. New York, NY: Verso.

Nieto, S., & Bode, P. (2008). *Affirming diversity: The sociopolitical context of multicultural education*. Boston, MA: Allyn & Bacon.

Orelus, P. (2011). *Rethinking race, class, language, and gender: A dialogue with Noam Chomsky and other leading scholars*. New York, NY: Rowman & Littlefield.

Ramis, H. (1993). (Director). *Groundhog day* [movie]. Culver City, CA: Columbia Pictures.

Rodriguez, D. (2009). The usual suspect: Negotiating White student resistance and teacher authority in a predominantly White classroom. *Cultural Studies ↔ Critical Methodologies, 9*(4), 483–508.

Said, E. (2002). *Reflections on exile and other essays*. Cambridge, MA: Harvard University Press.

Schick, C. (2010). By virtue of being White: Resistance in anti-racist pedagogy. *Race, Ethnicity and Education, 3*(1), 83–101.

Sleeter, C. E. (2001). Preparing teachers for culturally diverse schools research and the overwhelming presence of whiteness. *Journal of Teacher Education, 52*(2), 94–106.

Solórzano, D., Ceja, M., & Yosso, T. (2000). Critical race theory, racial microaggressions, and campus racial climate: The experiences of African American college students. *Journal of Negro Education, 69*(1/2), 60–73.

Solórzano, D., & Bernal, D. (2001). Examining transformational resistance through a critical race and LatCrit theory framework. *Urban Education, 36*(3).

Stanley, C. (Ed.). (2006). *Faculty of color: Teaching in predominantly White colleges and universities* (Vol. 69). San Francisco, CA: Jossey-Bass.

Sue, D., Capodilupo, C., Torino, G., Bucceri, J., Holder, A., Nadal, K., & Esquilin, M. (2007). Racial microaggressions in everyday life: Implications for clinical practice. *American Psychologist, 62*(4), 271–286.

Tatum, B. D. (2003). *"Why are all the Black kids sitting together in the cafeteria?" A psychologist explains the development of racial identity*. New York, NY: Basic Books.

Valenzuela, A. (1999). *Subtractive schooling*. Albany, NY: State University of New York Press.

Vera, H., & Gordan, A. (2003a). The beautiful American: Sincere fictions of the White messiah in Hollywood movies. In A. Doane & E. Bonilla-Silva (Eds.), *White out* (pp. 113–128). New York, NY: Routledge.

Vera, H., & Gordan, A. (2003b). *Screen saviors: Hollywood fictions of whiteness*. Lanham, MD: Rowman and Littlefield.

Wah, L. M. (Director). (1994). *The color of fear* [documentary film]. Oakland, CA: Stir-Fry Productions.

Willis, P. (1977). *Learning to labor*. New York, NY: Columbia University Press.

Williams, D., & Evans-Winter, V. (2005). The burden of teaching teachers: Memoirs of race discourse in teacher education. *The Urban Review, 37*(3), 201–219.

Yosso, T., & Garcia, D. (2007). "This is no slum!" A critical race theory analysis of community cultural wealth in culture clash's Chavez ravine. *Journal of Chicano Studies, 32*(1), 145–154.

"WHEN SAYING YOU CARE AIN'T REALLY CARING"

Emotions of Disgust, Whiteness Ideology and Teacher Education[1]
(with Michalinos Zembylas)

In the wake of the not guilty verdict in the U.S. murder trial of Trayvon Martin, Juror B37, a White female, appeared on CNN's *Anderson 360* to describe her thought process during deliberation. Responding to the credibility of the testimony of Rachel Jeantel, an African American teenage female, Juror B37 stated, "I don't think it was very credible ... because of her education and her communication skills. She wasn't a good witness." Juror B37 then described how "sad" she felt for Rachel, and argued that, for people like "them" that is "just everyday life, the type of life that they live and how they're living in the environment that they're living in."

Using Bonilla-Silva's (2006) theory of colorblind racism which unveils how Whites teeter between rhetorical arguments based on their dominant racial frame, this exasperated "concern" is often a rhetorical response, one which we coin an "emotional dimunitive" that strategically masks a deep-rooted disgust for African Americans. Disgust is a complex and multifaceted emotion, but in its simplest sense it means "bad taste" (Ahmed, 2004), a feeling of profound aversion for the Other that can be performed in a variety of overt – or not so overt – manners. Thus, since "Whites rely on diminutives to soften their racial blows" (Bonilla-Silva, 2006, p. 66), I argue that Juror B37's comments about "them" (code for Black people) and "the type of life they live" is an attempt to soften her feelings of disgust. Instead of displaying disgust, an emotion that is socially unacceptable and tantamount to racism, she displays pity for them, a more socially acceptable emotion that still objectifies and sentimentalizes the Black Other while deflecting racist culpability. In this release of racial responsibility, if disgust is masked with sentimentalized performances of pity, sympathy, and/or caring, how does it reify racist structures? Further – and most importantly – how can antiracist projects in education (and beyond) respond strategically and productively?

This chapter was originally co-authored with Dr. Michalinos Zembylas, a professor at Open University of Cyprus; thus, we share in this analysis here. The disguise of one emotion into another primarily concerns us because, as Zembylas and I work to train teachers with the ideals of social justice and equity, we are often confronted with responses from students, teachers, and faculty that display a variety of emotions such as care, empathy, and love. These are also emotions that are often advocated in the litany of research about teaching practices and anti-racist education (e.g., hooks, 2003; Nieto, 2003; Palmer, 2007). However, are these emotional responses from students and teachers truly "caring," "compassionate," and "loving," according to demands for *authentic care* (Valenzuela, 1999), and *active empathy* (Boler, 1999), or a stop to *false empathy* in teaching practices (Duncan, 2002)? The demands to reconsider the "truthfulness" of emotions are instructive because, as we delve deeper into their investigation, we begin to notice that the emotional responses of students and teachers are often associated with emotional diminutives which, although performed in one way, may in fact mask other emotions that are socially unacceptable or politically incorrect (see Matias, 2013a).

Additionally, both of us are interested in investigating the emotional ways in which our students (i.e., teacher candidates), who often have privileged identities, react to the study of race; yet, Zembylas and I come from totally different backgrounds: I grew up in a racially marginalized community, while Zembylas is White and had access to racial privileges. We hope that our different backgrounds, covering important aspects of the entanglement of emotions and whiteness ideology, will help us provide a critical interpretation about how the politics of disgust maintain whiteness in ways that are often taken as natural and innate.

This chapter investigates how racially diminutive emotions are entrenched in whiteness ideology and how this ideology perpetuates whiteness in a space where almost 90% of U.S. teachers and the teacher educators who train them are White females. Particularly, we use an IRB-approved study to explore how whiteness ideology among White teacher candidates in an urban teacher education program perverts their emotions of disgust to false claims of love, empathy, and caring. In an educational climate where antiracist projects are heralded, we hope to explicate how it is important for all educators to critically analyze and reflect on their (racialized) emotions, the ways in which these emotions are constructed through whiteness, and how their displays may counteract anti-racist endeavors.

THEORIZING RACIALIZED EMOTIONS: WHITENESS AND THE ROLE OF DISGUST

Fusing critical race theory (CRT), whiteness studies, and critical emotion studies, we begin by suggesting that whiteness as a social power and ideology normalizes white emotionality as nonracial and erroneously "translates" disgust for people of Color to false professions of caring and empathy (see Ahmed, 2004, 2012; Boler, 1999; Bonilla-Silva, 2006; Trainor, 2008; Valenzuela, 1999; Winans, 2010). Ahmed (2004, 2012), for example, explains how white subjectivities are constituted through certain modes of affectivity and embodiment. One of these emotions that has not received much attention is disgust. Ahmed analyzes the performativity of disgust, especially in contexts of racial relations, and argues that disgust works both individually and socially: feeling disgust is not simply a bodily state, but also psychic and constructed in social encounters and the boundaries (imaginary or real) between individuals and groups. Disgust, then, is about: the Other" from which we "pull away" with a movement that registers bodily and/or emotionally.

The feeling of being disgusted may also include an element of politics, as Ahmed (2004, 2012) points out, because it works to establish or confirm allegiances between certain individuals and against others. Disgust is then racialized and organizes the social and bodily space, creating powerful boundaries between "us" and "them" (e.g., Whites and non-Whites); thus, disgust comes to signify the danger of proximity with *them* (non-Whites), because *they* threaten to violate *our* space and *our* purity. Disgust, in other words, is not simply a means by which the subjectivation of the White individual and the white community is established; disgust also works to transform the bodies of others into "the disgusted" through a discourse that assumes injury to the White subject and its privilege (Leonardo & Zembylas, 2013).

As an affective formation, this relational interplay of proximity and distance, attraction and aversion, functions as a mode of white subjectification that is performed via a variety of discursive and bodily forms which are racist, although not always in blunt or overt ways (Hook, 2005); hence, they "disguise" socially inappropriate emotions into ones that are more acceptable (see also, Matias, 2013b). By understanding the operation of whiteness as an affective technology that maintains white emotional norms and structures, Hook (2005) suggests that we are provided with an important linkage among racism, racialized emotions, and whiteness. What this implies is that exclusion, abjection, and other emotions about non-White individuals are at once embodied, affective, and socially-produced. Whiteness, then, must be approached as a function of affective modes of constitution and affirmation through which feelings such as disgust for non-White individuals are systematically generated (Hook, 2005, Matias & Allen, 2014). Consequently, the issue of identifying and theorizing new and distinctive modalities of racism performed through various technologies of affect is a priority both for anti-racism activists (Hook, 2012) and for those interested in the political uses of emotions in public arenas, such as schools and institutions of higher education (Leonardo & Zembylas, 2013).

One of the modalities through which racialized emotions are performed in politically-correct and socially-accepted ways is the example of caring as hidden disgust. Theorists in political science (e.g., Whitebrook, 2002), feminist studies (e.g., Porter, 2006), cultural studies (e.g., Berlant, 2004), and education (e.g., Boler 1999, 2004) discuss how declarations of caring and empathy are often empty or inauthentic because they fail to be accompanied by action. The object of compassion exists primarily within an imaginary realm that sentimentalizes the Other and avoids any action that shows caring in practice. This means, in other words, feeling sorry for about those who suffer without necessarily taking action to alleviate their suffering (Chouliaraki 2010). Such benign feelings (caring, empathy, compassion, and even love) are grounded in a discourse of universal morality, often resort to a sentimental-oriented discourse of suffering that remains superficial, and engage in politically-correct performances (Boltanski 1999). In so doing, such feelings often disguise other feelings which are deeply rooted in one's subjectivity, yet must be soothed politically – such as disgust for the non-White Other. The sentimental framing of the Other's suffering, Berlant (2004) explains, remains at a superficial level and fails to acknowledge that this suffering is the effect of socio-economic relations of violence, oppression, and poverty. Most importantly, such expressions of caring fail to recognize how they are embedded in modalities of racism and social inequality perpetuated by assuming that declarations of caring are enough to alleviate the other's suffering.

An example of how the entanglement of racism and racialized emotions of disgust takes place in schools is found in Zembylas's (2011) study of the emotional geographies enacted in multicultural schools in the Republic of Cyprus. The 2011 study explicates how ethnically-dominant Greek-Cypriot teachers and students display emotional disgust for minoritized Turkish-speaking students. Although some teachers express feelings of sympathy and care for Turkish-speaking students, their negative emotions are manifested in everyday life at school. Emotions of disgust – often disguised in socially-appropriate forms, yet other times expressed bluntly – essentially "script" the emotional geographies of exclusion. The alignment of bodily and social space is evident in how disgust limits the movement of Turkish-speaking students in social space. Explicit and implicit expressions of disgust by Greek-Cypriot students work to secure social norms and power relations. This relates to Boler's (1999) feminist politics of emotions in that social control of emotions is in part an exertion of hegemony. If schools – with all their characters – are implicit in reinforcing emotions such as disgust, they are using the social institution of education to enact hegemonic social control. Emotions then become a larger process of how we consent to hegemony.

Considering how emotions might function as a site of perpetuating social control and hegemony, the work by Trainor (2008) and Winans (2010) is helpful in understanding how the emotional rules at home and school influence White students in ways that make racist speech persuasive or permissible. By attending to students' varied approaches to race through their emotional expressions (e.g., writing), Winans urges us to explore how emotional learning informs students' ideas about race and how these emotions may re-inscribe or challenge dominant social beliefs. Like Trainor and Winans, I am interested in understanding how whiteness ideologies are influential to students' approaches of race and racism. I depart from these theorists however, because I want to explore this issue in the context of teacher education, particularly in relation to how some emotional performances function to disguise others.

With respect to teacher education, the phenomenon of how disgust is often disguised as caring is particularly interesting because care, sympathy, compassion, and love are emotions that are routinely performed by teacher candidates (who are predominantly middle-class White females) and embedded in teacher education (see Fay & Funk, 1995; Palmer, 2007). Statements like, "I never owned slaves," or "Why are you making me feel like I am a racist?!" documented over the years are indicative of how racial angst gets projected onto another person rather than self-explored (Matias, 2013a). As Bonilla-Silva (2006) argues, "... projection is part of our normal equipment to defend ourselves" (p. 63) in situations of racial angst. However, instead of focusing on why one feels the need to defend oneself as "non-racist," projection averts the focus of the initial emotion. Thus, we argue that if we, as teacher educators, fail to investigate the complexity of these underlying emotions and the processes of masking one's "true" emotions for fear of being called a racist, there is a great possibility that our anti-racist endeavor is compromised and weakened.

Yet there is scant literature theorizing how these performative emotions by pre-service teachers are not exempted from the subjectivities and positionalities of their white identities (Leonardo & Zembylas, 2013). Ultimately, to engage in a genuine process of antiracism that acknowledges the emotional complexities of whiteness, we need to explore which emotions undergird teachers' race-related dispositions that mimic Juror B37. Since there exists an overwhelming presence of whiteness in teacher education (Sleeter, 2001), how does whiteness work in emotional ways that position urban students of Color poorly? Not interrogating plausibilities of disgust in teachers risks recycling their disgust for their students of Color and the families and communities that they come from, a disgust that students of Color internalize (Brown, 2003; DeCuir & Dixson, 2004; Pyke & Dang, 2003). This emotional geography is not much different from Zembylas's (2011) study on the emotional disgust of Turkish-speaking students by Greek-Cypriots. The bottom line is that the disguise of disgust by Whites and the internalization of disgust by students of Color reifies racist structures.

ANALYZING TEACHER CANDIDATES' EMOTIONS ON RACE AND WHITENESS

Racialized Emotions

Emotions are not estranged when it comes to their expressions in teaching and teacher education. I witness these expressions of emotion each day in teaching my course, mentoring my cohorts, and organizing programmatic functions for my U.S. urban teacher education program. Upon arriving to class, I regularly ask why my students want to become urban school teachers; for, becoming an urban school teacher entails a deepened understanding of poverty, students of Color, and multilingualism, ideas that my students – who are often monolingual-English, White middle-class, females – rarely experience. They reply using emotional expressions of "loving kids," "hoping to give back" and "passionately supporting education." Some even go as far as to write in their assignments that becoming an urban teacher is about how they "will promote unity, equity, peace, and love in [their] classroom."

Yet, when asked whether they believe themselves to be an antiracist educators – an essential component to social justice, equity, and urban education (Gillborn, 2008) – some students responded with answers that unveil a colorblind racist discourse. We provide three examples below:

> I don't believe myself to be antiracist. I believe we should all be color blind. It's in human nature to have to be better than someone else in some way.

> Racism is not an issue for me. Therefore, I have a hard time saying that I am an anti-racist educator, meaning I don't plan on going out of my way to show special treatment to students of color.

> I do not believe in race but in human character.

Racial Equity is Human Equity

These answers express a sense of normalized colorblind racist discourse, as if it is normal and natural that "human nature/character" has racial superiority. "But, as social scientists know quite well," writes Bonilla-Silva (2010), "few things that happen in the social world are 'natural,' particularly things pertaining to racial matters" (p. 37). When the second student responded with "I don't plan on going out of my way," s/he assumes that people of Color are given preferential treatment based on race, without acknowledging how Whites are the supreme benefactors of U.S. economics (Lipsitz, 2006), housing (Oliver & Shapiro, 1997), and education (Leonardo, 2009). According to Bonilla-Silva (2010), this is just another way of "calling Blacks 'nigger' softly" because it assumes much about the U.S. affirmative action policies that are viewed by American Whites as preferential treatment of people of Color (p. 54). Interpretively, although these White teacher candidates profess love, care, and hope for humanity, their students, and teaching, they nevertheless continue to make prejudicial assumptions. Interpretively, this unveils their deeply rooted aversion for people of Color and the necessary process to normalize whiteness.

In the course from which these statements were drawn, my teacher candidates explore CRT and how African American and Latino urban students experience a racialized and white supremacist U.S. education. Specifically, the students read about Ladson-Billings (1998), Lewis and Manno (2011), Hayes (2010), and Yosso and Garcia (2007). When learning about the material, one student admittedly revealed a sense of shame as a result of her feelings of disgust she had felt for African Americans.

> I've never thought of myself as racist, I've had many meaningful relationships with people of many ethnicities. However, I cannot deny the fact that I found African American behaviors annoying.

Another student revealed how he felt about African Americans. Instead of demonstrating his learning based on the course readings and lectures, he went out of his way to project his discomfort and disgust with African Americans by positing that he was a victim of reverse racism for being White:

> I feel racism is a learned behavior, whether they can admit it to themselves or not. If I were to walk into an all-Black barbershop, I would get stared at just as much as the reverse.

Both teacher candidates reveal their feelings toward African Americans as "annoying" or feeling as if Blacks use reverse racism. The latter even conflates systemic racism on people of Color (such as U.S. racial profiling and racial housing discrimination) to getting "stared at." Nonetheless, both sentiments suggest a similar "politics of disgust" as seen in Juror B37's comment about African American culture. The underlying concern here is that these are the very same teacher candidates who are initially professing a deep loving passion and commitment for social justice in urban education. Essentially, how can one continue to express emotional displays of love for urban teaching and urban schools while simultaneously carrying pejorative views of people of Color?

Racialized emotions are also expressed with whiteness ideology which presents itself as having an epistemology of ignorance (Mills, 2007). Another teacher candidate expressed how she was becoming aware of her white privilege, yet at the same time said things that questioned whether she truly understood her whiteness beyond professing that she was learning (about) it:

> I do understand that I have a very privileged position since I come from a middle-class, white background, but I do not know what exactly that means or how to move forward.

At first glance, identifying white privilege is a positive step, for how does one engage in antiracist projects if one cannot identify her/himself as a racialized being? Yet, this epiphanic moment is undermined when she described her actions, which are based on a politics of disgust for the Other:

> It is really tough for me to be honest with myself about my own biases. For example, on the light rail going home from class on Thursday, a young woman of color asked to borrow my phone to make a call. Beyond being a little uncomfortable about letting a stranger use my phone, I found myself jumping to conclusions about her background and why she didn't have a phone to begin with. Since I had just come from class, I was distinctly aware of how natural and easy it was for me to make those judgments, even though I did not know this young woman at all!

Importantly, one teacher candidate was open to reveal his disgust. After a class activity in which students visited an urban school to interview various people of Color, he reflected on his hesitation:

> I had to question whether it was "wrong" of me to be "disgusted" by the prospect of interviewing several types of individuals on the worksheet.

31

Here, the teacher candidate is so forthcoming with his emotional disgust for interviewing people of Color that he hesitated in completing the task. Instead of employing a strategic discursive maneuver (Bonilla-Silva, 2010) to feign white antiracism, he was critically reflective about his sense of disgust for people of Color. Needless to say, although this is problematic in many ways, it is a necessary step to understanding how teacher candidates may gradually develop a critical vocabulary for analyzing their own emotions, as well as emotions in their classrooms (Winans, 2010; Zembylas, 2012).

The Emotions of Whiteness Ideology

Some of the students used an emotional framework that hegemonically places whiteness at the center of racial discourse. This process erroneously recategorizes and redefines hegemonic meanings of race in favor of white interests, a co-option that keeps white emotions unfettered. For example, instead of recognizing the U.S. sociopolitical nature of being called "people of Color" as opposed to "colored" people, the following teacher candidate went on to belittle the terminology and re-classify people of Color as "non-White," which ultimately centers whiteness as normal. Another teacher candidate relied on the morality discourse of how Whites are not evil despite engaging in historical acts of racial discrimination, a discourse that once again focuses discussions of race on intent instead of impact:

> I have a hard time with the term "people of Color." I believe that everyone has a color as no one's skin is invisible. I understand that people use the term to be inoffensive, but I don't know if this term is a blanket term for everyone non-White, or if it's addressing a specific race, such as African American or Hispanic.

> Well I agree that White people have been terrible to a lot of different kinds of people – Black people, Muslim[s], homosexuals, and pretty much anyone different from us, but I'm far from an evil person.

Here, the two students engage in normative white rhetoric. The term *non-White* or normalizing whiteness as "not different" places whiteness at the center and all others in a "non" category. That is, other racial groups are deemed different to "us" and "we" are inherently the center, normal, and given. Although the first student professes that he believes everyone has skin color, which devalues the racialized experiences of those categorized as Black or Brown in America, and asserts that he is "definitely" an antiracist educator because he believes one should not "favor one race over another," he later assumes a female professor of Color to be impartial to him because of his White race. When asked how his learning about race, class, and gender might be differently taught by a female professor of Color who grew up in poverty, as opposed to a White, middle-class male professor, he responded with a presumed bias of reverse discrimination:

I might also feel judged based on the color of my skin, but would probably relax as I became more familiar with the professor.

Often engaged is the presumption that people of Color are racists to Whites in discussions of race (Leonardo & Porter, 2010). According to Bonilla-Silva (2010), this is the racial rhetorical tool of "they are the racist ones," which is defensive projection (p. 63). When projecting the presumed emotional bias and racial motivations onto the female professor of Color, one "avoid[s] the responsibility and feeling good about [oneself]" (p. 64). Similar to the racial attitudes about interracial marriage captured by Bonilla-Silva (2010), this student "couches" his concern by expressing the need for heightened sensitivity and consciousness. However, he does not recognize his own gendered and racial biases. In fact, he claims he would "relax" once he became more "familiar" with a female professor of Color, which thus suggests an assumed tension solely due to her presence as a person of Color. Centering whiteness as the victims and conveniently overlooking racial and gender biases are nonetheless apparent in the response of this student. All this is happening while he proclaims "I definitely believe myself to be an antiracist educator committed to racial equity."

This sentiment is not gender specific: many White females express a similar feeling. For example, during the class many White female teacher candidates discussed their commitment to antiracist teaching, often professing their desire for racial equity inside and outside of the classrooms. Four examples of this are captured below:

I am well on my way to become [sic] an antiracist and I am very committed to racial equity in and outside of the classroom.

I definitely believe myself to be an antiracist educator committed to racial equity. The most important part of teaching to me is helping my students learn something, no matter what their race or ethnicity.

I can say I am actively antiracist. However, I can also say there are times when I become a passive racist.

Absolutely, yes. I feel that I am not at all a racist educator.

These pageant-like antiracist responses starkly contrast with the feelings displayed throughout the course. Particularly, the first excerpt above comes from a White, female, middle-class teacher candidate who often spoke about her commitment to racial equity. However, this was undermined when she shared her experiences in taking an African American Periods and Personalities course as an undergraduate. She claimed that her Black professor talked much about white privilege and, because of that, she felt so uncomfortable that she dropped the class:

I felt like I was being called evil. I was so ashamed of who I was in that moment that I dropped the class; I probably should have stayed in it to get a genuine understanding to feel stereotyped and uncomfortable, but I didn't because I was so ashamed of being White in that class.

Here, this teacher candidate quickly announces that she had a Black professor and took an African American Studies course. However, she associates learning about systematic white privilege and supremacy from the professor's lecture to her personal identity as a White female. In doing so, she does not actualize her proclaimed commitment to racial equity because her emotions were too overwhelming to even learn about the mechanisms of white privilege, let alone engage in processes that challenge it. In fact, she dropped out of the course, claiming she now knew what it is like to be racially discriminated against. This misunderstanding perverts her understanding of race dynamics – as if hundreds of years of U.S. racial discrimination against Blacks is equivalent to feeling "evil" in a course on African American experiences. This has major implications on how teacher education is run.

In another instance, the same White, middle-class male who proclaimed his commitment to racial equity above revealed what he knew of race and racism:

> I really thought I was being singled out because I am White. And because I am White I felt like I was being blamed for all the problems in the educational and social systems. I thought all of this just because of the word "whiteness."

Here, white emotionality is expressed in guilt, defensiveness, and anger. Interpretively, this is revealed in his word usage of "being singled out" and "blamed" when merely learning about whiteness. This type of racial understanding once again promotes a whiteness perspective on race and racism, erroneously claiming that reverse discrimination hurts Whites more than racism hurts people of Color. Of most interest is how white racialized emotions are expressed upon merely reading the word "whiteness." If one claims to not see race, nor asserts that race is not an issue, then why the emotional response to the word "whiteness"?

Overall, the emotionality of whiteness is of grave concern for us as critical race educators. If the sensibilities of teacher candidates are such that they do not even want to learn about racism or white supremacy because it is emotionally discomforting to them, and/or refuse to be corrected about racial assumptions, then how can teacher educators expect teacher candidates to muster the emotional investment needed to engage in prolonged projects of antiracist teaching beyond a mere utterance of self-professing that they are?

More problematic is the fact that, although this course took place before the first above-mentioned female teacher candidate entered the urban-focused teacher education program, she still felt righteous in proclaiming she was "well on her way" to becoming an antiracist educator. Suffice it to say that someone who is not able to complete a course on race merely because it was too emotionally unbearable to her comfort in whiteness is *not* well on her way to becoming an antiracist educator. More interesting to note is that she engages an overall sentiment of innocence by disassociation. This can be seen her response about how the learning would be different on a course about race, class, and gender if the professor was a female woman of Color who grew up in poverty, as opposed to a White, middle-class male professor:

Well, for one, you have lived it. I don't know what it feels like to be a Black student, nor do I know what it feels like to be from a family of poverty, and if I had a White middle-class professor, he wouldn't either. But you can speak first-hand on your experience and I feel like I am going to get more out of a class with first-hand experience than a class that we read stories about people's experience.

In her response, this student relies on a normative rhetoric of whiteness which assumes a lack of white racial knowledge precisely because of one's white racial identity. This is seen again in a White male teacher candidate's question during the course: "I don't have the experience of growing up as a minority, [so] how is this going to affect my ability to teach a multicultural class?" As Mills (2007) so argues, Whites must stop feigning a racial epistemology of ignorance by virtue of being White, lest be complicit in recycling racism.

The Projection of Racial Angst on to People of Color

The focus on race, racism, and white supremacy in the course I teach is concrete. However, instead of critically reflecting on what whiteness means for the majority of White teacher candidates, many project their racial angst onto their future urban students of Color and even their female professor of Color. This can be seen in their line of inquiries or statements about their future career as teachers:

How, as a White male, am I going to educate the ethnic minority when they may see me as the oppressor?

How am I going to prove I am antiracist when people of Color are probably going to see me as a racist based on the fact that I am White and have probably benefitted from being White?

How will my urban student see me? Will they just see me as the White oppressor?

These statements project racial angst onto people of Color by assuming a reverse discrimination. Instead of self-interrogating whiteness, or even entertaining how it can manifest individually, the focus of race is again displaced onto people of Color. In the first statement, this male teacher candidate places the burden of race and racism on his students of Color, claiming that it is *they* who see him as an oppressor. Keep in mind, at this point in the program teacher candidates have yet to enter a student teaching context and therefore have not been actually exposed to an urban school. Instead of asking how his racially-privileged role might encourage enactments of his whiteness and how that may impact ways in which he teaches urban students of Color, he immediately deflects and projects the racial discomfort onto urban students of Color for blaming him for being racist.

In the second response, this teacher candidate again invokes her racial identity as White, yet instead of critically interrogating why people often see Whites as racist and how she might benefit from being White, she projects her racial angst onto her students. By claiming that she will not be able to reach her students because they will assume she is racist merely because she is White, she places the burden of race once again on people of Color and resists acknowledging her role in the systemic manifestation of whiteness. As Leonardo (2009) points out, in resisting, Whites "further their own supremacy" (p. 117). However, most interesting, is that all the responses engage in what Leonardo (2009) calls "throwing the White race card," an action used to "invoke race in a manner that maintains their 'innocence'" (p. 116). Opportunistically using their white racial identity to feign innocence and victimization becomes a process that maintains white supremacy. In fact, it becomes a collective white supremacist imagination that upholds the "white lies" so articulated by Daniels (1997).

As scholars of race who promote social justice with antiracism, what concerns Zembylas and me considerably is the fact that these teacher candidates use the terminology of equity and social justice to present themselves as socially-just urban teachers, yet have repressed their deepened feelings about people of Color until they are challenged, a process which surfaces their emotional discomfort and eventually their distaste – moreover their *disgust* – for people of Color. Interpretively, this emotional projection reifies the superiority of whiteness in that people of Color are deemed both the scapegoat and the symbolic reminder – and sometimes erroneously as the agitator – of the racial angst Whites may feel about race. Based on psychoanalytic racial interpretations of this phenomenon (see Fanon, 1967; Thandeka, 1999), shoving this racial "baggage" onto the shoulders of people of Color is done in part because of emotionally repressed notions of race. Yet in doing so, Whites release themselves of their own emotional culpability of race. This process then develops a deep shame in how Whites may experience humanity, hence Ignatiev and Garvey's (1996) assertion that "treason to whiteness is loyalty to humanity" (p. 10).

Conversely, if Whites avoid responsibility for their own racialized emotions, they not only purport whiteness to elevated status, they also engage in treason to humanity. For example, one female teacher candidate explained how she was committed to equity claiming, "I want my students to see themselves as equals to me, the teacher, and that their input is invaluable to the process of everyone's learning, including mine." This teacher candidate went as far as to profess America's prophetic "Golden Rule" wherein one does to another as one would want done onto oneself:

> I've always tried to live by the "Golden Rule" *per se*; we are all the same, and if a person was nice to me, I was nice to them. I have good friends of varying backgrounds; I embrace culture.

Although the language of this statement suggests a commitment to equity and even portrays a deep empathy for others, this student later shared a story about her feelings toward Muslims:

I've relied on a "single story" to dictate my feelings toward a group of people. Recently, on a flight to Las Vegas, I recall walking behind a Muslim family, and thinking, "I hope they aren't on my plane!"

Apparently, her professing of equity and empathy are tainted by her racist inner feelings toward certain racial groups, feelings that defy humanity. Specifically, her disgust for Muslims taints her disposition, a disposition or epistemology that nonetheless will enter the multicultural classroom with her. Another student wrote about his underlying disgust for Muslims:

I felt inspired to learn, but at the same time embarrassed that I'm a grown man and I don't know anything about Muslims. The only thing I really knew was that typically terrorists follow some form of this faith.

Both these students had an underlying racial disgust for Muslims, an emotion so repressed that it can rarely be acknowledged, let alone explored. Interestingly, because this disgust was so repressed, they felt proud to announce how they were committed to the program's socially-just philosophies. We provide two examples below:

The entire disposition of the program is to fight against social and racial injustice, which happens to involve education. When deciding last year what I wanted to do with my life, I wrote down some things that I am passionate about, things that I am good at, and my overall goal as a man. Essentially, everything I wrote down came back to teaching and giving students a chance at an opportunity of success and having a big impact along the way relationally. I want to fight the hard battles within education for justice. I want to make it my life's work because I am passionate about it and about the children it will affect.

I want to remember that I want to fight injustice and use education as a platform.

Apparently these teacher candidates were openly declaring commitment to the program by using language typically found in socially-just educational and teaching literature. Yet the genuineness that undergirds this open declaration is undermined when repressed feelings of disgust begin to be unveiled throughout the course.

SO WHAT NOW?

Based on the overarching action research project for the program and the epistemological lens of whiteness critique, the aims of this chapter were to: (1) show how professions of care and love in teacher candidates' discourses about people of Color often hide conscious or unconscious feelings of disgust; (2) examine how whiteness ideology is entangled with racialized emotions and racial angst; and, (3) consider the implications for teacher education, especially in urban settings. In general, our analysis from this ongoing action research project showed that the individual emotional experiences of the teacher candidates were connected with larger historical, political, and social structures (i.e., white privilege and whiteness ideology) which, in turn, supplied the meanings by which these individuals interpreted their emotional encounters with issues of race and racism.

Emotions like caring and love are commonplace in teacher education (hooks, 2003; Nieto, 2003; Noddings, 2003). However, caring, just like emotions of disgust and pity, is not exempt from the tentacles of power dynamics. That is, caring is value-laden in that power and hegemony, rendering definitive expressions of caring that are normalized and deemed appropriate, while subjugating other expressions. Our analysis here reiterates the argument made by Valenzuela (1999) that although teachers claim to be caring, they may lack an *authentic* care for their underprivileged students due to racial and cultural bias. In her words, caring is when teachers and other school personnel "depart from their penchant of *aesthetic* caring and embrace a more *authentically* caring ideology and practice," one that gets "ideologically wedded" (p. 263) to underprivileged groups' struggles for equal educational opportunity. Emotionally speaking, Valenzuela provides a critique of how emotions can present themselves *in appearance only* or sentimentalized as opposed to genuinely feeling them, leading to voyeurism and passivity (Boltanski 1999; Cohen 2001; Geras 1999). Similarly, in the accounts we offer in this chapter, we identify the emotional ambivalence of teacher candidates who profess feelings of caring for the underprivileged Other while at the same time express racialized emotions, repressed disgust, and racial angst for people of Color, as grounded in whiteness ideology (Leonardo & Zembylas, 2013).

For example, consider the racialized emotion of shame present in some accounts of teacher candidates who "admit" that they have been racist or when recognizing their white privilege. Undoubtedly, expressions of shame and the recognition of white privilege are notable because, as Thandeka (1999) suggests, Whites have experienced a racial trauma or abuse since childhood. This abuse forces White children to adopt a colorblind ideology (Trainor, 2008; Winans, 2010) despite bearing witness to racial reality, lest they be ostracized from their white community. Although Thandeka's psychoanalytic and emotional analysis of white racialization provides a framework to understanding the deep shame of whiteness, it does not articulate how that shame projects itself as disgust for people of Color – something that becomes evident, explicitly or implicitly, in some of the accounts shared here. Equally problematic is the disguise of disgust behind benign feelings such as caring, also seen in several emotional responses by teacher candidates. As it is shown in these accounts, adopting whiteness ideology becomes a shameful racial project and, when this is acknowledged, the emotions are projected onto those who remind the person of her or his white self. Since people of Color "wear" their racial identities literally on their skins, they serve as a constant reminder to those so inoculated in whiteness that they are living a lie of colorblindness. The psychological result for those who adopt whiteness ideology is that they despise people of Color and are in some way disgusted (Ahmed, 2004).

Furthermore, often invoked in teacher candidates' accounts is the reverse discrimination rhetoric. However, as Leonardo (2009) reminds us, people of Color "do not have the apparatus of power to enforce" (p. 119), therefore the notion of reverse racism is one that misconstrues the true operations of U.S. white supremacy. Yet not articulated in Leonardo's postulation is when such rhetoric engages what is happening to the individual emotionally. That is, by engaging a discourse of victimology, this strategy harbors resentment toward those whom Whites perceive to be the perpetrators. This harboring of resentment and disgust for the perpetrators concerns us deeply in that the majority of teacher candidates engage this discourse on topics of race, yet profess they are ready to teach urban students of Color with antiracist pedagogy.

The repression of raced emotions of shame (Thandeka, 1999), disgust (Ahmed, 2004), and emotional distancing (Matias, 2013a) are hindrances to cultivating deep emotional investment to antiracism. Herein lies the contradiction of our mission for racial justice. If we, as teacher educators, are to train the next generation of urban teachers with the ideas of social justice and equity, and ensure prolonged emotional investment to it, how can we guarantee their commitment if they repress their innermost feelings? That is, how do you help someone realize they aren't truly committing to a cause, if they refuse to admit that they are not emotionally committed in the first place?

Without dismissing the numerous and multifaceted challenges that have been pointed out about the disguise of disgust into caring and how teacher educators could respond strategically and productively, here we want to build on what Lindquist (2004) calls "strategic empathy" as a pedagogical strategy to respond to these incidents. Lindquist is concerned with how educators in higher education can instill a sense of criticality in those students who fail to recognize their conscious or unconscious racist or nationalist feelings towards others, thus she describes how she adopts a strategy of empathetic engagement with students' uncritical positions. Reflecting on this strategy, Lindquist writes, "What made this strategy work, I think, was my willingness to make myself strategically naïve in two moments: first, in seeking advice about *how* we should conduct discussions … and then later, when (working hard against my own emotional need to negatively evaluate some of the perspectives I was hearing …) I worked to communicate empathy for their positions *as affective responses*" (pp. 203–204).

The notion of strategic empathy is suggested here as a point of departure for teacher educators who want to delve into the hindrances that prevent a deep emotional investment to antiracism (see also Boler, 2004). This pedagogical strategy constitutes a way of recognizing that preservice teachers and teacher educators live within spaces of "troubled knowledge" (Jansen, 2009) – that is, knowledge which is emotionally discomforting for everyone involved in the process, yet in differential ways and for different reasons altogether (see also Albrecht-Crane, 2005,

Zembylas, 2013a, 2013b). This notion assumes that, in order to be truly effective, teacher educators have to be willing to use empathy strategically to engage in in-depth critical inquiry of their students' troubled knowledge, i.e., an emotional willingness to engage in the difficult work of empathizing with views that one may find unacceptable or offensive (Zembylas, 2012). Notably, while empathy involves recognizing the other's complex point of view, it does not require *adopting* the other's point of view (Halpern & Weinstein, 2004). This sort of empathy, which Zembylas (2012) calls "reconciliatory empathy," involves emotional openness to traumatic racial injury in whatever form it is manifested, and tolerates ambivalence for paradoxes as an enriching part of creating an ongoing workable relationship with the Other. In taking sides too early, the teacher educator will make it impossible to constructively navigate through and transform these troubled knowledges and emotions (Jansen, 2009). As Georgis and Kennedy (2009) write, "The truth of racial history and experience can be taught, but not in such a way that it forecloses our capacity to become new people in relation to this history, or indeed, to imagine the world altogether differently" (p. 20).

But for strategic empathy to succeed, a pedagogy of discomfort (Boler, 1999; Boler & Zembylas, 2003; Zembylas & Boler, 2002) may also be needed. A pedagogy of discomfort, as an educational approach, highlights the need for educators and students alike to move outside their comfort zones. Pedagogically, this approach assumes that discomforting emotions play a constitutive role in challenging dominant beliefs, social habits, and normative practices that sustain racism and social inequities, and in creating possibilities for individual and social transformation (see also Leibowitz et al., 2010; Matias & Allen, 2014). Most importantly, pedagogies of strategic empathy or pedagogies of discomfort suggest developing a mode of teaching and learning from troubled knowledge – a mode that produces a new ethical relationality and emotional culture in the classroom (Day, 2004; Liston & Garrison, 2004; Winans, 2010; Zembylas, 2010). Teacher candidates and teacher educators who struggle with traumatic racial injury bring different emotional histories with them to school; in tracing these histories of refusal, shame, anger, resentment, disgust and so on, it becomes clear that, in order to move beyond injury toward building emotional investment to antiracism, moralistic positions need to be avoided. Therefore, developing pedagogies that utilize strategic empathy and pedagogies of discomfort would mean being committed to develop affective connections and investments without dismissing the explicit and critical interrogation of past emotional histories, knowledges, and experiences (Zembylas, 2012). We, as teacher educators, have to be prepared to accept that this process is long and painstaking, and that it will be full of emotional landmines; but, it is of utmost strategic importance to expose the insidious emotional power of racism and its affective investments in White teacher candidates' identities. Perhaps it is more valuable to provide alternatives that do not alienate these White teacher candidates but gradually construct their emotional commitment to antiracist projects, rather than taking sides early on and making them feel guilty for the shame and disgust they experience.

Finally, with respect to the ongoing action research study, we encourage practitioners to ensure that the assessments used to appraise the teacher candidates' racial knowledge are continually amendable to address the nuances and ever-evolving dynamics of race. To capture personal affiliations of race, we recommend including the use of Jing[2] videos instead of solely relying on written session reflection. Doing so captures a visual representation of our teacher candidates' responses to the readings, discussions, and learning process. We also recommend the use of digital storytelling. Such a technique provides a medium for self-reflexivity, particularly on how the teacher candidate views her or his own emotional journey in understanding whiteness in teaching. Finally, the use of the "counterstory" method of CRT might be taken up productively to present an alternate point of view about what the experience of the teacher education classroom might be like for White students and teachers, vis-à-vis for students and teachers of Color.

CONCLUSION

In this chapter, I have argued that racialized emotions in urban teacher education settings need to be identified, exposed, and analyzed in both sensitive and critical ways if teacher educators want to break the cycle of sentimentalism and disgust. Like many other aspects of human life, emotions are value-laden, positional, and are not exempt from the power relations that structure its expression. When saying you care becomes a false profession of caring, the role of disgust must be interrogated, lest it be caught up in the painful cycle of emotional falsities. If, as critical educators, we commit ourselves to racial justice, then it would benefit us to begin with ourselves, our identities, and the very emotions we harbor in conjunction to the racial positionalities we occupy. Disgust is such a difficult emotion, yet one worthy enough for analysis. In this painful moment where the U.S. continues to mourn the death of Trayvon Martin, a young, African American teenage boy who was stalked, shot, then murdered in 2012 by a racist, we need to take a moment to grieve the disgusting situation of race; for our lives and the lives of our children need it.

NOTES

[1] This chapter was originally co-authored with Michalinos Zembylas, Ph.D. and is reprinted here with permission. Matias, C. E., & Zembylas, M. (2014). "When saying you care is not really caring": Emotions of disgust, whiteness ideology, and teacher education. *Critical Studies in Education*, 55(3), 319–337.

[2] See https://www.techsmith.com/tutorial-jing-record-video.html

REFERENCES

Ahmed, S. (2004). *The cultural politics of emotion.* Edinburgh, UK: Edinburgh University Press.
Ahmed, S. (2012). *On being included: Racism and diversity in institutional life.* Durham, NC: Duke University Press.

Albrecht-Crane, C. (2005). Pedagogy as friendship: Identity and affect in the conservative classroom. *Cultural Studies, 19*, 491–514.

Berlant, L. (2004). *Compassion: The culture and politics of an emotion.* New York, NY: Routledge.

Boler, M. (1999). *Feeling power: Emotions and education.* London: Routledge.

Boler, M. (2004). Teaching for hope: The ethics of shattering world views. In D. Liston & J. Garrison (Eds.), *Teaching, learning and loving: Reclaiming passion in educational practice* (pp. 117–131). New York, NY: RoutledgeFalmer.

Boler, M., & Zembylas, M. (2003). Discomforting truths: The emotional terrain of understanding differences. In P. Tryfonas (Ed.), *Pedagogies of difference: Rethinking education for social justice* (pp. 110–136). New York, NY: Routledge.

Boltanski, L. (1999). *Distant suffering: Morality, media and politics.* Cambridge, UK: Cambridge University Press.

Bonilla-Silva, E. (2006). *Racism without racists: Color-blind racism and the persistence of racial inequality in the United States.* Lanham, MD: Rowman & Littlefield.

Bonilla-Silva, E. (2010). *Racism without racists: Color-blind racism and the Persistence of racial inequality in America.* New York, NY: Rowman & Littlefield.

Brown, T. N. (2003). Critical race theory speaks to the sociology of mental health: Mental health problems produced by racial stratification. *Journal of Health and Social Behavior, 44*, 292–301.

Chouliaraki, L. (2010). Post-humanitarianism: Humanitarian communication beyond a politics of pity. *International Journal of Cultural Studies, 13*, 107–126.

Cohen, S. (2001). *States of denial: Knowing about atrocities and suffering.* Cambridge, UK: Polity Press.

Daniels, J. (1997). *White lies: Race, class, gender and sexuality in White supremacist discourse.* New York, NY: Routledge.

Day, C. (2004). *A passion for teaching.* New York, NY: RoutledgeFalmer.

DeCuir, J. T., & Dixson, A. D. (2004). So when it comes out, they aren't that surprised that it is there: Using critical race rheory as a tool of analysis of race and racism in education. *Educational Researcher, 33*(5), 26–31.

Duncan, G. A. (2002). Critical race theory and method: Rendering race in urban ethnographic research. *Qualitative Inquiry, 8*(1), 85–104.

Fanon, F. (1967). *Black skin, White masks.* New York, NY: Grove Press.

Fay, J., & Funk, D. (1995). *Teaching with love and logic: Taking control of the classroom.* Golden, CO: The Love and Logic Press.

Georgis, D., & Kennedy, R. M. (2009). Touched by injury: Toward an educational theory of anti-racist humanism. *Ethics and Education, 4*(1), 19–30.

Geras, N. (1999). *The contract of mutual indifference: Political philosophy after the Holocaust.* London: Verso.

Gillborn, D. (2008). *Racism and education: Coincidence or conspiracy?* London: Routledge.

Halpern, J., & Weinstein, H. M. (2004). Rehumanizing the other: Empathy and reconciliation. *Human Rights Quarterly, 26*, 561–583.

Hayes, K. (2010). Why teach in urban settings? In S. Steinberg (Ed.), *19 urban questions: Teaching in the city.* New York, NY: Peter Lang.

Hayes, C., & Juárez, B. G. (2009). You showed your whiteness: You don't get a 'good' White people's medal. *International Journal of Qualitative Studies in Education, 22*(6), 729–744.

hooks, b. (2004). *The will to change: Men, masculinity, and love.* New York, NY: Atria Books.

Hook, D. (2005). Affecting whiteness: Racism as technology of affect. *International Journal of Psychology, 16*, 74–99.

Hook, D. (2012). Theorizing "race trouble": On racism, racialing practice, and the question of affect. *Theory & Psychology, 22*(5), 707–712.

Ignatiev, N., & Garvey, J. (Eds.). (1996). *Race traitor.* New York, NY: Routledge.

Jansen, J. (2009). *Knowledge in the blood: Confronting race and the apartheid past.* Palo Alto, CA: Stanford University Press.

Kemmis, S., & McTaggart, R. (2005). Participatory action research: Communicative action and the public sphere. In N. K. Denzin & Y. S. Lincoln (Eds.), *The Sage handbook of qualitative research* (pp. 559–603). Thousand Oaks, CA: Sage.

Ladson-Billings, G. (1998). From Soweto to the South Bronx: African Americans and colonial education in the United States. In C. Torres & T. Mitchell (Eds.), *Sociology of education: Emerging perspectives* (pp. 247–264). New York, NY: SUNY Press.

Leibowitz, B., Bozalek, V., Carolissen, R., Nicholls, L., Rohleder, P., & Swartz, L. (2010). Bringing the social into pedagogy: Unsafe learning in an uncertain world. *Teaching in Higher Education, 15*(2), 123–133.

Leonardo, Z. (2009). *Race, whiteness, and education*. New York, NY: Routledge.

Leonardo, Z., & Porter, R. K. (2010). Pedagogy of fear: Toward a Fanonian theory of 'safety' in race dialogue. *Race Ethnicity and Education, 13*(2), 139–157.

Leonardo, Z., & Zembylas, M. (2013). Whiteness as technology of affect: Implications for educational theory and praxis. *Equity and Excellence in Education, 46*(1), 150–165.

Lewis, A., & Manno, M. (2011). The best education for some: Race and schooling in the United States Today. In M. Jung, J. Vargas, & E. Bonilla-Silva (Eds.), *State of White supremacy* (pp. 93–109). Palo Alto, CA: Stanford University Press.

Lindquist, J. (2004). Class affects, classroom affectations: Working through the paradoxes of strategic empathy. *College English, 67*(2), 187–209.

Lipsitz, G. (2006). *The possessive investment in whiteness: How White people profit from identity politics*. Philadelphia, PA: Temple University Press.

Liston, D., & Garrison, J. (Eds.). (2004). *Teaching, learning and loving: Reclaiming passion in educational practice*. New York, NY: RoutledgeFalmer

Matias, C. E. (2013a). On the "Flip" side: A teacher educator of color unveiling the dangerous minds of white teacher candidates. *Teacher Education Quarterly, 40*(2), 53–73.

Matias, C. E. (2013b). Check yo'self before yo' wreck yo'self and our kids: From culturally responsive White teachers? To culturally responsive White teachers! *Interdisciplinary Journal of Teaching and Learning, 3*(2), 68–81.

Matias, C. E., Viesca, K. M., Garrison-Wade, D. F., Tandon, M., & Galindo, R. (2014). What is critical whiteness doing in OUR nice field like critical race theory?: Applying CRT and CWS to understand the White imaginations of White teacher candidates. *Equity & Excellence in Education, 47*(3), 289–304.

Matias, C. E., & Allen, R. L. (2014). Loving whiteness to death: Sadomasochism, emotionality and the possibility of a humanizing love. *Berkeley Review of Education, 4*(2), 285–309.

Mills, C. (2007). White ignorance. In S. Sullivan & N. Tuana (Eds.), *Race and epistemologies of ignorance*. Albany, NY: State University of New York Press.

Nieto, S. (2003). *What keeps teachers going?* New York, NY: Teachers College Press.

Noddings, N. (2003). *Happiness and education*. Cambridge, UK: Cambridge University Press.

Oliver, M., & Shapiro, T. (1997). *Black wealth/White wealth: A new perspective on racial inequality*. New York, NY: Routledge.

Palmer, P. J. (2010). *The courage to teach: Exploring the inner landscape of a teacher's life*. San Francisco, CA: John Wiley & Sons.

Porter, E. (2006). Can politics practice compassion? *Hypatia, 21*, 97–123.

Pyke, K., & Dang, T. (2003). "FOB" and "whitewashed": Identity and internalized racism among second-generation Asian Americans. *Qualitative Sociology, 26*(2), 147–172.

Sleeter, C. E. (2001). Preparing teachers for culturally diverse schools research and the overwhelming presence of whiteness. *Journal of Teacher Education, 52*(2), 94–106.

Thandeka. (1999). *Learning to be White: Money, race and god in America*. New York, NY: The Continuum.

Trainor, J. S. (2008). *Rethinking racism: Emotion, persuasion, and literacy education in an all-White high school*. Carbondale, IL: Southern Illinois University Press.

Valenzuela, A. (1999). *Subtractive schooling: US-Mexican youth and the politics of caring*. New York, NY: SUNY Press.

Whitebrook, M. (2002). Compassion as a political virtue. *Political Studies, 50*, 529–544.

Winans, A. (2010). Cultivating racial literacy in white, segregated settings: Emotions as a site of ethical engagement and inquiry. *Curriculum Inquiry, 40*(3), 475–491.

Yosso, T., & Garcia, D. (2007). "This is no slum!" A critical race theory analysis of community cultural wealth in culture clash's Chavez ravine. *Journal of Chicano Studies, 32*(1), 145–154.

Zembylas, M. (2010). Teachers' emotional experiences of growing diversity and multiculturalism in schools and the prospects of an ethic of discomfort. *Teaching and Teachers: Theory and Practice, 16*(6), 703–716.

Zembylas, M. (2011). Investigating the emotional geographies of exclusion in a multicultural school. *Emotion, Space and Society, 4*, 151–159.

Zembylas, M. (2012). Pedagogies of strategic empathy: Navigating through the emotional complexities of antiracism in higher education. *Teaching in Higher Education, 17*(2), 113–125.

Zembylas, M. (2013a). Critical pedagogy and emotion: Working through troubled knowledge in posttraumatic societies. *Critical Studies in Education, 54*(2), 176–189.

Zembylas, M. (2013b). The 'crisis of pity' and the radicalization of solidarity: Towards critical pedagogies of compassion. *Educational Studies: A Journal of the American Educational Studies Association, 49*, 504–521.

Zembylas, M., & Boler, M. (2002). On the spirit of patriotism: Challenges of a "pedagogy of discomfort." Special issue on *Education and September 11, Teachers College Record Online*. Retrieved from http://tcrecord.org

LOVING WHITENESS TO DEATH

Sadomasochism, Emotionality, and the Possibility of Humanizing Love[1]
(with Ricky Lee Allen)

IN THE BEGINNING: WHAT'S LOVE GOT TO DO WITH IT?

What's love got to do, got to do with it
What's love, but a second-hand emotion
What's love got to do, got to do with it
Who needs a heart, when a heart can be broken (Britten & Lyle, 1984)

There exists a state of emotionality that has propelled human beings to build the Taj Mahal, write constitutions for newly-found nations, and engage in generations of religious warfare. Yet despite the grandeur of such emotion, its everyday saliency and essentiality are often dismissed. According to critics, the emotion of "love" is dismissed because it is merely an irrational sentiment left unquantifiable, nonobjective, and useless in terms of evaluating the social lay of the land. And, as society-at-large prematurely lays such a verdict on love, we have yet to understand that these negative depictions are evidence of a patriarchal and racist lens unable to lift itself from the depths of love's connotations. That is, heterosexual White men, blinded by their privilege of maleness, heterodominance, and whiteness, have analyzed and interpreted love in their favor for so long that the true gravity of love as a social force gets overlooked.

The argument here is that society should reject dominant notions of love and instead embrace a *humanizing love*, one where those involved in personal or collective relationships give love so as to foster the mutual growth and healing of one another depending on their respective relational needs within traumatizing systems of oppression (Fromm, 2000). Furthermore, to more fully interrupt normative notions of love (see Sumara & Davis, 1999), we, as a society, must entertain a more womanist definition of love, one that politicizes the tenderness, duty, and womanly strength found in Black feminists and feminists of Color who resist against racism, sexism, and classism (Collins, 1989; James, 1999; Walker, 1983).

Walker (1983) argues that a womanist is "committed to survival and wholeness of entire people" (p. xi). A womanist approach goes beyond an emotional self-indulgence in feeling feelings. Rather, in a womanist understanding emotions are more politicized because, in feeling these emotions, we can understand the possibilities of bettering humanity. Womanism is a counterspace wherein women of Color recover from internalized racism and patriarchy by relearning to love themselves. Love is seemingly an integral emotion of womanist thought, and although scholars in this field have not clearly defined it, love in this discourse underlies commonly talked about emotions like "caring," which serve as proxies for love. For instance, Beauboeuf-Lefontant (2002) argues that there is a distinct womanist definition of caring in teaching teachers that "embraces the maternal, political clarity, and an ethic of risk" (p. 71) and "seeks the liberation of all, not simply themselves" (p. 72). Since the maternal is present in womanism, it becomes beneficial for creating a womanist definition of love that builds on how a mother undeniably, unconditionally, and willfully experiences a more humanizing love with the expected painful labor process and ultimate birth of her child (see Darder, 1998). That is, beyond a superficial feeling of elation, mothers who willfully experience the burden of mothering and labor illustrate a womanist humanizing love. From a womanist perspective, love is an emotion that positively binds the humanity of one person to another. It can be employed in a process for liberating humanity when given proper consideration of its magnitude.

In our inquiry into love, we seek to disrupt social constructions that limit how we believe we feel and express love, especially with regard to race. Moving beyond the patriarchal social imaginary, so, too, should society be committed to experiencing a loving, painful process toward birthing a newly-liberated social world.

Seen in a new light, love becomes a formidable, rational, and powerful frame of analysis for interpreting Whites' emotional investment in whiteness. Often minimized, emotions are as key to political life as ideologies (Boler, 1999). We have feelings about what we think; our thoughts are not detached from our bodies. We have passions that drive us to connect or not connect, to engage or not engage, to respond or not respond. And these feelings are not simply innate or natural. They are constructed politically through social interactions. We are taught that some emotions are appropriate and some should be repressed. The emotions of some are belittled, and the emotions of others are taken as normal or exemplary. Some passionately feel pain when they hear about another child of Color beaten or shot by police, while others seemingly feel nothing. As Raymond Williams (1978) notes, there are "structures of feeling" that regulate the emotional world in favor of domination.

In this chapter, originally co-written with Dr. Ricky Lee Allen, a professor from the University of New Mexico, he and I look at a particular structure of feeling: that of love and whiteness. Allen and I seek to explicate not only how Whites feel about being white, but also where the emotions of Whites – i.e., *white emotionality* – emanate from and what the consequences are for both Whites and people of Color. If race is a social construction, as most believe, then there must also be an emotional dimension that binds those who become racialized as white to one another. To better understand whiteness, it is essential to venture into this emotional world of whiteness, for ir/rationality alone cannot explain its persistence. "Reason" detached from feeling cannot adequately tell us why Whites emotionally labor on behalf of the White race to produce not only tangible laws, policies, and systemic advantages, but also an enwhitened structure of feeling. The social and political construction

46

of white emotionality is just as real, complex, and problematic as are social constructions of patriarchal masculinity (hooks, 2004). A critical study of white emotionality thus looks at how the patterns, sources, and rules of feelings can be examined to deconstruct the normative expressions, understandings, and definitions of emotions – such as love – among White folks.

While we concur that feelings of hatred, apathy, greed, and fear are important emotional dimensions of white racism, we argue that an exclusive emphasis on them constitutes a normative discourse on white emotionality that minimizes love and takes for granted its fundamental role in the formation of social group attachments and senses of self and the Other. We focus on love because it offers the potential to reimagine how we can more genuinely and wholeheartedly engage in antiracist practices. Since plenty of existing antiracist literature focuses both explicitly and implicitly on the roles of fear (Galindo & Vigil, 2006), apathy (Forman, 2004), hatred (Godfrey, 2004), and greed (Lipsitz, 1998), it behooves us to entertain how the analytical power of a critical theory of love can benefit antiracist education. After all, fear, apathy, hatred, and greed are not human needs, but love is, and it is thus more deeply motivational (Darder, 2002).

Essentially, Allen and I want to understand the emotional aspects of Whites' commitment to whiteness, specifically their understanding of loving whiteness, and ultimately the White race, because we contend that it plays a major motivational role in perpetuating a system of white domination. Much like Tina Turner's query, "What's love got to do with it," we wonder what does love – or its distortion – have to do with how Whites refuse to undo their unhealthy racial coalition and unjust structural power? Are white commitments to the White race borne of love, or rather to some other psychic condition? Said differently, is the White race a loving community, meaning one that grows love for both Whites and people of Color? If the ontological opposite of love, hope, and humanity is apathy, despair, and monstrosity, then nowhere is the study of love more crucial than in theoretical postulations about Whites' loveless membership in the White race and the phobia of the painful possibility of finding love beyond whiteness.

In documenting the "bad romance" between Whites and their whiteness, this chapter expands on Eric Fromm's (2000) critical theory of love. Although educational scholars have employed love in various ways (see Duncan-Andrade, 2009; hooks, 1996, 2001), we take particular interest in Fromm's psychoanalytic framing of love because he critiques normative theories of it. Additionally, Fromm's (2000) portraiture of the sadist and masochist dynamic provides a framework for understanding the kinds of distortions of love that womanism deconstructs.

WHAT IS LOVE?

What is love?
Baby, don't hurt me
Don't hurt me, no more (Halligan & Torello, 1993)

Some may be surprised to hear that there are scholars who debate the social meaning of love. After all, isn't love something that just happens and we "fall into" it? Doesn't making it into an academic subject ruin its thrill and mystery? These may seem like commonsense reactions, but the real, everyday experiences many of us have with love tells us that it is often elusive, infuriating, and even traumatizing. To lessen its elusiveness, we need to examine the existing patterns associated with love and unearth their social meaning. By excavating the ways that normative notions of love construct our sub/conscious, we may reveal meaningful implications for how we think about both personal and social relationships.

Media popularizes our understanding of love. Consider for example how the love industry is replete with self-help experts ready to offer simple and quick fixes to our love problems. It is a thriving industry because our normative notion of love keeps us willing to pay for answers. Despite gross characterizations of Disneyfied love in romantic comedies, the public's Hollywood obsession over who will be the next "Brangelina," and skyrocketing sales of novelties that enhance, impart, or deflect love, we have yet to truly consider the gravity love has on human relations beyond a flirty wink and a happily-ever-after.

hooks (2001) notably contributed to the love industry when she wrote a national bestseller on finding various kinds of love, while positing that love itself is more an action than an emotion. hooks rightly argues what we must do to better understand love; but positing love as primarily an action again occludes its socially-constructed embodiment of its emotionality. In other words, emphasizing action means focus is placed on what the body does with love or to make love before an examination of *how* the heart feels love and *why* it feels it (or not). Additionally, hooks states that "love allows us to enter a paradise" (p. 147), yet it is this type of depiction we critique. Love has been problematically packaged in the form of romantic fantasies and burden-free utopian societies, where there is seemingly only joy and elation, even in the face of realities like the death of loved ones. The painful and vulnerable responsibilities and emotions of love cannot be avoided.

Consider as well the *New York Times* #1 Bestseller *The 5 Love Languages: The Secret to Love That Lasts* by Dr. Gary Chapman (2010). Chapman describes what he sees as the most pressing issue of love: one just needs to understand what he calls the five "love languages" (i.e., receiving gifts, quality time, physical touch, words of affirmation, and acts of service) that are essential in supporting the feeling of being loved in a relationship. Love, according to Chapman, is simply about learning one another's love language for the sole purpose of ensuring that their "emotional tanks" remain full. In this view, love is an object or a commodity that can be poured into our emotional tanks by another. His imaginary love would have us believe that our sense of feeling full of love depends on little more than some internal fluctuating tank in need of continual filling in order for us to feel superficially better. Chapman does not reveal *why* the tank is in need of continual refilling nor entertain the social and political conditions that might cause this mysterious dissipation.

In contrast to Chapman's and hooks's normative conceptualizations of love, those engaged in a humanizing love do not feel the fear of needing to be either "filled" or "entering paradise" because humanizing love is a constant state of fullness or, better put, of unconditional love. In truly loving humanity and feeling a part of that humanity, there never exists a state of separation from it: humanizing love is not a privatized, masculinized commodity framed by conditional love. Rather, it is similar to how a mother will never run out of love for her child. Therefore, those oriented toward humanizing love should never feel the need to refill their "love tank" because our mere existence as humanized beings provides an unconditional love as our baseline. That is, I love so that you feel loved, and that feeling of love intimately connects us as human beings. Conversely, when you hurt, I hurt; yet our hurt is felt only because we love.

One of our main suggestions is that we need a more critical analysis of normative constructions of love. We need to excavate the values of our everyday feelings of love and consider whether it brings us closer to humanization or makes us more dehumanized. As mentioned above, our critical theorization of love builds largely upon the work of Fromm, a prominent figure of the Frankfurt School. Fromm (2000) posits that most so-called "loving" relationships are not actually loving, much like how womanism posits that internalized racism and patriarchy are unloving relationships. He asserts that upon birth we long for the connectedness we experienced with our mothers in the womb. We spend our lives looking for that same type of unconditional, nurturing love. It is a primal, motivational force. Without this love we are prone to feeling alone, a severe consequence of lovelessness. As Fromm (1994) puts it, "to feel completely alone and isolated leads to mental disintegration, just as physical starvation leads to death" (p. 17).

Growing up in large-scale, bureaucratic systems of domination, humans are under great pressure to overcome aloneness by giving up their individuality to submit to the socially-constructed world that is; to do otherwise means that "one stands alone and faces the world in all its perilous and overpowering aspects" (Fromm, 1994, p. 29). So although modern forms of "democracy" promote the notion of individual freedom, the reality is that people are left to deal with their fundamental issues of love on their own, privately, leaving many feeling isolated and full of anxiety; love is neither seen as a matter of public concern nor as an underlying force of everyday social practice. To make matters worse, modern societies are fundamentally structured around conflict between groups, with one amalgamation actively seeking to dominate the others (see Bell, 1992; Bowles & Gintis, 1976; Collins, 1979).

In this context, the quests for individuality and the fundamental need for love are distorted. This means that we often are unable to create healthy, loving relationships, and we opt instead for what Fromm (2000) describes as a "sadomasochistic" relationship. Although many think of sadomasochism solely as a descriptor for certain sexual behavior, the term is also a way of referring to the normative unequal power dynamics of human relationships which may or may not involve sexual intercourse. Relationships between co-workers, family members, and lovers can all be scrutinized for their sadomasochistic tendencies, a dynamic that womanism reveals in its naming of everyday misogyny.

Sadomasochistic relationships arise from a neurotic compulsion that is as much social (i.e., structural) as much as it is psychological. According to Fromm (1994), "In neurotic strivings one acts from a compulsion which has essentially a negative character: to escape an unbearable situation" (p. 153). In a sadomasochistic relationship, two entities – the sadist and the masochist – compulsively fuse to overcome their aloneness, their "unbearable situation," and they do so in a way that furthers the damaging effects of the social structure. The sadistic individual connects through the domination of another. He seeks a partner and wishes to create an attachment with a follower, a submissive, who he can control.

Per Fromm (1994), the masochist in the relationship addresses his/her fear of aloneness by attaching to the sadist via the worship of an idol, allowing him/herself to be controlled by the sadistic partner:

> [T]he masochistic strivings are caused by the desire to get rid of the individual self with all its shortcomings, conflicts, risks, doubts, and unbearable aloneness, but they only succeed in removing the most noticeable pain or they even lead to greater suffering. The irrationality of masochism, as of all other neurotic manifestations, consists in the ultimate futility of the means adopted to solve an untenable emotional situation. (p. 153)

Masochists doubt their capabilities. They give up the freedom to decide for themselves, be responsible for their own fates, or contribute creatively to the betterment of humanity, all in the name of their compulsion to not be alone.

Essentially, both the masochist and the sadist are dehumanized, such as when women (masochists) and men (sadists) are dehumanized in patriarchy. The masochist believes she needs the sadist to survive in the world, and the sadist comes to believe he can only be loved by those who are willing to submit to his control, for he needs his "object just as much as the masochist needs his" (p. 157). Believing at some level they are unlovable, sadists do not believe they deserve the love of those who are more prone to humanizing practices of love. Hatred, greed, apathy, and fear arise from the mire of this psychosocial condition. Sadists and masochists do not learn how to love on equal human terms which, given our different situations in hierarchical systems of oppression, means we need to learn to love differently from our unequal locations.

Fromm (2000) states that the sadomasochistic relation is a "fusion without integrity." Conversely, a truly humanizing love exists when both entities contribute to the growth and development of the other. Through this type of fusion, each loves the other as they would love humanity itself. Unlike sadomasochistic relations, those in a humanizing relationship give love not to receive and fill a void, but to nurture and strengthen the other depending on their relational needs. This creates love for one's self as something different than merely waiting for love, but rather giving love as a lover of humanity.

Fromm (1994) goes on to argue that these notions of love apply to group relations in systems of oppression. The relationship between oppressor and oppressed is sadomasochistic. Or, as Freire (1993) informs us, "dehumanization, which marks not only those whose humanity has been stolen, but also (though in a different way) those who have stolen it, is a *distortion* of the vocation of becoming more fully human" (p. 26). One needs only to think here of Albert Memmi's (1965) classic depiction of the colonizer and the colonized. The oppressor seeks to connect through the submission of another, whereas the oppressed is often dehumanized to the point where they find themselves resigned to exist within the relationship. Conformity to the oppressor group means that one must take on a narrowly defined and distorted identity, make a kinship with others who have chosen privilege over justice, and mask over the original self that did not at the start of life see itself apart from the rest of humanity.

The kinship of the oppressor group is not one based on love. Rather, it is based on the surveillance of one another to uphold group norms and status interests (see Foucault, 1995). Some group members sadistically surveil the group's ideology in its members, whereas those who are surveilled in this way masochistically submit to this bankrupt relationship for fear of an unbearable condition of aloneness, of being shunned from the group. To illuminate, hooks (2004) relates this type of submission to patriarchy when she describes how her own brother gave up his freedom to express emotions. She claims he did so to "be accepted as 'one of the boys'" and for which he pays a psychic price (p. 12). Yet, freedom and justice are only to be had once members of this group are willing to break free and risk being alone. They need to take a chance on real love, i.e., fusion *with* integrity, rather than to submit to its opposite, sadomasochism. And, the more that members of the oppressor group take this action, less powerful is the coalition that gives the oppressor group its power (Allen, 2008). The essential sadomasochistic basis of the oppressor group can, in the end, only be rectified through the dissolution of the group itself, for that group was formed on unjust and unloving premises. In this way, individuals will feel less compelled to give up their original selves as a precondition for false love.

Another aspect of Fromm's (1994) analysis is how neurosis is normatively articulated as an aberrant personality disorder. In common discourse, most of society is positioned as "healthy" to the extent that they are able to conform to the functional order of things (Habermas, 1989). Fromm (1994) suggests that this discourse hides the general neurosis of mainstream society when he says, "from a standpoint of human values ... a society could be called neurotic in the sense that its members are crippled [sic] in the growth of their personality" (pp. 138–139). For instance, hooks (2004) states that "patriarchy promotes insanity" because "it is at the root of the psychological ills troubling men in our nation" (p. 30). According to Fromm (2000), he who is seen, in the normative lens, as "mentally stable" is "well adapted only at the expense of having given up his self in order to become more or less the person he believes he is expected to be" (p. 138). This process of becoming something one is really not in order to sadomasochistically fuse and overcome the unbearable feeling of aloneness produces pain because "[w]hether or not we are aware of it, there is nothing of which we are more ashamed than of not being ourselves" (p. 261).

Having ensnared oneself in this illusory trap of claiming to love freedom while at the same time pretending to be something one is not (e.g., a "superior" being, such as a "White"), the person of the oppressor group will respond neurotically to any attempts to expose this farce. When challenged with the realities of the social order that are plain for others to see, the neurotic oppressor group member will respond with defensiveness, anger, denial, absurdities, false or distorted facts, and other forms of deflection (Allen, 2004; Allen & Rossatto, 2009). For example, it is not uncommon for men to exhibit "random tantrums" when their patriarchal views are challenged (hooks, 2004). Individual oppressor groups make these moves compulsively to squelch the shameful dissonance between their idealized beliefs and the knowledge of their actual actions.

It should be no surprise then that neurotic behaviors are commonplace in classrooms where critical theories are used to challenge dominant ideologies and unjust power. In fact, there is a litany of educational research documenting the neurotic resistance of students to critical curricula in the classroom (see de Jesús, 2004; Matias, 2012, Williams & Evans-Winter, 2005). On the surface, many may attribute these behaviors to fear, hatred, greed, and apathy, and not pay much attention at all to the underlying motivational role of love.

In applying Fromm (2000) to a radicalized pedagogy, we understand how a critical praxis of love is born of a painful process. It requires the risk of isolation because succumbing to the "fear of isolation often acts as the mechanism to prevent males [in patriarchy] from becoming emotionally aware" (hooks, 2004, p. 71). It is about the creation of freedom and justice in a social system where hardly any exists. It is about taking a serious, critical look at what one is gaining from their social identity groups. For those in oppressor groups, it is about self-enlisting in a painful process of learning how one contributes to the sadistic infliction of trauma onto others. It is also about coming to terms with how being a part of an oppressor group and participating in its sadomasochism is traumatic to individual members such that they "forfeit their chance to be happy" (hooks, p. 73). Learning to replace dehumanization with love, a love that pays it forward with further and further humanization of all, is the goal. And, it may require those of the oppressor groups to love enough to walk away from their groups altogether in order to build more loving social arrangements and new forms of social being (Allen, 2011).

HOW DEEP IS YOUR LOVE?

How deep is your love
How deep is your love
I really need to learn
'Cause we're living in a world of fools
Breakin' us down

When they all should let us be
We belong to you and me (Gibb & Gibb, 1977)

Before we begin the specific analysis of love in white emotionality, Allen and I first vulnerably apply Fromm's (2000) critique to our own social constructions of love. We do so to illuminate possibilities of how something as intimate as our emotion of love is nonetheless influenced by structures of race, gender, and class. We illustrate how a critical theory of love can illuminate the meanings of our everyday lives. We also hope our readers find commonalities – or points of departure – to reflect upon on their own love stories. First, I offer my story in the next section, then, Allen offers his in the following section. We return to a unified voice to achieve these human commonalities.

LOVE: AN AMERICAN-BORN HETERO-NORMED MOTHERSCHOLAR OF COLOR

Growing up in America, I dreamt of love. I dreamt of Prince Charming and me running toward each other in slow motion with soft background music. He was "The One" who would use his last breath to profess his love for me before he sank into the dark cold ocean abyss, or save me with a kiss that would wake me from a life-threatening slumber. Expanding on Henry Giroux's (1994) critique of Disneyfication, this notion of heteronormed love is not organic; rather, it was co-constructed by images, films, and messages delivered by mass media. From "You had me at hello" to "Aaaaaas youuuuuu wiiiiiiish," my concept of love was not only corporately manipulated, just as whiteness is (Vera & Gordon, 2003), but also unrealistic. In fact, so unrealistic was my concept of love that it left me living in a perpetual state of disappointment wherein I searched for only that "ideal" love. Yet, nothing mirrored that superhuman, glamorized love so subliminally taught to me. Despite disappointment, I refused to let go of the dream of overly-romanticized love because it made me feel as if I was a part of something grander than my mere human existence, like a cosmic connection to another human being. Even if my subscription to such a dream meant living in a painful reality that would never produce such a kind of love, I latched onto it masochistically, for letting go meant to relinquish what I thought I knew about myself, my behaviors, and the emotions I associated with that ideal love.

Refusing to let go hindered my opportunities to feel a humanizing love precisely because I thought I would be left alone in finding a new meaning of it. Consistent with Fromm (2000), my identity was inextricably bound by the social construction of love that was nonetheless wrought with masochistic subtleties. Yet, I engaged in this sadomasochistic relationship with a socially-constructed notion of love because what else was I to latch onto if the alternative was unknown? I was ashamed to hold onto definitions I knew were falsities, but I refused to let go because I feared the unknown. These false definitions of oppressor groups are frozen in sadomasochism

53

too – to wit, men who desperately latch onto masculinities are inextricably bound to patriarchy (hook, 2004); their fear of being something other than the normative masculine is paralyzing.

It was not until I decided to have children that I mustered the courage to begin a process of re-understanding love from a womanist perspective, one wrought with expecting pain, sacrifice, and duty, and locating strength in my tears and commitment to my unborn twins. Like womanists, I learned to embrace my maternal and felt pain as a woman of Color. Simply put, I started to learn how to love myself again and take charge in redefining that love. And upon the expected birth of my twins, I could no longer selfishly put this humanizing love aside, despite my fear of not fully understanding it. So, I had a choice. I could recycle the dream of an overly-romanticized love, but subject my unborn twins to a false sense of love, or instead, I could model for them the courage it takes to learn anew. For me, a humanizing love became more than a string of happy, self-gratifying moments wrought with physical and emotional superficiality. Love, like when a mother loves her unborn child, cuts deeper than the surface glow of excitement. In this deepness, a humanizing love flourishes because it requires one to take a painful stance to better humanity despite facing embarrassment, guilt, shame, or fear. This is exactly what womanist theory acknowledges: that love, like caring, is not simply interpersonal, but profoundly political in intent and practice.

Personalizing the politics of taking a stance for humanizing love, I refused to prematurely deliver my unborn twins despite months of bed rest. During this time, my muscles atrophied and I could no longer walk or use the restroom alone. Yet despite the pending pain, I willfully underwent this process because I trusted that such a painful and fearful journey would help me learn a more humanizing love that extended beyond my superficial understanding. That is, I knew deep in my gut that this was not about love for myself, but about the love my children should have and what I could learn from that process of placing love beyond one's self.

Such a sentiment parallels the politicizing of womanist identity because the search for equity and justice goes beyond the self and into the community. Regardless of the fear of an unknown future and identity, I actualized a humanizing love the moment I first held my newborn twins. Hence, my understanding of love goes deeper than the yearn for physical beauty, finding my Prince Charming, or engulfing myself in fantastical, overly-romanticized notions of love that sadistically entrap me in a reality, intrinsically denies fruition of such a dream. For me, a humanizing love means to willingly engage in a renewed process of understanding what love is, and to learn how that love is rich with pain, loss, fear, selflessness, hope, solace, and humanity.

Being introduced to a more humanizing love, I am now better able to fully love another being. Instead of focusing on the needs and wants that were corporately dictated by what I believed I was physically, materially, and/or emotionally lacking, I learned that my pain, tears, sacrifices, and isolation are essential components for another to feel loved (see Beauboeuf-Lafontant, 2002; Knight, 2004; Said, 2002).

Love, then, is truly a cosmic connection when it is inextricably tied to how your love is felt by others and how they, in turn, express it further. To illuminate, I feel a humanizing love when I see my twins holding hands or kissing the forehead of their newborn cousin. This love I developed while carrying them is not about me; it is about how I modeled humanizing love and, in turn, how they now feel and express love beyond me. The true cosmicality of love is simply knowing that your love is beyond you, breathing life into the womanist commitment to shared responsibility.

I FOUND LOVE IN A HOPELESS PLACE: RICKY'S STORY

I, too, was taught a corporate, patriarchal, white supremacist, heteronormative ideology of love. As a White heterosexual male from the Midwest, I was supposed to play the role of "Prince Charming." To fulfill my potential beyond my socially-ascribed identities, I learned that I needed to have "game," a fat wallet, rockin' abs, and a flare for romance. Like George Bailey in the Christmas-time classic *It's a Wonderful Life*, I learned I had to be the superhero and lasso the moon for my girl. After all, that is what I was told that straight women wanted. They wanted the dream, the fairytale of having all of those material possessions that define success in capitalistic America. I had bought into the dream myself. In this way, the American Dream and the Dream of Love were one in the same. It was what I was supposed to desire. And I did. Thus, my sense of self was wrapped up in trying to be the one who could make the dream come true. To do otherwise would mean failure. Worse, it would mean that I am unlovable because love is accrued like capital – only under certain relational conditions.

But as a heterosexual male, I was not taught to desire "love" *per se*, not even the romanticized version. It was not something that I dreamt about as a child, nor was it something I spent much time discussing with anyone. I learned to perceive love as feminine and repress any conscious expressions of a desire for love. Since I had chosen to accept my socialization into a normative masculine role, I rejected deeper notions of love that might cast me as being feminine. My inculcation into patriarchy, into playing the normative role of sadist, was underway. Being a Prince Charming, at least in the male supremacist version of the story, did not mean creating love. It meant getting the "hot" girl to fall for you by any means necessary, including exploiting her insecurities. After all, "all is fair in love and war." And by her falling for you, and you marrying her, you would not be alone. Love was not about mutual growth and healing in the face of the traumas of systemic oppression and sadomasochistic norms. Love was conquest, with the vacuous emotional reward of avoiding aloneness. So, I learned to desire the absence of aloneness. Becoming a White heterosexual man meant always having someone else there who was loyal and faithful. The goal was not necessarily to feel some overwhelming sense of love for her, although that kind of talk existed in normative discourse and it painted love as a kind of mysterious presence. The greater most tangible goal it seemed was to not feel alone; that is, to desire a kind of fusion without integrity. Loyalty, faithfulness, and

55

trust were tied to the seemingly essential need to not be without someone. In short, I learned to fear aloneness more than I learned to fearlessly love.

This was the algorithm of a Match.com notion of love that I had internalized. Physical attraction, mundane compatibility, and sharing common interests were all that were required since the endgame was to avoid the fear of being unattached and, moreover, of not being an "alpha male." Love was not the equivalent of success. Rather, in white supremacist capitalist terms, "success" as normatively defined, gave love its (distorted) meaning. The fear of aloneness, of taking the risk of loving freedom enough to experience alienation, runs deep in many, and it drives people to do things and commit to things that are not loving, though they may tell themselves otherwise. In other words, romanticized love produces much misery and self-destruction, not to mention that it is an emotional reification for reproducing violent and hurtful social systems. After all, those who truly love would not stand for oppressive relations. They would have to do something about it or else lose integrity. And, they would be willing to risk aloneness.

For a few decades, I was rather lost when it came to love. When I was a young man, I sought women who adhered to the romanticized dream that I also had bought into. Consciously or not, I was seeking sadomasochistic relationships. I wanted whatever it was that this mysterious love was supposed to give me, so long as it included the American Dream. Later, as I grew critical of the corporatized enwhitened version of love, I sought those who also seemed critical. Yet, I still did not know what love was, and neither did they. I only knew that the dominant story about love was full of holes. Without a different, more critical theory of love, I oscillated back and forth between hating the normative imaginary of love and hating myself for not being able to fulfill its romanticized promise, which was a promise also connected to realizing the benefits of my maleness, heterosexualness, and whiteness. To be honest, I had given up on the whole notion of love, at least as I understood it at the time. Yet, I continued to pursue it compulsively. Something was wrong, but I did not know exactly what it was or why I could not figure it out.

My understanding of love began to change significantly when I took up antiracism as a personal and professional calling and became a professor. The academy can be an isolating environment. For those of us who identify as criticalists, especially those of us criticalists who challenge whiteness while inside the "ivory tower," the aloneness of the academy can be bone crunching. The political battles over the curriculum, research agendas, and institutional policy leave many wounds. Further, in an academic's desire to read and write, even more time is spent alone – at least when one finds that time. In the comfort of writing about one's ideas, the critical academic can imagine a new world with fair and just forms of connectivity. But realizing these possibilities in the institutions in which we work is another matter. The sad fact is that schools of education are as mired in dominant ideologies and petty turf wars as any other type of educational institution.

I never expected to find a new understanding of love in the academy, in what seemed to be a hopeless place. But to my surprise, my academic work as a White antiracist led me to a new meaning of love. When I was a new professor, I was bold and brash, willing to challenge anyone and say whatever I thought needed to be said to disrupt whiteness. But many Whites (and even some people of Color) pushed back. Initially, they discursively policed my ideas. Their surveillance eventually evolved into social shunning and distancing. There were even calculated acts of revenge aimed at getting me to stop what I was doing or leave the institution. I grew more isolated. Some colleagues said sadistically – most likely out of their own projected fears of isolation – "I think you just like being alone." But I did not relent. Although the subsequent isolation and shaming was painful, I persisted because I realized that my love for humanity was greater than my fear of being alone. Eventually, I also began to realize that I was *not* alone after all. There were supportive students and community members, as well as colleagues around the country, who shared the same vision and appreciated what I was doing. I had come to see that a truly humanizing project of love requires giving of oneself and not expecting in return. Overturning white domination in the world is an enormous, seemingly insurmountable task, yet I pursued it and I risked the consequences because I chose to love humanity.

So, here is what I have learned. A truly humanizing love can be realized once one is ready to accept the pain of isolation. I have learned the radical importance of vulnerability – that is, to be willing to risk feeling pain, to even find beauty in the pain, in order to love humanity, and thus myself, more. In fact, I now understand that pain is a necessary aspect of love. One can love so much it aches, yet not expect anything in return. I love humanity because it makes me feel whole. It helps me combat the sadistic forces of whiteness, capitalism, patriarchy, and heteronormativity that surveil my allegiances to force me to masochistically trade my humanity for a false sense of being. To be sure, there is joy to be found in creating a humanizing environment for another, to feel complete and unconditional love. And even if I doubt at times whether this love is true or authentic, as many people of Color may doubt that my efforts to undo whiteness and racism are legitimate, that is no reason for me to stop loving. I continue to love because that is what I want for humanity. Like my co-author, I am committed to building a type of love that pays forward. In this sense, I strive to be a critical agent of love.

WHITE LOVE OR BAD ROMANCE?

I want your ugly
I want your disease
I want your everything
As long as it's free
I want your love
(Love-love-love I want your love) (Germanotta & Khayat, 2009)

We now turn to a discussion of the title of this chapter: "Loving Whiteness to Death." We can say in one sense of the phrase that loving whiteness to death means that Whites seemingly love their whiteness so much that they are willing to undergo a kind of spiritual death to sustain it and reap what they believe are its material and psychic rewards (see Du Bois, 1935). The need for love and the fear of its ontological opposite, aloneness, cultivates a bad romance with whiteness, a sadomasochistic relationship with it, meaning Whites in many ways willingly and knowingly engage in the surveillance of a racialized social structure that sadistically inflicts harm onto people of Color. However, Whites also masochistically deny themselves the opportunity to experience humanizing love. Rather than dealing with this condition positively by undoing the racist social structure, Whites instead repress their racial knowledge, creating psychological defense mechanisms that allow them to continue reaping benefits (DiAngelo & Sensoy, 2012; Du Bois, 2005; Leonardo, 2009). As White group members ensure that this repression continues via social operations of surveillance (see Foucault, 1995), Whites are instilled with the sense that if they become traitors to whiteness, they will be alone, isolated, and, thus, without love (Thandeka, 1999). Fearing loneliness, Whites masochistically cling to the white polity, expecting to find some wholeness and love there.

Facing what they believe to be an unbearable condition, that is, to be without the White "race" and thus alone and racially vulnerable, Whites exhibit neurotic behavior when their contradictions are exposed. Living the lie of whiteness, they become angry, defensive, and agitated when the reality of their racial practice is shown to be incongruent with their racial idealism. Nowhere is this more obvious than in their embracing of colorblind ideology. As Bonilla-Silva (2009) has shown, Whites articulate the ideals of abstract liberalism – that is, we all ought to live together, go to school together, and intermarry – but they know that, for the most part, they do not actually do these things. Rather than being honest about it, many Whites conjure up stories to distance themselves from taking responsibility. For example, "I would send my kids to a school with mostly Black kids, but the curriculum wouldn't be challenging enough and the schools are just a bit rough around the edges"; "I would live next door to a Native American family, but sometimes they don't take care of their property very well"; "I love Latinas because they are feisty and full of life, but our cultures are too different for marriage and would be too difficult for our mix-raced children"; or, "I believe in diversity in the workplace but my Filipina boss is just not collaborative with us." These offensive deflections are more than just passive stereotypes or active rhetorical moves. Instead, they are lies produced by a psyche that does not wish to be revealed for all to see. They are behavioral symptoms of the deep shame Whites feel for pretending to be something they are not (i.e., "White") and inflicting pain and trauma onto people of Color (see Ignatiev & Garvey, 1996a). Underneath all of their protestations about the reality of white privilege, there is an original self that gave up its independence in order to get the conditional love of the white community, a "love" that remains only if they fall in line with white racial talk and maintain the façade of racial superiority (Thandeka, 1999).

In this state, Whites communicate without integrity whether through icy cold indifference or red-hot rage, as we often see in the antiracist classroom. Cross-racial dialogue can only occur once Whites feel a humanizing violence, which is necessary for countering white tendencies to control classroom dialogue, and they come to understand the impact of their whiteness on students of Color (Leonardo & Porter, 2010). We also argue that only when the pain of what one gives up to become white is revealed and accepted can a dialogical interaction take place. At that point, Whites will truly have a stake in antiracism and in giving up whiteness.

Applying a theory of humanizing love to whiteness, it becomes clear as to why Whites emotionally invest in whiteness. Just as how romanticized love is socially produced with capitalistic or corporate intentions, so too are race and racism intertwined with our notions of love. The American dynamics of race produce a state of meaning for people dependent on their racial categorization (Bonilla-Silva, 1996; Collins, 2000; Haney López, 2006). That is, everyone experiences race and makes meaning of it under a system of race, but does so very differently. For people of Color, an oppressive system of race disenfranchises their stories, experiences, histories, identities, languages, and cultures inasmuch as it propels, highlights, and substantiates those things for Whites (Gilroy, 2000; Ladson-Billings & Tate, 1995; Leonardo, 2009).

Just like our (the authors') emotionally-adhered-to distorted definitions of love are borne of a fear of aloneness, Whites emotionally invest in the need for whiteness for fear of ostracism. Inherent in this emotional investment are senses of belonging, self-understanding, and distorted love as tied to a group identification. One thinks, *I am not alone because my emotional investment in whiteness demonstrates my acceptance into a larger group.* However, unrecognized or suppressed is an understanding of their sadomasochistic relationship with whiteness, which is iterative of a fear of isolation and loneliness that so compels Whites to never leave whiteness. In other words, they do not cling to whiteness out of love; rather, they take up whiteness for fear of being expelled and powerless in the face of white racial domination. For example, consider how racially discriminatory housing covenants were implemented to protect whiteness (Brodkin, 2006; Haymes, 1995; Lipsitz, 1998). Although U.S. public policy and practice once openly barred people of Color from residing in places like the suburbs, Whites willingly entered these communities hoping whiteness would flourish without the alleged "contamination" of, as well as the "risk" associated with, people of Color (Conley, 1999; Massey & Denton, 1993; Oliver & Shapiro, 1997). In acts like these, Whites acknowledge they have an emotional investment in their whiteness in that their yearning for acceptance from such a community is seemingly more important than the harm they do to people of Color (Ignatiev & Garvey, 1996a).

Yet, loving whiteness also hurts Whites themselves, just as clinging onto over-romanticized notions of love hurts people who want to feel love (Thandeka, 1999). Take for example the effect that the racialization of housing has had on the white psyche. By opting to emotionally invest in whiteness, White people spiritually and materially isolate themselves from the rest of humanity and, in doing so, limit their own experiences, much like women who choose not to have children solely out of fear of labor pains. At the same time, Whites justify their emotional investment in whiteness by stereotyping and denigrating urban communities, which, due to pro-white housing policy, are populated mostly by people of Color. Therefore, adhering to whiteness stifles Whites' ability to have pride and strength in a group identification or community because they commit to a group that seeks only their conformity in a quest for domination (Ignatiev & Garvey, 1996b) or, in other words, unity without integrity. While Whites reap the benefits of white privilege as the wages for their willingness to relinquish their individuality and sense of pride, they pay for it in terms of shame for pretending to be a White person, which they know occupies an unjust "superior" status (Baldwin, 1999). Love is non-existent in such a scenario. Besides, *how is love "love" if it hurts others*? In conditions barren of love, it is not too hard to see how hatred, apathy, greed, and fear can thrive. As Ignatiev and Garvey (1996b) famously said, "Treason to whiteness is loyalty to humanity" (p. 10). For Whites, committing treason and rejoining humanity is work that is not only material and ideological, but also emotional and spiritual. A critical focus on love reminds us of that.

As we described above, loving whiteness to death also produces a fearful state of loneliness for Whites. Why leave when rejecting whiteness clearly marks a state of impending loneliness? Can loving whiteness make Whites fear loneliness so much that they are willing to accept any type of love (regardless of its sadomasochistic quality)? Loving whiteness then becomes nothing but a death sentence that limits Whites' potential understanding of a love that does not use the fear of loneliness as a way to entrap Whites in whiteness and leave them emotionally frozen when it comes to the racial pain of others (and themselves).

Whites are fearful of the impending pain of rejecting whiteness, as if somehow the feeling of discomfort is incompatible with love. A more humanizing love embraces painful feelings because to feel them is to inherently recognize we still care about being connected with one another. Consider how many critical whiteness scholars explicate the role white guilt plays in obtaining an antiracist white racial identity (Brodkin, 2006; Howard, 1999; Matias, 2013). Anticipating the impending discomfort of white guilt in an antiracist process and choosing not to embrace it stagnates Whites' ability to feel and utilize it as an emotional tool for continuing toward a racially-equitable human condition. In fact, what Whites typically try to do is avoid feeling it altogether (Matias, 2014). How then are Whites ready to divorce their whiteness if they fear feelings of pain and discomfort? Conversely, people of Color have been living in discomfort all their lives due to the oppressiveness of white supremacy (Fanon, 1967; hooks, 1996; Solórzano & Yosso, 2002). Yet, by mutually feeling pain, people of Color better empathize with each other which ultimately demonstrates the humanizing love they have for themselves and humanity as a whole (Leonardo & Porter, 2010).

If not just for the fear of being lonely, what else compels Whites to emotionally latch onto whiteness? Since whiteness is historically, politically, and socially instituted, the system of whiteness gives Whites little encouragement to leave. For example, if U.S. history (Acuña, 2000; Roediger, 1999; Takaki, 1993), court cases (Haney López, 2006), immigration laws (Haney López, 2006; Pierre, 2004), schooling (Bell, 1980; Lewis, 2003; Love, 2004), and economy (Lipsitz, 1998; Oliver & Shapiro, 1997) all reinforce the superiority of Whites and the centrality of whiteness, then letting go of whiteness would mean a loss of identity, one built upon such falsities (Matias, 2012). The elusive question of "Who am I?" becomes too much to bear when acknowledging that in answering such a question Whites must unlearn their emotional investment in whiteness. Such an active agency places a proprietary burden on Whites, a historical burden that has been thrust upon the backs of people of Color for far too long. More recently, Whites' admonition of racial ignorance, or colorblindness, has left to people of Color the burden of revealing the inherent contradiction of a society that practices systemic racism while claiming to be racially-open (Bonilla-Silva, 2009; Morrison, 1992). Whites turn a blind eye to it and claim it is not their problem (Tatum, 2003). Instead, they subscribe to the sadomasochistic "love" of whiteness that numbs them from their human responsibility to shoulder their fair share.

CONCLUSION: TRUE LOVE WILL FIND YOU IN THE END

True love will find you in the end
You'll find out just who was your friend
Don't be sad, I know you will
But don't give up until
True love will find you in the end (Johnston, 1984)

In summary, we presented a theoretical critique of love and how it applies to social conditions such as Whites' emotional investment in love. Such ruminations have implications for the state of antiracist education. Specifically, they show how understanding the emotionality of love and whiteness aids Whites in moving beyond emotional discomfort (i.e., anger, guilt, sadness, and fear) and into the prolonged emotional investment in humanity, so necessary to undoing racism.

The antiracist implications of realizing a humanizing love are manifold. In a humanistic sense, Whites would not see race as a problem of the Other (i.e., people of Color), but rather as a white problem because hurt embedded in racism becomes a collective hurt, which ultimately brings us together in a shared mission. Sharing in this burden would demonstrate a collective sign of strength wherein Whites finally learn how to be responsible for their share of the emotional burden of white supremacy. And through feeling this painful, discomforting burden, Whites may finally experience a more humanizing love that releases them from their neurotic compulsions and sadomasochistic tendencies. Whites may perceive that going through the necessary emotional process of undoing white power and privilege would be an unbearable situation, a form of emotional chaos.

But what Whites need to realize is that remaining in whiteness is even more unbearable because it is a living death. Yes, it will be a painful process for Whites, just as labor is a painful process of motherhood, or social justice is a painful process of academia, but the reward of real love is ultimately much greater than the reward for kowtowing to whiteness out of fear. Plus, how can Whites be lonely when they finally realize that humanizing love, wrought with juxtapositions of pain, joy, sadness, and happiness, is intimately married to our humanity as a whole? After all, Whites who authentically undertake this painful burden and struggle with people of Color against white domination will be more likely to have people of Color as close friends and allies. They will not be alone.

When Whites become courageous enough to feel and accept humanizing love, they will finally learn that they can never be without love or be alone since we have existed together as a human family before the social construction of race fractured our understanding of our essential ties. Metaphorically speaking, the humanizing love we are talking about, that which predates the birth of manufactured racial categories and hierarchies, has been a long-standing river. In creating the social institution of race, Whites metaphorically devised paths away from that river, so much so that the original path to the river has been overgrown and seemingly lost. Yet, the river was never lost. It has always been there, obscured. Through their own actions, Whites have lost the path to the river, and finding a way back should entice Whites to take up a humanizing love in order to heal the human family so broken by race. As we suggested in our personal stories, love then is more than a superficial need to self-gratify; rather, it is a state of existence, a way of being in the world that leads us back together. It is a feeling that is paid forward in the interconnectedness of our humanity and its capacity to produce more just conditions. Plainly stated, if Whites actively leave their emotional investment in whiteness, then they not only leave behind a sadomasochistic notion of love, they also open the doors to experiencing humanity.

Therefore, in order for Whites to experience this humanizing love, they must abandon the whiteness that has all along abandoned them, and has left them longing for love and a release from their shame (see Zembylas, 2008). This brings us to the other meaning of "loving whiteness to death." If treason to whiteness really is loyalty to humanity (Ignatiev & Garvey, 1996b), then the greatest act of love Whites can show humanity is to end whiteness itself, to love so much as to send whiteness to its grave. Given that whiteness is mainly a sadomasochistic construction, Whites need to not only undo racist ideologies and organize acts of racial disobedience, but also bear the emotional pain necessary to lovingly end the White race as a sociopolitical form of human organization. Let us be clear, we believe that Whites have the capacity to actually muster up the tremendous emotional strength and courage to love humanity as it should be loved. And when they do, waiting for them is a more loving humanistic community ready to embrace them.

Educationally speaking, almost 90% of the U.S. teaching force is White (Sleeter, 2001). This severe overrepresentation has profound implications for how whiteness impacts curriculum, pedagogies, standards, and policies (Gillborn, 2005; Ladson-Billings, 2009; Lewis & Manno, 2006). In order to disrupt the normality of whiteness so that the ideals of antiracist education can be realized, we must consider how teachers, educational policy makers, districts, and academia can disinvest in whiteness such that the discomfort in talking about race becomes less violent (Leonardo & Porter, 2010). In understanding that emotionally investing in whiteness is sadomasochistic, critical educators can explore the possibilities of confronting the emotional discomfort in antiracism so needed in prolonged projects of racial justice. For example, the overwhelming presence of White teachers and teacher educators in the teacher preparation pipeline (Sleeter, 2001) has produced a condition where discussions of race, diversity, and white supremacy are resisted (Rodriguez, 2009, Yoon, 2012). In emotionally refusing to *feel* discomforted by understanding race, teachers and teacher educators disingenuously engage in antiracism. *For how can one wholeheartedly engage in a cure if s/he cannot emotionally bear talking about the problem?* As such, critical ruminations of how to re-understand our commitment to love and humanity can provide a new way of thinking about how White teachers and teacher educators can emotionally reinvest in the possibilities of antiracist projects.

Finally, more critical conceptualizations of emotionality and whiteness are needed. For example, there must be more pedagogical practices that engage emotional theories of whiteness lest the genuineness of antiracist education be questioned. After all, students may learn the scripts we provide them and say all the right things, only to later demonstrate that their hearts weren't really in it. Specifically, antiracist educators and antiracist educational programs must ask their White students some of the following questions: What does love mean? Do you feel anxious, guilty, apathetic, or angry when talking about race? Why or why not? Do you love being White? Why or why not? Do you love people of Color? Why or why not?

Too often educational rhetoric relies on the need to "save" urban students of Color, advocate for social justice in urban education, and serve and protect underrepresented populations. Yet, rarely are White educators asked *why* they feel that need to save, advocate, serve, or protect, and why they believe they are the rightful ones to do such things. Further interrogating the social constructions of emotions provides a greater context to understand to whom we intimately tie our racial hearts. By doing so, we reveal how we limit our humanity when we blindly accept normative social constructions of emotionality that wrongly direct our hearts.

In the end, love, like other emotions, is felt. Beyond a simple unquestioned feeling, love is a human need that leads us to feel other emotions like anger, guilt, fear, and loneliness. Whose pain are we angry about? Whose misdeeds do we feel guilt for? Whose loneliness do we seek to comfort? These emotions are expressions based upon whether one feels a humanizing love, or doesn't. And, amidst the historical relics of the Taj Mahal, wars of Helenian proportions, and doctrines of nationhood, it becomes apathetic of humanity to disregard love's full power. For when we wholeheartedly love humanity, the possibilities become endless.

NOTE

[1] This chapter was originally co-authored with Ricky Lee Allen, Ph.D. and is reprinted with permission given by the publishers. Matias, C. E., & Allen, R. L. (2013). Loving whiteness to death: Sadomasochism, emotionality, and the possibility of humanizing love. *Berkeley Review of Education*, *4*(2), 285–309.

REFERENCES

Acuña, R. (2000). *Occupied America: A history of Chicanos* (4th ed.). New York, NY: Longman.

Allen, R. L. (2004). Whiteness and critical pedagogy. *Educational Philosophy and Theory, 36*(2), 121–136.

Allen, R. L. (2008). What about poor White people? In W. Ayers, T. Quinn, & D. Stovall (Eds.), *The handbook of social justice in education* (pp. 209–230). New York, NY: Routledge.

Allen, R. L. (2011, April). *From sadomasochism to humanization: An abolitionist theory of white guilt*. Paper presented at the 2011 meeting of the American Educational Research Association, New Orleans, Louisiana.

Allen, R. L., & Rossatto, C. (2009). Does critical pedagogy work with privileged students? *Teacher Education Quarterly, 36*(1), 163–180.

Baldwin, J. (1999). On being "White"… and other lies. In D. Roediger (Ed.), *Black on White: Black writers on what it means to be White* (pp. 177–180). New York, NY: Schocken Books.

Beauboeuf-Lafontant, T. (2002). A womanist experience of caring: Understanding the pedagogy of exemplary Black women teachers. *Urban Review, 34*(1), 71–86.

Bell, D. (1980). *Brown v. Board of Education* and the interest-convergence dilemma. *Harvard Law Review, 93*(3), 518–533.

Bell, D. (1992). *Faces at the bottom of the well: The permanence of racism*. New York, NY: Basic Books.

Berman, L. (1991). Normative inquiry: Dimensions and stances. In E. Short (Ed.), *Forms of curriculum inquiry* (pp. 225–241). Albany, NY: State University of New York Press.

Boler, M. (1999). *Feeling power: Emotions and education*. New York, NY: Routledge.

Bonilla-Silva, E. (1996, June). Rethinking racism: Toward a structural interpretation. *American Sociological Review, 62*, 465–480.

Bonilla-Silva, E. (2009). *Racism without racists: Color-blind racism and the persistence of racial inequality in the United States* (3rd ed.). Lanham, MD: Rowman & Littlefield.

Bowles, S., & Gintis, H. (1976). *Schooling in capitalist America: Educational reform and the contradictions of economic life*. New York, NY: Basic Books.

Britten, T., & Lyle, G. (1984). What's love got to do with it. On *Private Dancer* [CD]. Los Angeles, LA: Capitol Records.

Brodkin, K. (2006). *How Jews became White folks and what that says about race in America*. New Brunswick, NJ: Rutgers University Press.

Capra, F. (1943). (Director). *It's a wonderful life* [Film]. New York, NY: RKO Radio Pictures.

Chapman, G. (2010). *The 5 love languages: The secret to love that lasts* (New ed.). Chicago, IL: Northfield Publishing.

Collins, P. (1989). The social construction of Black feminist thought. *Signs, 14*(4), 745–773.

Collins, P. (2000). *Black feminist thought* (2nd ed.). New York, NY: Routledge.

Collins, R. (1979). *The credential society: An historical sociology of education and stratification*. New York, NY: Academic Press.

Conley, D. (1999). *Being Black, living in the red: Race, wealth, and social policy in America*. Berkeley, CA: University of California Press.

Darder, A. (1998, April). *Teaching as an act of love: In memory of Paulo Freire* [Paper]. Presented at the Annual Meeting of the American Educational Research Association, San Diego, CA.

Darder, A. (2002). *Reinventing Paulo Freire: A pedagogy of love*. Boulder, CO: Westview Press.

de Jesús, M. (2004). R.A.W.: "Raunchy Asian women" and resistance to queer studies in the Asian Pacific American classroom. *The Radical Teacher, 70*, 26–31.

Delgado, R., & Stefancic, J. (2001). *Critical race theory: An introduction.* New York, NY: New York University Press.

DiAngelo, R., & Sensoy, O. (2012). Getting slammed: White depictions of race discussions as arenas of violence. *Race, Ethnicity, and Education, 17*(1), 103–128. doi:10.1080/13613324.2012.674023

Du Bois, W. E. B. (1935). *Black reconstruction in America.* New York, NY: Simon & Schuster.

Du Bois, W. E. B. (2005). *The souls of Black folk.* Stilwell, KS: Digireads.com Publishing.

Duncan-Andrade, J. M. (2009). Note to educators: Hope required when growing roses in concrete. *Harvard Educational Review, 79*(2), 181–194.

Fanon, F. (1967). *Black skin, White masks.* New York, NY: Grove Press.

Forman, T. A. (2004). Color-blind racism and racial indifference: The role of racial apathy in facilitating enduring inequalities. In M. Krysan & A. Lewis (Eds.), *The changing terrain of race and ethnicity* (pp. 43–66). New York, NY: Russell Sage Foundation.

Foucault, M. (1995). *Discipline and punish: The birth of the prison.* New York, NY: Random House.

Freire, P. (1993). *Pedagogy of the oppressed* (Rev. ed., M. B. Ramos, Trans.). New York, NY: The Continuum Publishing Company. (Original work published in 1970)

Freire, P. (1994). *Pedagogy of hope: Reliving pedagogy of the oppressed* (R. R. Barr, Trans.). New York, NY: Continuum.

Fromm, E. (1994). *Escape from freedom.* New York, NY: Holt Paperbacks. (Original work published 1941)

Fromm, E. (2000). *The art of loving.* New York, NY: Perennial Books. (Original work published 1956)

Galindo, R., & Vigil, J. (2006). Are anti-immigrant statements racist or nativist? What difference does it make? *Latino Studies, 4*(4), 419–447.

Germanotta, S., & Khayat, N. (2009). *Bad romance. On the fame monster* [CD EP]. Santa Monica, CA: Interscope Records.

Gibb, B., & Gibb, M. (1977). *How deep is your love. On Saturday night fever: The original movie soundtrack* [Record]. London: RSO.

Gillborn, D. (2008). *Racism and education: Coincidence or conspiracy?* London: Routledge.

Gilroy, P. (2000). *Against race: Imagining political culture beyond the color line.* Cambridge, MA: Harvard University Press.

Giroux, H. A. (1994). Animating youth: The Disneyfication of children's culture. *Socialist Review-San Francisco, 24*, 23–23.

Godfrey, P. (2004). "Sweet little (White) girls"? Sex and fantasy across the color line and the contestation of patriarchal White supremacy. *Equity & Excellence in Education, 37*(3), 204–218.

Habermas, J. (1989). On hermeneutics' claim to universality. In K. Mueller-Vollmer (Ed.), *The hermeneutics reader: Texts of the German tradition from the enlightenment to the present* (pp. 293–319). New York, NY: Continuum Publishing Company.

Halligan, D. D., & Torello, J. (1993). *What is love. On what is love* [CD single]. Cologne, Germany: Coconut Records.

Haney López, I. (2006). *White by law: The legal construction of race* (Rev. ed.). New York, NY: New York University Press.

Haymes, S. (1995). *Race, culture, and the city: A pedagogy for Black urban struggle.* Albany, NY: State University Press of New York.

hooks, b. (1996). *Killing rage: Ending racism.* New York, NY: Holt Paperbacks.

hooks, b. (2001). *All about love: New visions.* New York, NY: William Morrow Paperbacks.

hooks, b. (2003). *Teaching community: A pedagogy of hope.* New York, NY: Routledge.

hooks, b. (2004). *The will to change: Men, masculinity, and love.* New York, NY: Atria Books.

Howard, G. (1999). *You can't teach what you don't know: White teachers, multiracial schools.* New York, NY: Teachers College Press.

Ignatiev, N., & Garvey, J. (1996a). Abolish the White race. In N. Ignatiev & J. Garvey (Eds.), *Race traitor* (pp. 9–14). New York, NY: Routledge.

Ignatiev, N., & Garvey, J. (1996b). When does the unreasonable act make sense? In N. Ignatiev & J. Garvey (Eds.), *Race traitor* (pp. 35–38). New York, NY: Routledge.

James, J. (1999). *Shadowboxing: Representations of Black feminist politics.* New York, NY: St. Martin's Press.

Johnston, D. (1984). *True love will find you in the end. On retired boxer* [CD]. Austin, TX: Stress Records.

Knight, M. G. (2004). Sensing the urgency: Envisioning a Black humanist vision of care in teacher education. *Race, Ethnicity and Education, 7*(3), 211–227.

Ladson-Billings, G., & Tate, W. (1995). Toward a critical race theory of education. *Teachers College Record, 97*(1), 47–68.

Leonardo, Z. (2009). *Race, whiteness, and education.* New York, NY: Routledge.

Leonardo, Z., & Porter, R. (2010). Pedagogy of fear: Toward a Fanonian theory of "safety" in race dialogue. *Race, Ethnicity and Education, 13*(2), 139–157.

Lewis, A. (2003). *Race in the schoolyard: Negotiating the color line in classrooms and communities.* New Brunswick, NJ: Rutgers University Press.

Lewis, A., & Manno, M. (2011). The best education for some: Race and schooling in the United States today. In M. Jung, J. Vargas, & E. Bonilla-Silva (Eds.), *State of White supremacy: Racism, governance and the United States* (pp. 93–109). Stanford, CA: Stanford University Press.

Lipsitz, G. (1998). *The possessive investment in whiteness: How White people profit from identity politics.* Philadelphia, PA: Temple University Press.

Love, B. (2004). Brown plus 50 counter-storytelling: A critical race theory analysis of the "majoritarian achievement gap" story. *Equity & Excellence in Education, 37*(3), 227–246.

Massey, D., & Denton, N. (1993). *American apartheid: Segregation and the making of the underclass.* Cambridge, MA: Harvard University Press.

Matias, C. (2012). "Who you callin' White?!": A critical counterstory on colouring White identity. *Race, Ethnicity and Education, 16*(3), 291–315.

Matias, C. E. (2013). Check yo'self before you wreck yo'self and our kids: Counterstories from culturally responsive white teachers?… to culturally responsive white teachers. *Interdisciplinary Journal of Teaching and Learning, 3*(2), 68–81.

Matias, C. E. (2014). "And our feelings just don't feel it anymore": Re-Feeling whiteness, resistance, and emotionality. *Understanding and Dismantling Privilege, 4*(2).

Memmi, A. (1965). *The colonized and the colonizer.* Boston, MA: Beacon Press.

Morrison, T. (1992). *Playing in the dark: Whiteness and the literary imagination.* Cambridge, MA: Harvard University Press.

Oliver, M., & Shapiro, T. (1997). *Black wealth/White wealth: A new perspective on racial inequality.* New York, NY: Routledge.

Pierre, J. (2004). Black immigrants in the United States and the "cultural narratives" of ethnicity. *Identities: Global Studies in Culture and Power, 11*(2), 141–170.

Rodriguez, D. (2009). The usual suspect: Negotiating White student resistance and teacher authority in a predominantly White classroom. *Cultural Studies ↔ Critical Methodologies, 9*(4), 483–508.

Roediger, D. (1999). *Wages of whiteness: Race and the making of the American working class* (Rev. ed.). New York, NY: Verso.

Said, E. (2002). *Reflections on exile and other essays.* Cambridge, MA: Harvard University Press.

Sleeter, C. (2001). Preparing teachers for culturally diverse schools: Research and the overwhelming presence of whiteness. *Journal of Teacher Education, 52*(2), 94–106.

Solórzano, D., & Yosso, T. (2002). A critical race counterstory of race, racism, and affirmative action. *Equity & Excellence in Education, 35*(2), 155–168.

Sumara, D., & Davis, B. (1999). Interrupting heteronormativity: Toward a queer curriculum theory. *Curriculum Inquiry, 29*(2), 191–208.

Takaki, R. (1993). *A different mirror: A history of multicultural America.* Boston, MA: Little, Brown and Company.

Tatum, B. D. (2003). *"Why are all the Black kids sitting together in the cafeteria?" and other conversations about race* (Rev. ed.). New York, NY: Basic Books.

Thandeka. (1999). *Learning to be White: Money, race and god in America.* New York, NY: Continuum.

Vera, H., & Gordon, A. (2003). *Screen saviors: Hollywood fictions of whiteness*. Lanham, MD: Rowman & Littlefield.

Walker, A. (1983). *In search of our mothers' gardens: Womanist prose*. New York, NY: Harcourt.

Williams, D., & Evans-Winter, V. (2005). The burden of teaching teachers: Memoirs of race discourse in teacher education. *The Urban Review, 37*(3), 201–219.

Williams, R. (1978). *Marxism and literature*. London: Oxford University Press.

Yoon, I. H. (2012). The paradoxical nature of whiteness-at-work in the daily life of schools and teacher communities. *Race, Ethnicity and Education, 15*(5), 587–613.

Zembylas, M. (2008). The politics of shame in intercultural education. *Education, Citizenship and Social Justice, 3*(3), 263–280.

NOT I

The Narcissism of Whiteness

In my years of advocating for racially-just education, I have done quite a few lectures, invited talks, and panel discussions. In them I explicate the need to address whiteness lest we collectively be at the mercy of recycling it. Especially in a field like education, predominate with White female teachers, it becomes even more necessary that we stop playing the "I don't see race" game just because it unfetters white fragility (DiAngelo, 2011). Beyond the discomfort there lies a truth that must be exposed, deconstructed, and honestly re-examined if we are to proclaim ourselves as antiracist teachers, racially-just teachers, or even socially-just teachers. As such, in my talks I always impress upon the audience the need to critically interrogate whiteness and go beyond celebrating the racial epiphanies of Whites who have become racially aware. In fact, I focus specifically on theoretical ruminations of whiteness, such as the emotionality of whiteness and how it dominates space. This hegemonic emotional domination renders the emotions of people of Color as subordinate to the emotions felts in whiteness. That is, because of the hegemonic power of whiteness, racial dialogues falls short when emotionalities of whiteness such as guilt, defensiveness, silence, or sadness are held above emotionalities of anger, frustration, sadness, and humiliation felt by people of Color when deconstructing race (Leonardo & Porter, 2010).

In my classes, for example, many of my students are White teacher candidates and once the dialogue of race gets down and dirty, their tears appear. Though it is only natural to feel, it is unnatural to place more weight on the tears of the racially-dominant and thus structure our behaviors, discussion, and emotions around it. This is seen when the crying White teacher candidate expects to be coddled for feeling bad. Such comfort is not given to the humiliated teacher candidate of Color who has just revealed how racism continues to harm her identity. Needless to say, there is an emotional dominance of whiteness that undergirds racial discussions, one which I reveal in my talks.

So, during these talks I spend hours explicating the need to decenter whiteness, especially the emotionality of whiteness, from the canonical philosophies, pedagogies, and curricula that frame modern educational thought. As taxing as it is to do this – because often times, I am the only person of Color on the panel – what I find most taxing is what happens after the talks. Typically after the talks we engage in a Q & A period whereby audience members ask questions about the ideas brought up during the talk. One by one I witness a familiar response from the predominantly White audience membership. Don't get me wrong – these individuals see themselves as White allies and are attending such a panel precisely because they are aware of whiteness and want to contribute to racial justice by learning more about it. Meritorious as their mere attendance may be, the routine emotional expressions after the talks are not. In fact, the reactions and comments received after my panels are so routine that they demonstrates a pattern of whiteness in a discussion that is specifically trying to deconstruct it. Instead of questions that engage deconstruction and decentering whiteness, the mainly White audience members shift the focus back onto enacting hegemonic whiteness. This is done in four ways.

For one, since the talk hits right at the heart of one's racialized emotions, some audience members react by presumably feeling guilty. To assuage this guilt, they attempt to reaffirm themselves during Q & A. Therefore, instead of questions regarding the ideas promulgated by the discussion, they shift the gaze to their racial heroism by listing the many things they do to combat racism. In fact, after presenting in Puget Sound, Washington, I had two White females who, although they did not know each other, tag team back and forth about their own supposed antiracist actions. Instead of addressing their comments to me, they fixed their gazes onto other White audience members. Nodding their heads, as if egging the rest of the crowd on, they took turns talking about what organizations they are a part of, what movements they have participated in, and one even talked about how her partner was a man of Color. In the end, they re-centered hegemonic whiteness by virtue of co-opting the space as a platform for their self-glorification.

A second response I often get after my talks is that of helplessness and what Mills (2007) would call the performance of racial ignorance that relinquishes racial culpability. "Well, then what am I supposed to do?" is a common question asked, though rarely in isolation. Instead, it is paired with a long soliloquy of who the respondent is, how s/he is a good person, and includes a list all past actions that portray an antiracist persona. I often respond with a similar soliloquy: "Do you have a checklist or handbook to deal with your mother? How about your partner? Okay, how about your friends? Then why are you asking for a handbook on how to deal with people of Color? Isn't a part of teaching also about developing relationships with your students? Then develop a mutual relationship – one that you already have experience with by virtue of having friends, partners, and a family." In the end, this type of behavior once again centers white emotionality, i.e., "I feel bad after hearing what I heard and thus want to prove to everyone I am a good person. After doing that I will place the burden of undoing hegemonic whiteness on the person of Color who made me feel bad in the first place instead of doing the emotional work myself."

The third response is a form of self-victimization seen through the comments that shift the focus of how hegemonic whiteness impact people of Color and humanity to how it impacts the speaker. Although whiteness does impact those who racially benefit from racism, it does so from a different point of departure, namely it bequeaths privilege. In this book I have discussed at length how Whites are impacted by whiteness; however, such an impact should never be equated to that of people of Color. In the same vein, men who partake in feminism can never equate their experiences under patriarchy to women. Though both men and women do experience patriarchy; men are affirmed at the expense of denigrating or subjecting women. In fact, hooks (2004) describes the impact of patriarchy on men in her book *The Will to Change: Men, Masculinity, and Love.* She tells how men lose their humanity when they partake or are complicit in patriarchy. They no longer feel and therefore lose their humanly capacity to connect with other human beings.

The same can be said for race and whiteness. Ignatiev and Garvey (2006) corroborate this by claiming that loyalty to whiteness is treason to humanity. As such, Whites do experience whiteness, albeit from a position of privilege. Therefore, when I receive comments and questions that reframe the entire talk on "What about me?" diss-course, they once again center on the emotionality of whiteness. Let me be clear: because listening to my talk often makes my audience feel discomforted, the only way for Whites to restore the emotional equilibrium of whiteness is to re-position themselves once again as the victims. This is nothing different than presuming that one who feels guilty is just another victim of an angry Brown woman. In doing so, emotionalities of whiteness are upheld.

The final response I often received in Q & A sessions is blatant disrespect. At a recent talk in New Mexico, I had time for a couple more questions. A White woman stood up in the back but she did not have a question; rather, she wanted a soapbox for a defensive reaction that had nothing to do with the ideas from the talk. Instead, her monologue was an emotional reaction to the discomfort she felt from ideas of the talk. The moderator for the event tried to stop her diatribe twice, but she was relentless. It was obvious that she had developed so much emotional angst from learning about whiteness that her incoherent rhetoric (Bonilla-Silva, 2006) started spewing out like – as the vernacular goes – "verbal vomit." In fact, her words were directly disrespecting my talk by not addressing the topic, my presence, or the moderator of the entire event. Instead, she vomited her emotional reactions onto the audience without regard to the explicit direction to self-analyze one's own emotions. After almost ten minutes of "Colombus-ing"[1] or "Bogart-ing"[2] my Q & A, she looked to the rest of the 150 audience members and took the liberty to close the session out with, "Thank you all for coming. So here is the final question …" and continued with her reactionary commentary (no real question was actually offered). She then began packing up her belongings, knowing full well we still had 20 minutes of Q & A remaining. With regard to the emotionality of whiteness, this was just another tactic to remove the power away from someone who critiques whiteness and put it back into the hands of whiteness itself.

I share stories like this not to demonize those who become too emotionally unfettered to deal with their own emotionalities of whiteness. Indeed, it does show how resolute, manipulative, and obstinate whiteness can be. Rather, I share these experiences to highlight one thing about whiteness: it is narcissistic. It will continue to position itself at the center of discourse, especially when one is trying to push it to the margins. This chapter focuses on the emotionality of narcissism in whiteness because to overlook how whiteness hegemonically positions itself as the apex of humanity will continue to oppress people of Color while distorting who is *actually* getting oppressed.

EMOTIONALITY OF NARCISSISM

Before delving straight into narcissism, one must first look into the power structure of emotions for, unlike popular beliefs, emotions are not simply innate; indeed, they are also socializing projects that are still systematized under a power structure. Emotions, as Boler (1999) so cogently argues, comprise a web of complex political relations dependent on the social hierarchies of who is expressing the feeling, who is receiving the feeling, the surrounding structures, and the power relations within that structure. For example, Fanon (1967) details how a simple phrase, "Look, a Negro," spoken by a White boy is in and of itself an interpellation between whiteness and Blackness. Ahmed (2004) corroborates this by stating that the emotion of fear that is embedded in such a phrase "allows the white body to be constructed as a part of the black body" (p. 63). Thus, emotionalities, like the fear felt by the White boy, are also interpellations of white supremacist racial hierarchy and are thus worthy of deconstruction, especially in a field like education whereby most educators are still overwhelming white (National Center for Education Statistics [NCES], 2012) and the production of whiteness continues to emotionally inoculate curricula (Ladson-Billings, 1998), teacher education (Sleeter, 2001), educational policy (Gillborn, 2005), and educational thought (Allen, 2004; Leonardo, 2009). Needless to say, deconstructing the emotionality of whiteness and its interpellation to that of the many students of Color, teachers of Color, and people of Color, writ large, is a necessary component for education to move its pontifications for antiracist education into a full-scale embodiment of racial justice. Meaning, instead of "claiming" to be about antiracist education, perhaps educators – many of whom are White – must "do the emotional work" of deconstructing their discomfort with whiteness, which in turn will lead to stronger possibilities for whole-hearted engagements of racially-just educational projects. Plainly, one cannot expect to withstand a prolonged commitment to racially-just projects in education if one's whole heart is not "in" it. Thus, an emotional fortitude must be cultivated with respect to racial studies.

Yet, to develop an emotional fortitude to withstand the emotional unfetteredness experienced in white fragility (see DiAngelo, 2011) – so often experienced in racially-just projects – interrogations as to why the emotionality of whiteness persists must first be explored. Since Bell (1980) argues that racism is intimately tied to narcissistic personality disorder, which Fanon (1967) corroborates by claiming that the narcissism of White men sustains colonial racism, these considerations beg education toward considering to what extent narcissism plays in the maintenance of the emotionality of whiteness in education and how does it impact the interpellations between teacher and students? Ultimately, *how does narcissism curtail the pedagogical futurity for racial justice?*

NARCISSISM OF WHITENESS

To begin answering this question, one must first examine the role of narcissism. Freud (1914) offers much to think about with respect to narcissism. First, he defines it within the confines of sexual identity development, claiming that narcissism is nothing other than "the attitude of a person who treats his own body in the same way in which the body of a sexual object is ordinarily treated – who looks at it, that is to say, to stroke it and fondles it until he obtains complete satisfaction" (p. 3). Though Freud's love affair with sexualization is often criticized, he does point out a key factor in narcissism: it idolizes one's self and structures one's entire life around behaviors, emotions, and discourses that stroke or fondle the idolized self. One does this because it becomes the only way one finds complete satisfaction in life. Said in reverse, he who is narcissistic believes he is unable to exist in the world if that world does not bow down to his supreme being and continually uplift his presence. Beyond the self, this is compelling in many ways. If, for example, a narcissistic man graces our society, he will engage in self-affirming behaviors, associate with people who cater to his needs, and partake in dialogues that stroke his ego. Hence, his super ego – the id – becomes the basis for the interpellations of conversations, behaviors, and policies for all of society.

Let me offer a new viewpoint for narcissism, one that explicitly accounts for race and whiteness. It is easy for one to say someone is individually vain, self-absorbed, and/or all about him/herself. On the surface, this acknowledges that a narcissistic person engages in life in self-gratifying ways. That is understood. However, what is not so readily understood is that accepting that a narcissistic person is self-gratifying and will engage in self-gratifying behaviors, also ontologically assumes that narcissism is an individualistic characteristic, meaning is confined to the realms of one personal identity – an individual process, so to speak. Alas, we are social beings with social identities that have social interactions based upon those social identities. So when the narcissist engages in the world and society in self-gratifying ways, he does so with respect to interactions, interpellations, and interconnections with other beings. Seen this way, narcissism then moves beyond a process of individualism and instead actively flirts with a process of socialization, for whom will the narcissist befriend to stroke, uplift, and affirm his God-like qualities?

The narcissist then draws society into his psychosis when he interacts with the world; that is, he will need a Sancho Panza to his Don Quixote status. This relates to films of today. Vera & Gordon (2003) argue that leading actors in Hollywood films, often White, have a Black sidekick to provide comic relief while affirming whiteness. Whether it is through the mammy or Sambo stereotypical characterization of African Americans that stem from racist minstrels of yesteryear, many films are complicit in spreading whiteness. To extend this postulation, films also are complicit in perpetuating narcissism because what gets transmitted to the rest of society is the *need to have that sidekick* who will stroke and fondle the White lead's ego.

Let us return to the notion of the narcissist. There are many routes the narcissist will engage in in order to socialize his narcissistic identity. One route, as described above, is how he befriends those who will coddle his identity. Like an abusive relationship whereby the parties are a sadist and a masochist, both dependent on each other's identity to inform their own, the relationship between a narcissist and his cheerleader is that of mutual psychosis: they both find something intrinsically and extrinsically rewarding about their roles within the relationship. The narcissist will further socialize his identity by finding and validating histories, media, topics, and discourse patterns that hold him to high esteem. However, when he is confronted with language, images, and/or facts that contradict his self-assumed Elysian[3] identity, he will either avoid, defend, or silence it. Take, for instance, Don Quixote, who, upon his own reality believed himself to be riding along the countryside on his gallant steed. When confronted by others about the reality of riding nothing but a *burro*, Don Quixote dismisses the notion, justifying his actions because those people counter his narcissistic identity.

Applied to postcolonial theory, Memmi (1965) asserts that colonizers who justify their colonization are usurpers who legitimize their position by "upsetting the established rules and substituting his own" (p. 9), i.e., manipulating the events, discourse, or situations in order to affirm their elevated sense of self. Like Don Quixote, the colonizer refuses to believe he is riding a burro, which in fact is the established reality, and instead supplants his fantastical belief of riding the steed as a necessary means to match his overinflated sense of self. Needless to say, the colonizer is much like the narcissist in that they both usurp a sense of superiority over others and find ways to manipulate situations so that their identities are affirmed. Bear in mind that a narcissist only feels completely satisfied if his identity is put on a pedestal, and he will go to great lengths to secure the belief that his identity is superior. The great lengths in this case are to refute reality or established rules regardless to reality or truth simply because to accept such a reality would demoralize his sense of self: thus he would cease to understand his existence.

But what of those who are confronted with a narcissist? How does it impact their identities? Though those who placate narcissistic individuals have their own issues as to why they succumb to such self-absorbing tendencies, those who resist the interpellations between the narcissist and themselves are confronted with a different dilemma. For one, the narcissist can refuse to befriend such resistant people, thus causing a sense of alienation between certain groups, mainly between the narcissist and those who refuse to bow down to his supremacy.

Another case acknowledges conflict on both sides. The narcissist may get angry or defensive when engaging in practices with people who do not succumb to his narcissistic identity. This causes grief on both sides because the narcissist becomes removed from his social space because the situation does not affirm his identity. On the other hand, the resistant person can feel either justified for refusing to be complicit in narcissism or frustrated for having seen a reality that the narcissist refuses to acknowledge. This is tantamount to shaking Don Quixote and screaming,

"You ain't on a horse!" to which his narcissistic response would be "Yes, I am." This puts the dynamics of power between the narcissist and anyone beyond him, and, in doing so, the process becomes a socializing one because everyone is involved in a constant battle of whether to affirm or deny the identity of the narcissist. Despite that a narcissist may not agree with this precisely because he focuses on the self, narcissism, in its totality, is beyond him and spills into society.

Having explored the individualistic dimensions and the socializing projects of narcissism, I return to the hint I brought up earlier: if narcissism can be a socializing project in a given society, then the power structures in that society must be considered. For example, it is ridiculous to assume a child's preference of where to go on a Saturday is on equal standing of their parent's preference. This is acknowledged and readily accepted primarily because what happens in the family, whether it is dialogue or action, will be structured under the power dynamics that parents have over their children. Thus, to examine interactions and interpellations between parents and children without acknowledging the power dynamics therein would be to overlook how those interactions are structured.

To use another example that often happens in urban education, I employ the relationship between a White teacher and her urban students of Color. In this classroom, the White teacher claims she "loves kids" and "wants to give back" to "disenfranchised" or "marginalized" youth and communities. Like the many movies that capture this sense of morality and altruism (see Chapter 2), she believes herself to be someone who can "save" these students of Color. Essentially, she has a narcissistic sense of purpose because who is she to assume the role of savior in urban classrooms, especially since she most likely never had a meaningful relationship with a person of Color, nor has lived in a community that resembles those from which her students hail. Frankly speaking, she narcissistically named herself Jesus without ever doing the work or experiencing the risks it takes to save a community, let alone a people. Just like a narcissist, she is only completely satisfied when she is acknowledged as an all-benevolent and altruistically-giving superior being.

However, in moving this sense of narcissism beyond the individual and into the socializing process, the White teacher, a self-proclaimed savior, impacts her students when her ways, beliefs, and decisions reflect *her* reality and not that of her students, much like Don Quixote does to Sancho. The students may feel imposed on, manipulated, lied to, and silenced because the narcissist will do anything to justify her elevated status; it is what makes her completely satisfied in life. This is how the process becomes a socializing dynamic. However it gets more complex when overlaying the power structure of whiteness because whiteness is hegemonic and exerts Whites above people of Color; it influences any speech, actions, emotions, and/or beliefs between the two groups. Instead of merely acknowledging that the dynamics between the narcissist and others can be one of personal discontent, frustration, and/or placation, the factor of power makes the dynamics beyond the personal; it becomes a systemic oppression that bequeaths white privilege at the expense of the beliefs, realities, truths, experiences, and speech of people of Color.

75

For example, a teacher and her students may be talking about racism in the class. If the teacher uses her power to stop the conversation or structure it toward dominant rhetorical of whiteness, she is enacting her power structure of race and as a teacher with authority over her students. Yet, her insistence to not talk about race because she believes race is not real in all of her interactions in society – from her college graduate courses to her classroom – becomes a systemic silencing of knowledge. Like Foucault's (1977) argument that knowledges are also competing for power for the stamp of truth while subjugating other knowledges, upholding the knowledge of whiteness (which includes colorblind racism) ultimately upholds a systemic power structure of race.

THE NARCISSISM OF WHITENESS IN EDUCATION

Bell (1980) asserts that "racism (the belief of racial superiority, and thereby, the right to dominate other races) is one psychic derivative through which narcissism may manifest itself" (p. 665). Using the third *Diagnostic and Statistical Manual of Mental Disorders*, Bell defines the medical characteristics of narcissists and parenthetically relates them to racists as follows (p. 662):

a. Grandiose sense of self importance or uniqueness (this fits the racist's supposed racial superiority).
b. Preoccupation with fantasies of unlimited success, power, brilliance, beauty, or ideal love (clearly, the wish to dominate another racial group fits here as well as the Malthusian principles of the rightness of whiteness and the Teutonic standard of white beauty).
c. Exhibitionistic: requires constant attention and admiration (such as wearing white sheets or swastikas).
d. Responds to criticism, indifference of others, or defeat with either cool indifference or with marked feelings of rage, inferiority, shame, humiliation, or emptiness (the phenomena of white backlash and the feeling that blacks are being pushy).
e. Two of the following:

1. Lack of empathy: Inability to recognize how others feel (racists could not possibly recognize how their "inferiors" feel otherwise they would not behave in such an unempathic manner).
2. Entitlement: expectation of special favors with reactions of surprise and anger when others don't comply (racists are always surprised and angry when the "inferiors" don't accede to their wishes).
3. Interpersonal exploitiveness: takes advantage of others to indulge his own desires or for self aggrandizement, with disregard for the personal integrity and rights of others.
4. Relationships characteristically vacillate between the extremes of over idealization and devaluation (the characterization of blacks as being primitive and yet extreme amounts of cultural plagiarism, i.e., sun tan phenomenon).

Though these characteristics of a narcissistic racist are indeed instructive in how we view individual characteristics behind the emotionality of whiteness, Bell (1980) also reminds us that there is socializing aspect to the narcissistic racist, i.e., "the need for a sense of absolute control which the racist feels justifies his self-given right to violate another's 'territory'" (p. 662). Plainly, the need for absolute control by any means necessary from someone who is already in power can be quite dangerous because it ultimately violates others. Hence, narcissism becomes a powerful controlling element of the emotionality of whiteness; when applied to education, the impacts can be deleterious.

To illustrate this point, let's look at the U.S. educational system. The majority of U.S. K-12 teachers are White. The majority of the teacher educators who train teachers are White. The majority of the deans who manage the teacher educators who train the teachers are also White. And the majority of chancellors, college presidents, administrators, university regulation office members, and college board members who oversee the deans who manage the teacher educators who train the teachers are also White. Yet, I am not finished. Whites also write the majority of the textbooks that White teachers use in classrooms predominated by students of Color. Whites also write the majority of the teacher education articles and books which teacher educators employ in the training of their teachers. Though there are teacher educators of Color, as well as White teacher educators who engage in topics of race, racism, and white supremacy in teaching, the articles written by these two types of teachers are rarely used in college classrooms. If anything, the topic of race, let alone whiteness, is reduced to one session, inside one semester-long diversity course, and rarely ever delves into the power dynamics of racism. Yet the topic of whiteness is rarely given credence, especially in a field where the members, the curricula, and the policies are all developed, maintained, and enforced by one particular group.

To illustrate this I draw from a recent experience in teaching whiteness. I was encouraged to create the first ever whiteness course in my community because of the many talks and guest lectures I had delivered throughout my career and due to my role as faculty advisor for many race-related student groups. Because my university is one of three local colleges housed on one campus, my research assistant and I thought it would be most equitable to cross-list the course on all campuses. Doing so would give all students access to the course. Being that it was the first course to ever focus on whiteness on all three college campuses, my research assistant and I sought out various departments that might be interested in offering the course. Our initial inclination was to find programs or faculty whose work delves into culture, diversity, ethnicity, or race. We immediately found a teacher education program that focused on culturally and linguistically diverse education. In fact, the program's website claimed that "[t]he courses, field experience, and student teaching are built upon current research in the field of cultural and linguistic diversity," and that "[t]he importance of culture and the role it plays in the education of linguistically diverse students is emphasized in the program." We were ecstatic, thinking this would be a perfect venue to cross-list an education course entitled "Problematizing Whiteness: Educating for Racial Justice." Yet when my research assistant and I approached the chair with the possibility, she was quick to show her disinterest with the ideas of the course and render it irrelevant to her program. In a program that claims to see the importance of the role of culture in education, she chose to render white culture – the one that impacts the curricula, policies, and pedagogies in education – stealthily invisible, yet powerful, again. This is the narcissism of whiteness.

To the extent that any program can self-proclaim its cultural and linguistic diversity without looking into how whiteness maintains this entitled sense, and be the determiners of a field of study, becomes suspect. It is tantamount to a situation whereby men preside, teach, coordinate, and write the articles and books inside a Women's Studies department, focusing only on women's cultural experience of oppression without ever addressing how the power structures of patriarchy and male privilege influence those cultural experiences, while aggrandizing itself as "the" feminist program that benefits women. How are women to trust such a program? In the same vein, if a program dominated, taught, and coordinated by a majority of White professors self-proclaim to be culturally diverse without ever acknowledging whiteness, how are people of Color and White allies to trust such a program? The more burning question is, who is this self-aggrandizing, this display of grandiose self-importance, really for?

This leads us back to notions of narcissism. If the intent is to truly promote culturally diverse education by promoting the importance of culture in society, then it should also speak to why such cultures were not given credence in the first place and thus need promoting. Without doing so, this becomes yet another example of how whiteness institutionalizes itself in narcissistic ways. To draw from Bell (1980), a program that markets itself as culturally-diverse by exploiting the racialized oppressions of students of Color (e.g., closing the racialized achievement gap), preoccupies itself with fantasies of success, and responds to criticism with the ease to render such criticism irrelevant is in and of itself an exemplar of narcissism. In addition, by refusing to look into whiteness as a privilege, this (in)action yet again reinforces a power structure whereby Whites have control and power to be the determiner of what constitutes cultural diversity.

Yet these same narcissistic trends happen in U.S. classrooms and teacher education programs on a more personal level. Take for example a guest lecture I gave to Roberto's (my doctoral student's) teacher education course. The class had just read one of my articles published in the premier international journal on race and education. While talking about how difficult it is to teach whiteness, I was abruptly stopped by a nineteen-year-old, White female teacher candidate. She stood up and said, "When I read this thing about whiteness I was like, 'Who the fuck does this bitch think she is?'" Upon her comment, the entire auditorium grew tense and quiet. I noticed some students looking down, others shifting in their chair, and Roberto stood up. Although her comment was outright rude and unprofessional, it was more instructive to examine it under lens of narcissism. Here I was a professor, who earned her doctorate focusing on race and ethnic studies in education, whose "thing" in question was published in an internationally reputable academic journal, and was the professor of the course. Despite my roles of power, this student's emotional unfetteredness of whiteness outweighed those roles, meaning she felt entitled to make that comment despite later admitting she had "never learned about race." This is how whiteness is narcissistic. And this narcissism made her feel grandiose and self-important. In fact, her admission to have had never learned about race before – a topic that causes great harm to her narcissistic identity – revealed her narcissism the second she stood up, like an exhibitionist who requires constant attention. Her narcissism was further revealed when she responded to criticism (i.e., the studying of whiteness) with rage and a lack of the empathy for the others in the room who had to interact with her entitled behavior (p. 662).

Yet what strikes me as even more concerning is that this teacher candidate is becoming a classroom teacher and will graduate a program that heralds itself on social justice, urban education, and culturally and linguistically diverse education. She will be considered a *master*, an expert on all things diversity without ever having checked her own narcissism in whiteness. True to narcissism, a person who is a narcissist will enter that classroom with an air of self-importance, believing to be a superior being with the god-like ability to "save" students. In her interactions with her students, she will again use her power in whiteness and as a teacher in ways that affirm her own identity. She will do this while self-aggrandizing herself as an altruistic, all-moral, and caring teacher because instead of going to a White suburban school, she opted to teach at a urban school. In fact, in teaching in a school of education, I often have veteran teachers – again, mainly White – come back for master's degrees and make it a point to announce that they are "urban" teachers, "Title 1" teachers, teachers in schools where "all students are on reduced lunch," or teacher in "poor, diverse communities," when they introduce themselves to me. This need to profess a sense of sainthood dispels the notion that they are caring people, a moral quality that affirms their sense of identity. Yet rarely do they consider how narcissism plays a role in this display.

This is particularly important because emotional interpellations can impart false sentimentalization (Matias & Zembylas, 2014) and inadvertently reinforces a white supremacist racial hierarchy. In fact, in my work with Zembylas, we found that most White teachers often professed sentiments of caring in a particular urban teacher education program, yet also held pejorative sentiments about people of Color. One such teacher talked about how she believed herself to be an antiracist teacher, but then later revealed she does not like people of Middle Eastern descent on the plane with her. Another also claimed to be an antiracist teacher but divulged she had negative thoughts about African Americans. Clearly, there is a politics of disgust here, one disguising itself as care, yet still negatively impact students of Color.

CONCLUSION

In the eternal pursuit of racial justice, shouldn't we, as educators, dig deeply into the core of what emotionally motivates us to teach? Is it really for the public good, or is it merely to affirm a narcissistic sense of self? When it comes to race, the narcissism of whiteness will exert itself by attempting to refute, ignore, and make relevant the study of whiteness, especially in programs dominated by White individuals, white curriculum, and policies that protect whiteness. Yet some of these are the very programs or individuals who self-proclaim their ideals of social justice, urban education, and cultural and linguistically diverse education.

For those narcissists who parade their badge of antiracism in soliloquies after Q & A sessions, or make it a point for people to know they are indeed "urban" teachers, I employ Hayes & Júarez (2009): "You don't get a 'good' White people's medal" for doing antiracist things; you should be doing all along.

NOTES

[1] Slang term for when White people swoop in and take something that is not theirs, especially when it belonged to someone else for generations.
[2] Popular slang phrase which means to take something of someone's but do nothing useful with it. See: www.urbandictionary.com/define.php?term=bogart
[3] In reference to the beauty of the Elysium Fields in Greek mythology.

REFERENCES

Ahmed, S. (2004). *The cultural politics of emotion*. UK: Edinburgh University Press.
Allen, R. L. (2004). Whiteness and critical pedagogy. *Educational Philosophy and Theory*, *36*(2), 121–136.
Bell, C. C. (1980). Racism: A symptom of the narcissistic personality. *Journal of the National Medical Association*, *72*(7), 661.
Boler, M. (1999). *Feeling power: Emotions and education*. East Sussex, UK: Psychology Press.
Bonilla-Silva, E. (2006). *Racism without racists: Color-blind racism and the persistence of racial inequality in the United States*. Lanham, MD: Rowman & Littlefield.
DiAngelo, R. (2011). White fragility. *The International Journal of Critical Pedagogy*, *3*(3).
Fanon, F. (1967). *Black skin, White masks* [1952] (C. L. Markmann, Ed.). London: Pluto Books.
Foucault, M. (1977). *Discipline and punish: The birth of the prison* (A. Sheridan, Trans.) New York, NY: Vintage.
Freud, S. (1914). On narcissism. In J. Sandler, E. Person, & J. Fonagy (Eds.), *On narcissism – An introduction* (2012 Reprint). London: Karnac Books.
Gillborn, D. (2005). Education policy as an act of white supremacy: Whiteness, critical race theory and education reform. *Journal of Education Policy*, *20*(4), 485–505.
Hayes, C., & Júarez, B. (2009). You showed your whiteness: you don't get a "good" White people's medal. *International Journal of Qualitative Studies in Education*, *22*(6), 729–744.
hooks, b. (2004). *The will to change: Men, masculinity, and love*. New York, NY: Washington Square Press.
Ignatiev, N., & Garvey, J. (Eds.). (1996). *Race traitor*. East Sussex, UK: Psychology Press.
Ladson-Billings, G. (1998). Just what is critical race theory and what's it doing in a nice field like education? *International Journal of Qualitative Studies in Education*, *11*(1), 7–24.
Leonardo, Z. (2009). *Race, whiteness, and education*. New York, NY: Routledge.

NOT I: THE NARCISSISM OF WHITENESS

Leonardo, Z., & Porter, R. K. (2010). Pedagogy of fear: Toward a Fanonian theory of "safety" in race dialogue. *Race, Ethnicity and Education, 13*(2), 139–157.

Matias, C. E., & Zembylas, M. (2014). "When saying you care is not really caring": Emotions of disgust, whiteness ideology, and teacher education. *Critical Studies in Education, 55*(3), 319–337.

Memmi, A. (1965). *The colonized and the colonizer*. Boston, MA: Beacon Press.

Mills, C. (2007). White ignorance. In S. Sullivan & N. Tuana (Eds.), *Race and epistemologies of ignorance*. New York, NY: SUNY Press.

National Center for Education Statistics. (2012). *Fast facts: Teacher trends*. Institute of Educational Sciences, U.S. Department of Education. Retrieved from http://nces.ed.gov/fastfacts/display.asp?id=28

Sleeter, C. E. (2001). Preparing teachers for culturally diverse schools research and the overwhelming presence of whiteness. *Journal of Teacher Education, 52*(2), 94–106.

Vera, H., & Gordon, A. M. (2003). *Screen saviors: Hollywood fictions of whiteness*. New York, NY: Rowman & Littlefield.

CHAPTER 6

WHITE SKIN, BLACK FRIEND

A Fanonian Theorization of Racial Fetish in Teacher Education

Fanon's (1967) psychoanalytic investigation of Blackness posits a psychosocial condition whereby Blacks are forced to wear white masks in order to survive the neurotic and irrational state of whiteness. "It was up to the white[1] man to be more irrational than I," Fanon declares (p. 123), and thus renders whiteness a condition wherein Whites are "incapable of straight thinking" (p. 85). Such an irrational condition, Fanon then contends, leads to the production of neurosis in the Black man:

> His reality as a man has been challenged. In other words, I begin to suffer from not being a white man to the degree that the white man imposes discrimination on me, makes me a colonized native, robs me of all worth, all individuality, tells me that I am a parasite on the world, that I must bring myself as quickly as possible into step with the white world, "that I am a brute beast, that my people and I are like a walking dung-heap that disgustingly fertilizes sweet sugar cane and silky cotton, that I have no use in the world." (p. 98)

In this seemingly cathartic repudiation of that which racially denigrates Black men, Fanon not only unveils the pain of white supremacy, he also inadvertently suggests a psychosocial connection between the psychological dimensions of Whites and Blacks. As Fanon argues, "not only must the black man be black; he must be black in relation to the white man" (p. 110); ergo, Whites can only be white in juxtaposition to Blacks. Instead of understanding the dimensions of whiteness separately from Blackness, Fanon presents the relationship between the White man and Black man as interconnected because "it is The Other who corroborates [the white man] and his search for self-validation" (p. 213).

Instead of utilizing a discursive analysis of whiteness, which is often used in the field of education and teacher education, I opt for Fanon's psychoanalytic approach to investigate the psychosocial attachment some Whites feel in befriending – or professing to befriend – Blacks as a means to assuage "white guilt." By doing so, I seek to provide a renewed application of racial analysis used by past scholars such as Fanon. Also, as discussed in Chapter 1, Bonilla-Silva (2010) already analyzes how the parlance of "but I have a Black friend" stands as a discursive maneuver to feign kinship with people of Color and so promotes colorblind racism. Others analyze the stilted relationships between people of Color and Whites (Hayes & Juárez , 2009; Thompson, 2003), false empathy between White teacher candidates and urban students of Color (Duncan, 2002), and the servant/served paradigm found among Black and White feminists (hooks, 1994). However what these discursive analyses do not explore, however, is *why* Whites feel compelled to draw upon this discursive practice in the first place. What are the racialized psychoanalytic forces behind why those with white skin exaggerate false relationships with Black friends? What theoretical role does *racial fetish* play in this phenomenon? In applying such a psychosocial condition to teacher education, an area that is predominately white and promotes itself as "serving" students of Color, how does teacher education become an *institutional fetish* of the racial Other by promoting "white skin, Black friend"? Therefore, although discursive analysis unveils the impact of whiteness enacted in speech and/or behavior, psychoanalysis investigates the underlying context which renders such speech and behaviors. In order to truly engage in ways that dismantle systemic racial oppression, one must not only understand the social impact of one's speech and behaviors which contribute to racial oppression, one must also learn what lies at the root of these behaviors and speech individually. Furthermore, although researchers can simply ask Whites why they employ the "Black best friend" rationale, emotionalities often get sentimentalized, masking the underlying emotions of disgust (Matias & Zembylas, 2014). That is, "Whites teeter between rhetorical arguments based upon their dominant racial frame, this exasperated 'concern' is often a rhetorical diminutive, one which we coin an emotional diminutive, that strategically masks a deep-rooted disgust for African-Americans" (p. 319).

As a critical race teacher educator, I am preoccupied with this psychosocial condition precisely because I must cultivate genuine antiracist approaches in my teacher candidates – especially in those who wish to teach in U.S. urban schools predominated by students of Color (e.g., African Americans, Latinos/Hispanics, and Asian Americans). In this context of urban teacher education, a psychosocial state of whiteness exists when White teacher candidates believe they have "authentic" relationships with urban students of Color that are, at times, problematic. Suffice it to say that whiteness is a pre-existing psychosocial condition which makes those who subscribe to it feel humanistically empty, therefore, by emotionally attaching to people of Color – and specifically Blacks as the symbol of racialized pigmentocracy – Whites feel they have successfully avoided whiteness, erroneously presuming they are no longer humanistically empty.

As Fanon (1967) suggests, Whites "turn to men of color and ask them for a little human sustenance" (p. 129), an example of which is being their "Black friend." However, as Freire (1993) posits, it is not until the oppressor – in this case the *racial* oppressor – fully realizes the state of oppression that s/he can "begin a process of re-humanization." If a path toward whiteness leads to treason against humanity (per Ignatiev & Garvey, 1996), then a path *away* from whiteness is loyalty to humanity, ergo, a process of re-humanization.

I coin this process *racial re-humanization*, a concept particularly interesting in teacher education. Almost 90% of the U.S. teaching force is comprised of middle-class White females (NCES, 2012), many of whom have little to no experience nor previous relationships with people of Color, let alone people of Color living in urban communities. In my experiences as a teacher education professor, many of these students say they are drawn to urban teaching because they want to "give back" or "help disadvantaged urban students of Color." Many express how this "mission" has a significant meaning to their self-named "privileged White identities." The overarching ideal, according to these students, is to create a "friendship" between themselves (the White saviors) and the urban students of Color (the racialized Other) whom they will "save." This need for attachment becomes a process for racial re-humanization, albeit via fetishism.

Yet, within these articulations exist problematic attachments between the teacher candidates' identities as White persons to those they impose upon people of Color. If whiteness – and white identity development – caters to this "narcissistic racial privilege," how then does narcissism play out in Whites' fetishized attachment to urban students of Color? Take for example my own experience as the only faculty of Color at an urban teaching program: I am often used as "a toy in the white hands" (Fanon, 1967, p. 140) of my colleagues when they ask to include my face on brochures or other publicity acts. The presence of my darkened face provides a comforting fetish for the scopophilic gaze of my White onlookers, hoping that my mere presence is enough to fulfill some psychological sense of human deficiency. Thus, I "cannot dissociate myself" (Fanon, 1967), for I am nonetheless fetishized by the brownness of my skin and my Spanish surname (Bhabha, 1996; Espiritu, 2001; Hook, 2005; hooks, 2006; Johannson, 1999; Schroeder & Borgerson, 2003).

I strategically implement critical whiteness studies in this chapter because the subject "expose[s] [the] white lies, maneuvers, and pathologies that contribute to the avoidance of a critical understanding of race and racism" (Leonardo, 2013). Additionally, CRT's use of counterstorytelling dispels the oft-recycled and unquestioned majoritarian stories (Solórzano & Yosso, 2002), so I utilize these methods to illustrate scenarios in which the interrelation between whiteness exerted and whiteness felt. I further highlight this crossroads by employing my own counterstories as a female motherscholar of Color working within a university department consumed by whiteness.

I then fuse these psychoanalytic theorizations of whiteness with various theoretical perspectives on fetishism (see *colonial fetish* or *racial fetish* in Bhabha, 1996, and hooks, 2005). Of specific interest is how, when used together, the individual lenses of whiteness theories and fetish literature conceptualize *racial fetish*, a racial condition in which the racially-dominant attaches a narcissistic sense of racial superiority onto the accumulation of bodies of Color.

I then overlay racial fetish onto the everyday workings of teacher education, not solely for critique's sake, but rather to match the ideological footings of antiracism to the ever-evolving states of race, racism, and white supremacy in education. Finally, I end the article by outlining the dangers and hopes for deconstructing the psychosocial dimensions behind the relation of "white skin, Black friend."

85

PSYCHOANALYTICS OF WHITENESS IN EDUCATION

> The white man has found a poetry in which there was nothing poetic. The soul
> of the white man was corrupted ... (Fanon, 1967, p. 129)

Fanon's (1967) words indicate that a psychosocial process racially corrupts the White man's soul; he then provides a psychoanalytic answer as to the effect of such a process:

> The white man wants the world; he wants it for himself alone. He finds himself
> predestined master of this world. He enslaves it. An acquisitive relation is
> established between the world and him. (p. 128)

For Fanon, corruption is a result of *colonial racism*, the act of one race enslaving and mastering another. A corrupted soul that unjustifiably perches itself at the apex of racial relevancy is nevertheless a psychosis of some sort because such mentality loses contact with racial reality (see Bell, 1992, on *racial realism*). If *psychosis* is characterized by a "loss of contact with reality"[2] then accordingly Fanon's assertion that the White man's "Hidalguismo" (i.e., 'son of God') relationship with the world puts him out of touch with its racial reality is very true. These "latent forms of psychosis ... [then] become overt as a result of a traumatic experience" (p. 85).

This overt result has interesting applications for two reasons. First, it renders psychosis as narcissistic racial superiority, that which is overindulgent and "perpetuates a systematic relation of violence" for people of Color (Leonardo & Porter, 2010, p. 148). For example, Fanon (1967) argues that the White man believes himself to be the "predestined master of this world," obliging us to believe that "sin is Negro, as virtue is white" (p. 139). Whites can then psychologically internalize and validate whiteness as "virtuous," "orderly," and "natural" by reason of violently presenting Blackness as its ontological opposite: Blackness is "parasitic," "dung-heap," and "disgusting" (p. 139). The systematic relation to violence then befalls Blackness and Black peoples for, "in order to achieve morality, it is essential that the black, the dark, the Negro vanishes from consciousness" (p. 194). However, such a systematic racial violence is only hegemonically surveilled (Foucault, 1977) by the white racial psychosis that narcissistically advances the agenda of whiteness.

Delving deeper, Bell (1980) argues that racism, i.e., the belief of racial superiority, and thereby the right to dominate other races, is "one psychic derivative through which narcissism may manifest itself" (p. 665). Although Bell relates narcissism to racism, he does not recognize that racism is upheld by white supremacy – as CRT so asserts – and that white supremacy is maintained by the hegemonic naturalization of whiteness – as critical whiteness studies asserts. The trifecta of racism, white narcissism, and white supremacy characterizes white racial psychosis and reveals how racial oppression operates and maintains itself. For Fanon (1967), a Black man's "first encounter with a white man oppresses him with the whole weight of his blackness" (p. 150), yet his blackness is only made inferior by the White man who ultimately enacts his white racial psychosis.

Secondly, Fanon (1967) avers that the manifestation of psychosis is produced by one's experience with trauma, that *white racial narcissism* (Corbett, 1995), otherwise known as a "racial superiority complex," is a phobogenic response to the racial trauma Whites experience throughout their lives. What are these traumas that give rise to a psychosocial projection of heighten Hidalguismo? Doesn't such trauma reside more acutely in people of Color (see Matias, 2013b)? True that people of Color incur continual racial trauma via racial microaggressions, racial battle fatigue, and racial bias (see de Jesús & Ma, 2004; Fasching-Varner, Albert, Mitchell, & Allen, 2014; Cleveland, 2004; Williams & Evans-Winter, 2005), but if *all* people are racialized under a system of race – albeit differently – then Whites, too, undergo the trauma of racialization. Though their unique process bequeaths racial privilege unlike the racial trauma of people of Color, it does so at a different psychic cost. If colonial racism leaves the Black man "forever in combat with his own image" (Fanon, 1967, p. 194) because "he is made inferior" (p. 149), then white racial narcissism leaves the white man in a state of "collective catharsis" (p. 145) and/or a "victim of his unconscious" (p. 175).

I depart somewhat from Fanon's discussion of other psychoanalytics of the White man. Although I agree that the subscription to whiteness allows for a collective catharsis that becomes emotionally expressed through shame, guilt, or defensiveness, I do not agree that those who adhere to the whiteness ideology are "victims of their unconscious." On the contrary, I see them as willing participants in a system they know will benefit only them. Although some actively participate in whiteness for economic and political protection (Lipsitz, 2006; Oliver & Shapiro, 1997; Roediger, 2005), others argue that one's complicity in repressed forms of whiteness is also a form of active ignorance of race (Mills, 2007; Thandeka, 1999). Said another way, those who bear witness to bullying and do nothing are just as complicit in the act of bullying as those who are actively bullying.

Consider the common racialized parlance of "You can't bring home a Mexican boyfriend!" or "That's a Black movie!" Both of these commonplace phrases not only demonstrate racialized sentiments about people of Color, but how whiteness operates through active surveilling of white behaviors (see Matias & Allen, 2013). Though the litany of antiracism literature in education often engages white privilege as a "moment of racial epiphany" (Picower, 2009), I disagree that whiteness is unconscious or just about white privilege (see Leonardo, 2004). Rather, whiteness is so actively repressed that it becomes a subconscious and latent aggressive act of enforcing racial superiority. As Mills (2007) points out, an epistemology of racial ignorance is not to be misconstrued as "passive"; indeed, it is an *active suppression* of knowledge that deliberately represses awareness in order to feign racial innocence and unawareness, a process that then releases racial culpability. The dimensions of whiteness, particularly white racial psychosis, are cultivated in part by the surfacing of white racial traumas and by assuming their perpetuation is inactive, the underlying causes of whiteness are ignored, leaving only the resulting psychosis.

Yet, these are the very traumas that *must* be psychoanalytically explored. Thandeka (1999) provides a psycho-emotional interpretation of white racial trauma that sheds light onto that which sustains the white narcissism embedded in white racial psychosis. When exploring the emotionality of whiteness, the emotional expressions of *white guilt* or ambivalence (Leonardo & Porter, 2010), *white resistance* (Matias, 2012), and *white anger* (Godfrey, 2004) are often endorsed in the literature. Yet the emotionality of whiteness is not that limiting; rather, its definition must include the identification of emotions, processes of how these emotions are expressed, repressed, and projected, and theorizations as to why they are expressed in regard to the power structure of race. Just as the notion of "safe spaces" in interracial race dialogue is undermined when the power of whiteness is maintained (Leonardo & Porter, 2010), the presumed neutrality behind the emotionality of whiteness undermines the permanence of white supremacy (Allen, 2004; Leonardo, 2004).

Fanon (1967) "rejected all immunization of the emotions" (p. 113); yet, I affirm that, in order to do so, we must seek to investigate the functions and derivatives of commonly expressed emotions of whiteness. Take the example of shame: if *white shame* functions as a psychological guard, then what are the implications of this emotion on the maintenance of white supremacy (Thandeka, 1999, p. 27)? Shame becomes an emotion noteworthy to analyze, for it reveals "the self's failed attempt to live up to its own notion of an *ideal self*" (Thandeka, 1999, p. 108). If in whiteness the ideal self is one that internalizes narcissism, entitlement, and false racial kinship with other Whites, then nothing is more shameful than when that false ideal is threatened by reality.

But the cultivation of this white shame does not happen instantaneously; rather, it is slowly taught and learned throughout childhood (Thandeka, 1999). Since the White child is raised to be "a figment of the parent's imagination" and is one who "conforms uncomplainingly to what others think," the cost of such ideological adoption is "brokenness" due to the lack of "self-coherency and integration" (pp. 107–108). That is, whites "feel *white* shame because the persons who ostensibly loved and respected them the most actually abused them and justified [that abuse] in the name of race, money, and God" (p. 134). This abuse comes in the form of surveilling the White child's behaviors, thoughts, and curiosities about race, such that the colorblind racism that inoculated the parent is recycled in the child.

Bonilla-Silva (2010) argues that white racial discourse embeds colorblind racism through the use of "rhetorical maneuvers," thoughts, and actions that had to be learnt and practiced in order be mastered. A disturbing pedagogical praxis of whiteness exists in education, which burrows itself in the mindsets of children exposed to, and expected to reify, whiteness. Considering that Fanon (1967) acknowledges that the supremacy of whiteness cultivates in some Blacks an "inferiority complex," it is then not far-fetched to accept that this pedagogical process can happen in reverse: "[H]ate is not inborn; it has to be constantly cultivated, to be brought into being" (p. 53). Whites live in an environment where they are taught and learn how to perform whiteness in order to maintain white supremacy, just as Blacks are taught to assume the inferior role in a state of whiteness.

CONCEPTUALIZING RACIAL FETISH

While I was forgetting, forgiving, and wanting only to love, my message was flung back in my face like a slap. The white world, the only honorable one, barred me from all participation. A man expected to behave like a man. I was expected to behave like a black man – or at least like a nigger. I shouted a greeting to the world and the world slashed away my joy. I was told to stay within the bounds, to go back to where I belong. (Fanon, 1967, pp. 114–115)

Using the scenario in which a White boy points and shouts, "Look! A Negro," Fanon (1967) explicates the interconnected psychoanalytics of whiteness and Blackness. The White boy asserts his whiteness and its inherent superiority, something Fanon claims "burns" the Black man and makes it impossible for him "to get away from an *inborn complex*" (pp. 114–115). Such an act likewise embeds within him a sense of Blackness that categorically labels "Negroes as savages, brutes, and illiterates" (p. 117). When Blackness is called out, whiteness is reified.

Under such conditions, the relationship between Whites and people of Color cannot be divorced from colonial racism, the historically-repeated servant/served correlation seen in the myriad of racial and patriarchal dynamics. Key players of this enterprise are that of colonizers (Whites) and the colonized (people of Color), and the state of colonization indeed cultivates various portraitures of those who assume these polarities (Memmi, 1965) including *racial fetishization*. Such a phenomenon is promulgated in the oft-spoken excuse "But I have a Black friend," as discussed in depth in Chapter 1. However, in order to unveil this dynamic, we must first begin with a psychoanalytic deconstruction of Whites as racial colonizers.

Psychoanalytic Portraiture of Racial Colonizers

Whites, like colonizers, have used the systemic mechanisms of white supremacy to strategically uphold racial privilege (Allen, 2002; Daniels, 1997; Gillborn, 2006; Roediger, 2005). In this enactment, several considerations maintain this pseudo-performance of whiteness. First, Whites have to justify their position as racially-privileged through social and personal identity negotiations. For example, White children can perceive racial dynamics as early as the age of three (Clark & Clark, 1939); thus, as Thandeka (1999) asserts, they are racialized into whiteness through the adoption of colorblind ideology. Although White children bear witness to race, their acceptance into the white community and into whiteness in general is predicated by rejecting race perceptions and feigning colorblindness. Like "someone who is living a lie" (Thandeka, 1999, p. 34), accepting whiteness then becomes a commodity, if you will, that provides benefits, albeit at a cost (Matias, 2014). Thandeka writes:

The price for the right to be white had already been exacted: wholeness. What remained was a self that was conflicted and fearful of another racial assault. (p. 87)

Per Igantiev and Garvey (1996), the acceptance into whiteness leads one *away* from humanity. Furthermore, by exacting the price of wholeness, the whitened individual may feel disconcerted and "unwhole" per his whitened privileged identity. Memmi (1965) writes:

> [A]ccepting the reality of being *colonizer* means agreeing to be a non-legitimate, privileged person; that is, a usurper. To be sure, a usurper claims his place and, if need be, will defend it by every means at his disposal. This amounts to saying that at the very time of his triumph, he admits that what triumphs in him is an image which he condemns. His true victory will therefore never be upon him... For this he would have to convince the others, if not himself. In other words, to possess victory completely, he needs to absolve himself of it and the conditions under which it was attained. This explains his strenuous insistence, strange for a victor, on apparently futile matters. He endeavors to falsify history, he rewrites laws, he would extinguish memories – anything to succeed in transforming his usurpation into legitimacy. (p. 52)

Thus, adopting whiteness into one's racialization is to give up a human victory that is rightfully legitimate – the colonizer feels compelled to constantly justify his usurped positionality. The strategic implementation of rewriting history and laws whilst engaging in hegemonic discourse that further denigrates people of Color becomes, as Leonardo (2009) posits, a white racial knowledge that refuses to acknowledge itself and thus is "nothing but false and oppressive" (p. 108). As such, the constant need to justify one's racial privilege is simply a defensive mechanism to mask the shame of usurping power in a racist structure while turning a blind eye to the reality of this usurpation.

Second, in acknowledging this portraiture of whiteness, the emotional, psychological, and spiritual states of the White colonizer then become suspect because he is constantly finding ways to justify usurpation while repressing racial reality. A state of emotional and human emptiness manifests itself inside the White colonizer, leading to his need for constant comforting in order to feel whole (Matias, 2014). The White colonizer then emotionally attaches to someone of Color in order to find comfort and reclaim wholeness: "But, you see, I have Black friend!" This is where fetishism begins.

In defining whiteness in opposition to Blackness, an extricable tie between White bodies and identities to Black bodies and identities emerges, even if this mechanism involves denigrating the latter to uplift the former: one cannot define oneself without the other. If "race is a form of pleasure ... achieved through humiliation of the Other," then Whites who partake in "denying their fetishism of race" (Farley, 1997, p. 464) mask the process of white racialization, positioning their identities through the attachment to Black identities. When Whites become excessively attached to Blacks – more accurately, to people of Color – this attachment defines their whiteness. Farley (1997) maintains that the "white body is created and maintained by decorating black bodies with disdain, over and over again … whites return and return and return again to this fetish in order to satisfy a self-created urge to be white" (p. 463). As such, one beginning point of fetishism – and thus the cost of becoming white – stems from the need to feel whole again. By attaching oneself to the Other, the White colonizer feels defined by his juxtaposition to Blackness.

Emotionality becomes another point of departure from which racial fetish manifests. Fanon (1967) argues that Blacks develop a dependent inferiority complex because white supremacy has all but amputated the Black man, crippled him through the state of racial subjugation. What Fanon does not consider is that, although Black men have black skin and opt to wear white masks in order to survive a racist state, Whites who falsely believe such a skin affords "justified privilege" wear their white masks up front, shaming themselves. Whites then form fictive kinships with people of Color in order to alleviate the shame of race, particularly the assumption to whiteness. As Bonilla-Silva (2010) argues, those who claim fictive kinships by stating "my best friend is Black," do so as a strategic maneuver to deflect deeply-embedded racist attitudes.

Yet, beyond this phenomenon is an emotional underpinning: in order for White colonizers to feel justified in feigning fictive kinship with people of Color, the shameful practice of emotionality must be sentimentalized in order to mask true emotionality toward people of Color. For example, in Chapter 3, Zembylas and I argue that this emotionality of whiteness can be performed as caring for people of Color, yet it is actually a sentimentalization masking a disgust for people of Color (Matias & Zembylas, 2014). Disgust then is not only about feeling a sense of aversion toward an object or subject deemed lower, but also is about maintaining a sense of aboveness from that disgusted subject (Ahmed, 2004). Therefore, in emotionally deeming the racially-colonized as humanly disgusting, the White colonizer is inadvertently situated as humanly attractive, desirable, and/or fascinating. The emotion of shame becomes a strong precursor to racial fetish. Shame, as Ahmed (2004) suggests, "feels like an exposure – another sees what I have done that it is bad and hence shameful" (p. 103). The exposure of white racialization thus surfaces shame, for when White colonizers feign colorblind ideology, claiming they do not see race, they "suddenly speak volumes about [race] when their racial ideology is challenged" (Leonardo, 2009, p. 114). This contradiction becomes one White colonizers must confront: they are aware of race dynamics and, according to Mills (2007), must "actively participate in a process of epistemological racial ignorance." Such a process allows White colonizers to release racial culpability while "further[ing] their own supremacy" (p. 117).

Shame can also become a process of self-awareness, something "crucial to the process of reconciliation of the healing of past wounds" (Ahmed, 2004, p. 101). In fact, Ahmed (2004) argues that, with respect to Australia and its indigenous peoples, the declaration of shame can be a process to "acknowledge past wrongdoings" (p. 101). Although Ahmed (2004) describes how a national acknowledgement of shame can be a praxis for racial connectivity and reconciliation, she also asserts that it leads to other performative behaviors. That is, she argues that a national recognition of shame may "cloak" individual shame which, for the purposes of this chapter, prevents one from taking onus of one's individual emotionalities. If such critically self-reflective stages are not experienced in full acknowledgement of the role white supremacy plays in society, then the shamed individual can reinvent a performance as racially-aware without any self-sacrifice of their privileged identity (Igantiev & Garvey, 1996). For example, hooks (2006) describes how White males profess their sexual desire to be with women of Color:

> [T]o seek an encounter with the Other does not require one to relinquish forever one's mainstream positionality. When race and ethnicity become commodified as resources for pleasure, the culture of specific groups, as well as the bodies of individuals, can be seen as constituting an alternative playground where members of dominating races, genders, and sexual practices affirm their power-over an intimate relations with the Other. (hooks, 2006, p. 367)

Although these White men believe their desire to have sex with women of Color is "a progressive change in white attitudes towards non-whites" and do "not see themselves as perpetuating racism" (p. 369), they are fetishizing women of Color as objects to be used for sexual pleasure, i.e., they are "eating the Other" (hooks, 2006). Just like Fanon's (1967) alarming claim that "the Black man is a penis" forever fetishized by the White onlookers, more generally speaking, sexual desire for a person of Color is an objective to fulfill a racial desire (p. 170). Relating to the psychoanalytics of white narcissism, fetishizing the racially-colonized becomes an indirect way to uphold whiteness because it placates the need for the overindulgent super ego. If the colonized can be used as an object that provides pleasure for the colonizer, then fetishizing becomes affirmation of the narcissistic identity of White colonizers. From White missionaries who piously throw candy to impoverished children, to White teachers seeking to save urban students of Color, fetishization can be psychoanalytically interpreted as a performance of whiteness that facilitates one's narcissistic need to feel humanly fulfilled as a process of atonement for white racialization.

TEACHER EDUCATION: INSTITUTIONALIZING RACIAL FETISH?

Although a litany of literature in U.S. teacher education critiques the overwhelming presence of whiteness in the K-12 teaching force (Picower, 2009; Sleeter, 2001; Solomona, Portelli, Daniel, & Campbell, 2006), less explicitly described is how this same whiteness exists inside the U.S. teacher education professoriate of higher education through filtering socially-just pedagogies and curricula through the ocular of whiteness (Matias, 2013a). After years of teaching in U.S. teacher education programs, I observe that the K-12 teaching pipeline from teacher candidates to teacher education professors is (still) predominately heterosexual, White, middle-class, and female. I see white culture, white mannerisms, white emotions, white euphemisms, and white diss-courses commonly employed and uncontested. The normalcy of whiteness then becomes commonplace, a breeding ground of recycled hegemonic whiteness.

Whiteness then sets the prevailing context for which U.S. teacher education exists and operates. The context of White-teacher-as-savior (see Chapter 2) is aligned with the teachers' psychosocial experiences with race and whiteness despite their lack of diverse racial and socioeconomic upbringing. Many of my teacher candidates have explained that their desire to become an urban-focused teacher hinges on their privilege of whiteness and thus they feel the "need to give back." Yet nearly all cannot articulate *why*: *what makes them feel compelled or guilty enough to give back*? What racialized processes have they undergone that leads them to believe they are apt to teach urban students of Color? And, most importantly, how will this impact urban students of Color?

I theorize that these White teacher candidates seek to fill an emptiness, for whiteness exacts a loss of humanity, ergo one logically seeks atonement and redemption through giving back to those from whom humanity was taken. About the White man who is thus ensnared by whiteness, Fanon (1967) writes: "What about dignity? He had no need to achieve it: It was injected now into the labyrinth of his arteries, entrenched in his little pink fingernails, a solidly rooted, white dignity" (p. 52).

Yet, when the falsity of whiteness is exposed, how is dignity to be restored? Herein lies the excessive attachment which precipitates racial fetish. If a Black man is "black in relation to the white man," a White man is equally white in relation to the Black man (Fanon, 1967, p. 110). Whites must then attach to Blackness in order to find meaning and to restore their sense of wholeness. Thus, White teacher candidates in the urban-focus program believe they will be fulfilled by teaching K-12 students of Color and by acquiring these students as their "Black friends." Such a friendship will at once solidify the colonizer/colonized (teacher/student) relationship while perpetuating their safety in whiteness by not fully confronting it.

Interestingly, these White teacher candidates resist making "Black friends" of their professors of Color, a practice I've encountered first-hand with my White colleagues as well (see Matias, 2013a). The White-student-to-Black-professor or White-professor-to-Black professor relationship morphs into the servant/served paradigm: now the professor of Color, one with higher status in the relationship, becomes a threat to whiteness, white narcissism, and the student's white colorblindness (see Duncan, 2002; Thompson, 2003). The power shift, perhaps never present in their lives before, reveals that they are, in fact, not antiracist after all, a problematic issue if they are to teach urban students of Color and profess themselves to be antiracist teachers.

DANGERS AND HOPES IN "WHITE SKIN, BLACK FRIEND"

> If the white man challenges my humanity, I will impose my whole weight as a
> man on his life and show him that I am not that 'sho good eatin' that he persists
> in imagining. (Fanon, 1967, p. 229)

Vera and Gordan (2003) describe how media and film often depict Black
characters and other people of Color as sidekicks to White heroes, simply adding
comic relief and a "fantasy of racial harmony" (p. 171). Yet, beyond enabling
us to "laugh [racial hostility] all off" (p. 171), film characters of Color play a
strategic role in reifying whiteness. Just as Fanon (1967) argues the falsity of the
"good Negro" image, Vera and Gordan (2003) identify "the tame Black man"
as a strategically-included figure to assuage white racial tensions, for Whites
needed to decipher the "safe" Blacks from those that are unsafe. If the media is
a reflector of a society (Kellner, 1995) that has pedagogical applications, then
having the Black friend sidekick in real life works in the same manner. The act of
Whites publically claiming association with Black friends reveals the dangers and
hopes that divert or align the hope of antiracism. Unless exposed, a false sense
of racial unity is promoted. Certainly, merely having a Black friend, a Latina or
Filipina (Pinay) girlfriend, or a biracial child does not preclude one from having
racist ideologies: the behavior of Donald Sterling, owner of the Los Angeles
Clippers and his exposed comments about keeping African Americans away
from his arena despite having a mixed race (African American and Mexican)
girlfriend demonstrates that. But the pontification of the "White skin, Black
friend" dynamic without consideration of its inherent fetishization threatens true
antiracist sentiment. A White teacher who truly engages in antiracism would not
need to either promote her perceived Hidalguismo in teaching urban students of
Color or affirm her own narcissism by pegging a "friend" as a Black one. Further
– and perhaps most importantly – a truly antiracist teacher would recognize that
the relationship between White adults and children of Color is not enough to
proclaim a commitment to antiracism since the power dynamic still perches
White teachers over students of Color.

The hope of antiracism exists simply in increasing contacts with people of Color
(Helms, 1990). Yet, to begin to emotionally detach themselves from the racial fetish
dynamic, Whites must first accept that they are, at best, "antiracist white racists."[3]
Only within this detachment will Whites have the opportunity to engage in the *burden
of race* themselves without relying on the support and guidance from people of Color.
Self-assuming the burden of race forces Whites to realize their own complicity in
whiteness and white supremacy. In order to release their psychoanalytic attachment
to people of Color, Whites must self-critically ask and answer for themselves,
"Why I am feeling so guilty, angry, defensive, and/or uncomfortable?" instead of
projecting onto people of Color the defensive questions of "Why are you making
me feel bad? *I* never owned slaves!" With respect to Zembylas' (2013) theorization

of critical pedagogies of compassion, the process of de-fetishizing cannot only stem from understanding the stories of suffering, pity, and false empathies. Rather, it must also entertain the depth of quality relationships between teacher and students. Such a relationship can only deepen if the teacher self-investigates her/his own emotional need to attach to students of Color.

TO BE A FRIEND: A NEW BEGINNING

As a woman of Color – moreover, a motherscholar of Color – nothing is more frustrating than being strategically employed as *that* friend whose browned melanin brings forth credibility to a White person. Instead of treating our relationship as a form of white credibility, I demand, as Fanon (1967) does, that we acknowledge the "human behavior from the other" (p. 229). In this recognition of humanistic behavior, I demand to be seen as a person with humanistic qualities in order to forge truer relationships. Like Fanon, "I want the world to recognize, with me, the open door of every consciousness" (p. 232). Yet that cannot be done until Whites dig deeply into their psyches and consider how society continues to socialize racism and white supremacy, as it does Black identities, in ways we all have repressed and/or have actively refused to understand for fear of surfacing painful emotions. Until we have the ovaries – and I use this body part specifically (see Chapter 4) to confront these painful emotions, and until this psychoanalytic racial burden has been feverishly excavated, honestly applied, and deeply considered, those with white skin cannot finally and fully become, simply, a friend.

NOTES

[1] Though the structure I use for this book is to capitalize race names, e.g., "Black" and "White," while I maintain "whiteness" as lowercase to describe it as a state of being, Fanon did not utilize the same capitalization structure. However, we both capitalize "Blackness" to illuminate and honor the particular state of being felt by people of Color.
[2] Per http://thefreedictionary.com/psychosis
[3] Derived from personal communication with critical whiteness studies scholar Dr. Ricky Lee Allen.

REFERENCES

Ahmed, S. (2004). *The cultural politics of emotion*. London: Edinburgh University Press.
Ahmed, S. (2013). *The cultural politics of emotion*. New York, NY: Routledge.
Allen, R. L. (2002). *Pedagogy of the oppressor: What was Freire's theory for transforming the privileged and powerful?* [Presentation]. Paper presented at American Educational Research Association, New Orleans, LA.
Allen, R. L. (2004). Whiteness and critical pedagogy. *Educational Philosophy and Theory, 36*(2), 121–136.
Bell, C. C. (1980). Racism: A symptom of the narcissistic personality. *Journal of the National Medical Association, 72*(7), 661.
Bell, D. A. (1992). *Faces at the cottom of the well: The permanence of racism*. New York, NY: Basic Books.

Bhabha, H. (1996). The other question: Difference, discrimination, and the discourse of colonialism. In H. A. Baker, Jr., M. Diawara, & R. H. Lindeborg (Eds.), *Black British cultural studies: A reader* (pp. 87–106). Chicago, IL: University of Chicago Press.

Bonilla-Silva, E. (2010). *Racism without racists: Color-blind racism and the persistence of racial inequality in America*. New York, NY: Rowman & Littlefield.

Clark, K. B., & Clark, M. K. (1939). The development of consciousness of self in the emergence of racial identification in Negro pre-school children. *Journal of Social Psychology, 10*, 91–597.

Cleveland, D. (Ed.). (2004). *A long way to go: Conversations about race by African American faculty and graduate students* (Higher Education, Vol. 14). New York, NY: Peter Lang.

Corbett, M. M. (1995). *The relationship between White racial identity and narcissism* (Doctoral dissertation). Proquest Information & Learning.

Daniels, J. (1997). *White lies: Race, class, gender and sexuality in White supremacist discourse.* New York, NY: Routledge.

de Jesús, M. L., & Ma, S. M. (2004). R.A.W.: "Raunchy Asian women" and resistance to queer studies in the Asian Pacific American studies classroom. *The Radical Teacher, 70*, 26–31.

Duncan, G. A. (2002). Critical race theory and method: Rendering race in urban ethnographic research. *Qualitative Inquiry, 8*(1), 85–104.

Espiritu, Y. (2001). Ideological racism and cultural resistance: Constructing our own images. In M. Andersen & P. Collins (Eds.), *Race, class, and gender: An anthology.* Belmont, CA: Wadsworth Publishing.

Fanon, F. (1967). *White skin, Black masks.* New York, NY: Grove Press.

Farley, A. P. (1997). Black body as fetish object. *Oregon Law Review, 76*, 457.

Fasching-Varner, K., Albert, K. A., Mitchell, R. W., & Allen, C. A. (2015). *Racial battle fatigue in higher education: Exposing the myth of post-racial America.* Lantham, MD: Rowman & Littlefield.

Freire, P. (1993). *Pedagogy of the oppressed* (Rev. ed.). New York, NY: Continuum.

Foucault, M. (1977). *Discipline and punishment.* New York, NY: Pantheon.

Gillborn, D. (2006). Rethinking White supremacy: Who counts in 'Whiteworld'? *Ethnicities, 6*(3), 318–340.

Godfrey, P. (2004). "Sweet little (White) girls"? Sex and fantasy across the color line and the contestation of patriarchal White supremacy. *Equity & Excellence in Education, 37*(3), 204–218.

Hayes, C., & Juárez, B. G. (2009). You showed your whiteness: You don't get a 'good' White people's medal. *International Journal of Qualitative Studies in Education, 22*(6), 729–744.

Helms, J. E. (1990). *Black and White racial identity: Theory, research, and practice.* Westport, CT: Greenwood Press.

Hook, D. (2005). The racial stereotype, colonial discourse, fetishism, and racism. *The Psychoanalytic Review, 92*(5), 701–734.

hooks, b. (1994). *Teaching to transgress: Education as the practice of freedom* (Vol. 4). New York, NY: Routledge.

hooks, b. (2006). Eating the other: Desire and resistance. In M. Durham & D. Kellner (Eds.), *Media and cultural studies keyworks.* Malden, MA: Blackwell Publishing.

Igantiev, N., & Garvey, J. (1996). *Race traitor.* New York, NY: Routledge.

Johansson, P. (1999). Consuming the other: The fetish of the western woman in Chinese advertising and popular culture. *Postcolonial Studies: Culture, Politics, Economy, 2*(3), 377–388.

Kellner, D. (1995). *Media culture.* New York, NY: Routledge.

Leonardo, Z. (2004). The color of supremacy: Beyond the discourse of 'White privilege.' *Educational Philosophy and Theory, 36*(2), 137–152.

Leonardo, Z. (2009). *Race, whiteness, and education.* New York, NY: Routledge.

Leonardo, Z. (2011). After the glow: Race ambivalence and other educational prognoses. *Educational Philosophy and Theory, 43*(6), 675–698.

Leonardo, Z. (2013). *Race frameworks: A multidimensional theory of racism and education.* New York, NY: Teachers College Press.

Leonardo, Z., & Porter, R. K. (2010). Pedagogy of fear: Toward a Fanonian theory of 'safety' in race dialogue. *Race Ethnicity and Education, 13*(2), 139–157.

Lipsitz, G. (2006). *The possessive investment in whiteness: How White people profit from identity politics.* Philadelphia, PA: Temple University Press.

Matias, C. (2012). "Who you callin' White?!": A critical counterstory on colouring White identity. *Race, Ethnicity and Education, 16*(3), 291–315.

Matias, C. E. (2013a). On the "Flip" side: A teacher educator of color unveiling the dangerous minds of white teacher candidates. *Teacher Education Quarterly, 40*(2), 53–73.

Matias, C. E. (2013b). Check yo'self before yo' wreck yo'self and our kids: From culturally responsive white teachers? To culturally responsive white teachers! *Interdisciplinary Journal of Teaching and Learning, 3*(2), 68–81.

Matias, C. E. (2014). "And our feelings just don't feel it anymore": Re-Feeling whiteness, resistance, and emotionality. *Understanding and Dismantling Privilege, 4*(2).

Matias, C. E., & Zembylas, M. (2014). "When saying you care is not really caring": Emotions of disgust, whiteness ideology, and teacher education. *Critical Studies in Education, 55*(3), 319–337.

Memmi, A. (1965). *The colonizer and the colonized.* Boston, MA: Beacon Press.

Mills, C. (2007). White ignorance. In S. Sullivan & N. Tuana (Eds.), *Race and epistemologies of ignorance.* New York, NY: SUNY Press.

National Center for Education Statistics. (2012). *Fast facts: Teacher trends.* Institute of Educational Sciences, U.S. Department of Education. Retrieved from http://nces.ed.gov/fastfacts/display.asp?id=28

Oliver, M. L., & Shapiro, T. M. (1995). *Black wealth/White wealth.* Urbana, IL: University of Illinois Press.

Picower, B. (2009). The unexamined whiteness of teaching: How White teachers maintain and enact dominant racial ideologies. *Race Ethnicity and Education, 12*(2), 197–215.

Roediger, D. (2005). *Working toward whiteness: How America's immigrants become White.* New York, NY: Basic Books.

Schroeder, J. E., & Borgerson, J. L. (2003). Dark desires: Fetishism, ontology and representation in contemporary advertising. In T. Reichert & J. Lambiase (Eds.), *Sex in advertising: Perspectives on the erotic appeal* (pp. 65–89). Mahwah, NJ: Lawrence Erlbaum Associates.

Sleeter, C. E. (2001). Preparing teachers for culturally diverse schools research and the overwhelming presence of whiteness. *Journal of Teacher Education, 52*(2), 94–106.

Solomona, R. P., Portelli, J. P., Daniel, B. J., & Campbell, A. (2005). The discourse of denial: How white teacher candidates construct race, racism and 'white privilege.' *Race Ethnicity and Education, 8*(2), 147–169.

Solórzano, D. G., & Yosso, T. J. (2002). Critical race methodology: Counter-storytelling as an analytical framework for education research. *Qualitative Inquiry, 8*(1), 23–44.

Thandeka. (1999). *Learning to be White.* New York, NY: Continuum.

Thompson, A. (2003). Tiffany, friend of people of color: White investments in antiracism. *International Journal of Qualitative Studies in Education, 16*(1), 7–29.

Vera, H., & Gordon, A. (2003). *Screen saviors: Hollywood fictions of whiteness.* New York, NY: Rowman & Littlefield.

Williams, D. G., & Evans-Winters, V. (2005). The burden of teaching teachers: Memoirs of race discourse in teacher education. *The Urban Review, 37*(3), 201–219.

Zembylas, M. (2013). The "crisis of pity" and the radicalization of solidarity: Toward critical pedagogies of compassion. *Educational Studies, 49*(6), 504–521.

CHAPTER 7

GRIEF, MELANCHOLIA, AND DEATH

Beyond Whiteness?

Who am I to be?
Foundation wrought with whiteness
Sprouting a new self

While teaching about whiteness to my mainly White college students, I was once asked, "Well, then how can I shed this white-ist identity? Who will I become after I do?" Such exasperation is no less different than the proverbial need to ask, "Who am I?" or, as my poem above suggests, "Who am I to be?" The quandary over understanding the self is of great interest in many fields. Philosophy, for one, ruminates over the meaning of life merely because life is what the "self" experiences. Education, on the other hand, preoccupies itself with developing, improving, and educating the self for the hopes that such enlightenment will give rise to the creation of a better society. As opposed to the social sciences, the physical sciences, such as biology, are entranced with understanding how the self works, hurts, and heals. Needless to say, the understanding of the self is of grave importance; indeed it is a forever quest for knowing, reacquainting, and re-conceptualizing the self.

In this chapter I focus on the white self and the emotional labor one must undergo to begin a therapeutic process of de-racializing the whiteness embodied in that white self. Employing the emotional process of grief, melancholia, and death provides an emotional roadmap, so to speak, of what one will experience in trying to let go of their whiteness. This paper uses psychoanalytical approaches to theorize what happens to those individuals – whose identities are self-defined by whiteness – when they attempt to let go of their whiteness. Entertaining Cheng's (2000) psychoanalytic analysis of melancholia, grief, mourning, and trauma (but in reverse), this chapter unveils the emotional process that Whites must undergo in order to wrestle with their own whiteness.

Though this chapter does not contend that whiteness is something that can be "given up" or "released" in a society that continually institutionalizes white supremacy, it does assert that a process toward racial awareness is beyond the mere acquisition of racial awareness, racial knowledge, and/or racial terminologies. Rather, the process must therapeutically consider the deeply-embedded ways which whiteness emotionally informs identities and people's sense of core values.

THE UBIQUITY OF WHITENESS

Leonardo (2009) asserts that whiteness permeates every structure of education such that even radical pedagogies, such as Critical Pedagogy, cannot be divorced from the hegemonic ideals of whiteness (Allen, 2004). This spread of whiteness then "overwhelms" educational fields from teacher education (Sleeter, 2001) to educational policy (Gillborn, 2005) and, with respect to individuality, our own individual identities (Tatum, 1997). Sleeter (2001), for one, claims that teacher education programs are "predominantly White institutions [that] have generally responded very slowly to the growing cultural gap" (p. 95). This becomes gravely important in that these White teachers then superimpose their white beliefs onto students of Color and also impart "stereotypic beliefs about urban children" (p. 95). Gillborn (2005) corroborates the deleterious nature of whiteness when he claims "one of the most powerful and dangerous aspects of whiteness is that many (possibly the majority) of white people have no awareness of whiteness as a construction, let alone their own role in sustaining and playing out the inequities at the heart of whiteness" (p. 490). He further posits that such whiteness weaves itself into the fabric of educational policies which ultimately "alter[s] how schools operate, placing a premium on those subjects that will count in the school tests"; subjects that are typically white (p. 494).

Both Sleeter and Gillborn explicate how whiteness embeds itself in the infrastructure of education and how that can have devastating effects on students, let alone students of Color. However, Tatum (1997) takes the notion of whiteness to an individual level. She posits that whiteness "reopens a person's wounds" to a point where "frankly, people of color don't necessarily want to hear about it" (p. 111). In fact, she argues that people of Color are too busy having to "resist negative societal messages and develop[ing] an empowered sense of self in the face of a racist society" (p. 94). As such, Whites have the task of understanding their own whiteness. What Tatum brings to the table is a reflexive understanding of how whiteness impacts both people of Color and Whites themselves precisely because whiteness is a figment of our existence continually superimposing its hegemonic domination upon us. Suffice it to say that we are "colored" based upon our social proximity to whiteness.

To illuminate this, let me engage my own identity. As a brown-skinned Pinay I am often racially misinterpreted as Latina. My interactions with those who misidentify me are based on the racist and sexist stereotypes and biased assumptions of Latin@s.[1] From "Ya, I love Latina women because they are feisty," to "Your English is so good," the communiqués I receive from them reflect their presuppositions of Latinos – specifically Latinas – and thus I have to navigate that space with regard to maintaining, reaffirming, and defining my own Filipina identity. That is, in that seemingly minor racial microaggressive moment, I have to metacognitively work through the racial tensions of a society: *What are the racial features that make people mistake me for Latina? What does it mean to be Latina? If Latinos are Hispanics, then am **I** Hispanic knowing that the Philippines were under Spanish* *rule for 300 years? Wait a minute! I thought I was American?! If I'm not considered American, then why are **they** considered Americans? Where does my racial identity fall next to Whites?*

Conversely, if one were to racially interpret me as Asian American, I am confronted with a different set of behaviors, norms, and communiqués. From presumed submissiveness to racially fetishizing me as a "Dragon Lady" (Espiritu, 2001), the behaviors presented nonetheless rely on racial misconceptions, stereotypes, and the pejorative labeling of Asian Americans, specifically Asian American females. Yet, regardless of the two kinds of interactions I receive, they are structured by the hegemonic control of whiteness, i.e., I deal with others' racial misidentification of me *precisely because* whiteness runs rampant. This process exemplifies how my identity as a brown-skinned Pinay continues to be structured by whiteness.

In educational settings, curricula, pedagogies, and instructional approaches often cater to white culture. Lewis and Manno (2011), for instance, argue "White cultural hegemony, including the institutionalization of white cultural norms and the demographic dominance of white middle-class teachers in schools, set the context for much of what takes place in public schools" (p. 96). Schools, in this sense, are merely reproducing racial hierarchies whereby Whites remain at the apex. Ayers and colleagues (Ayers, Ladson-Billings, Michie, & Noguera, 2008) corroborate the notion that there exists an underlying hegemony of whiteness by asserting that multicultural education is a "response to reality" and so posit "What would schooling be if we rejected multiculturalism education for white supremacy?" (p. 8)? Acknowledging the institutionalization of white supremacist thought in schooling practices, the authors offer "reports from the front row" by urban students, classroom teachers, and beyond, hoping that such stories will "provide context for understanding the challenges and possibilities of education" (p. xxxi). The stories indeed provide a comprehensive understanding of the challenge and possibilities in education as lived by students, teachers, and scholars, yet they do not interrogate whiteness or white supremacy itself. That is, the challenges of urban schools are commonly thought to be issues with achievement gaps, poverty, inequitable funding sources, and/or anything related to "disadvantaged" students such as being identified as multilingual, overrepresented in special education, and underrepresented in gifted and talented education.

Yet rarely do we, as a society, engage in an interrogation of the "advantaged" and how they are socially positioned to assume such an advantage. Clearly, if one is to delve into who is disadvantaged, then shouldn't there be literature to explicate those who are deemed *advantaged*? Such a one-sided approach belies the hope for racially-just education, for how can one talk about the dynamics of a racialized schooling system if one overlooks how Whites are positively positioned within it? Again, the invisibility of whiteness is maintained when we, as educational scholars, pin the problem on those most marginalized. Though it is absolutely necessary to understand the impacts of racism by excavating the daily and structural experiences of people of Color, it is equally important to *not ignore* the latent expressions of whiteness that precede those experiences. Needlessly to say, the problem of the "colorline" DuBois (2007) so cogently argued over a hundred years ago is also about the spread of invisible whiteness.

THE PSYCHOLOGICAL IMPACTS OF WHITENESS

Fanon (1967) details how whiteness negatively impacts Black men by claiming they have developed an inferiority and dependency complex under the constant pressure of white colonial racism. This process of internalization leads to psychological damage because, as whiteness is imposed, the only message taught to Blacks is that a "good" Black is "a Negro who serves with a smile" (p. 72). In fact, James Baldwin's "A Talk to Teachers" (1963) corroborates this by claiming that under white supremacy Blacks have to position themselves as "happy, shiftless, watermelon-eating darkies who loved Mr. Charlie and Miss Ann, that the value he has a black man is proven by one thing only – his devotion to white people" (p. 1).

Though different in racialization processes, Cheng (2000) makes a similar argument for Whites, claiming "dominant white identity in America operates melancholically – as an elaborate identificatory system based on psychical and social consumption-and-denial" (p. 11). Suffice it to say, that under a racist system, just as Blacks have to redefine their "otherness" in juxtaposition to Whites, Whites too must define who they are by demeaning, degrading, inferiorizing, and justifying the belittlement of Others. Although racialization processes are similar among racial groups under a White supremacist system, there is yet one major difference: when Whites experience their racialization under a system that benefits their whiteness, they receive favorable experiences. Conversely, when people of Color experience their racialization under that exact same system, they receive unfavorable experiences.

The difference between the two distinct racialized experiences is not happenstance. When looking at a colonial system of race, there are those who are deemed "racial colonizers" and those who are deemed the "racially-colonized." Yet, despite their distinct label, both parties experience a process of colonization. Memmi (1965) explains this as a process by which those who are deemed colonized in an enterprise of colonization find themselves unable to "acknowledge belonging to himself" (p. 68). He further contends that "the result is that the colonialist is unsure of his true nationality" (p. 68). The underlying theme here is that when a person of Color internalizes the whiteness that is constantly imposed onto her, she can develop an internalized racist's depiction of herself. Alas, the notion of the self is again engaged. Essentially, under a white supremacist system that continually exerts whiteness, people of Color are then made to become Whites' counterparts or, as Fanon (1967) suggests, only "black in relation to the white man" (p. 110).

This is seen again in the Clark & Clark (1939) doll study in which Black and White children were to listen to a series of questions and answer by picking a Black or White doll. One question was, "Show me the doll that is bad"; remarkably, both Black and White children often selected the Black doll. When asked which doll they were, Black children would slowly pick up the Black doll, which they had just designated as the "bad" doll per the previous question. But more telling are the psychoanalytics behind such a choice. As Cheng (2000) asserts, the doll study reveals more about the psychological state of race, namely that "these interior patterns of grief and how they both constrain and are constrained by subjectivity" (p. x). Plainly stated, people of Color internalize a demoralizing perception of themselves based on the hegemony of whiteness and thus live in a perpetual state of grief, needing to both rectify their identity and defend it.

This internationalization process is again seen in educational schooling practices. Recently I published an article entitled, "Why Do You Make Me Hate Myself: Whiteness, Abuse, and Love in Urban Teacher Education," (2015) in which I describe the processes by which students of Color are made to hate themselves based on the constant expressions of whiteness made by their White teachers. bell hooks (1994) argues that she, herself, "lost her love for school" as a young Black child when forced to being bussed to Whites' schools. She explains how her White teachers feared her intelligence and her wit to deconstruct their racist assumptions. Her strategy for survival was to pretend obedience to the curricula and pedagogy that were wrought with racist stereotypes of Blacks. She claims to have done this because "too much eagerness to learn could easily be seen as a threat to white authority" (p. 3). Like hooks, students of Color are confronted with daily acts of racial microaggression or, as Ladson-Billings (1989) suggests, psycho-cultural assaults on their racial identities.

In fact, I began my article with words I painfully remember coming from a White teacher colleague (who I will call Ms. R) to our Brooklyn middle school students back in 2005. Though there were other White allied teachers, this particular teacher proclaimed herself to be "down" with people of Color. Often times Ms. R re-appropriated Black English vernacular, otherwise known as "African American Language," and would use it to perform an allied identity. She would boast about her love of rap and hip-hop and would often "bump it" on her iPod Mini so we could all hear.[2] This performance became oddly confusing when, in front of her mainly White friends she reverted to "white ways." Now, I am sensitive to the research on code-switching and language brokers,[3] yet what I observed in my two years of teaching with her was a confused identity hoping to gain acceptance in realms not her own. And though she did teach with me in Bedford-Stuyvesant, Brooklyn and proclaimed a deep connection with the Black community, she would apparently yell at her mainly Black and Latino students to "look out the window and see those crackheads. That's what you will be if you don't listen to me!" I remember her proudly relaying the story to all of us and inviting us to do the same thing. However, it never felt right with me that she did that and boasted about it. Not only was it crass and inappropriate; something struck at me deeper.

Having grown up in public schools predominated by White teachers in the east side of Los Angeles, I was instantly transported to my experiences as an urban student of Color. I felt sick. I remembered having to find pride in my racial and ethnic identity on the streets since the schools were so silent on issues of race and multicultural contributions to U.S. Education. I remembered my second grade teacher, Ms. Pekuri, who changed the label on my Filipino food from "lumpia" to "eggroll," and how much that pained me because she overlooked my identity and homogenized it with her conceptualizations of Asian Americans. I still struggle with her action because, not only did it show poor judgment by a teacher – my professional identity – but it revealed what she really thought of us students of Color: she gave herself the authority to so easily change our identities – our personal, individual "labels."

Again, taunting me are the racial quandaries from my experience with Ms. R. For example, would she easily associate me with some mail-order bride, only useful to the pleasures of straight White men if I had not been so masterful in code-switching between whiteness and reality? Did she see herself above me since I was a woman of Color? These are the internalized inferiorizations and constant questioning of our racial identity that people of color undergo (see Yancy, 2008). Just as Memmi (1965) describes that the colonized who submits to colonial racism develops "feelings ranging from shame to self-hate" (p. 121), so too can students of Color develop the same sentiments.

But what of Whites? Whites are also racialized, albeit in favorable ways. If whiteness is so ubiquitous and thus influences the way Whites experience race, then why aren't scholars rethinking what they thought about race, racism, and white supremacy? How can we even study race without realizing the etiolated tendency of whiteness left unchecked? Relatedly, if, as Leonardo (2009) suggests, whiteness is everywhere and yet simultaneously recognized nowhere, then how do we conceptualize our identities free from a notion of whiteness? More importantly, what happens when one realizes one's identity was built upon the lie of whiteness (see Thandeka, 1999)?

As described in other chapters, Whites have also developed a psychological condition towards their whiteness. Opting for Fanon's (1967) terminology, Whites have developed a dependency on a white supremacist system because such a system constantly reinforces, uplifts, and purports their existence, identity, mentality, and behaviors above people of Color. Yet the focus on the dependency complex is not often explored and this lack of exploration has great implications. For one, to focus only on racial victims' dependency complex over that of racial perpetrators' overlooks the inter-dynamics of how one influences the experiences of another. Cheng (2000) corroborates this by claiming "that is why trauma, so often associated with discussions of racial denigration, in focusing on a structure of crisis on the part of the victim, misses the violators' own dynamic process at stake in such denigration" (p. 12). Eventually, this purposeful oversight leaves Whites not responsible for their own complicit behaviors in the structure of white supremacist society. To be clear, in order to undo white supremacy, Whites need to first interrogate themselves and not deflect their racial misunderstandings by focusing solely on how people of Color are impacted by race.

A GLIMPSE AT GRIEF, MELANCHOLIA, AND DEATH

The thought of grief, melancholia, and death conjure up popularized definition of despair, loss, loneliness, depression, and emptiness. These become strong words in that they are clearly sentiments that social beings, like ourselves, most fear. Who would want to be isolated from society for entirety? Who would want to be excommunicated from a group which has a strong hand in developing who you believe you are? What happens to you if you are beyond the protection of such a community? Who do you become? These are just a few of the ponderings one reflects on when engaging in a process of renewal. To illuminate this phenomenon, I draw from my own experiences.

In winter 2014, I found I was pregnant. Having delivered twins seven years prior, I recognized the initial feeling a woman gets when she redefines her identity as a mother. It was exciting, adventurous, and jubilant; though an identity I had experienced before, it nonetheless provided me with a renewed sense of commitment that I was more than willing to dive into once again. Plainly, becoming a mom again defined who I believed to be, how I needed to act, and how I engaged with the world. During my first trimester, I picked up books that affirmed my "new mother" identity. I read nightly to see the development of my baby, even if it was the same chapter over and over again. I changed my behaviors. No longer did I run my five miles every day. Instead, to accommodate my new identity, I ran three, making sure I stopped any time I felt I was overexerting myself. I also changed my discourse and emotional patterns. Instead of my usual healthy pessimism regarding society's ills, I began to re-hope anew, believing I could give birth to a child in a society much better than it was yesterday. Ultimately, I evolved my identity to match my circumstances. And who wouldn't? The possibility of giving birth once again reminded me of who I self-define myself to be. That is, life is such a miracle that the thought of it all happening inside me was beyond mere superficial incorporations. Indeed, I saw my new identity as a deeply-embedded way to incorporate who I was with whom I would evolve into.

But beyond my own self-gratification, it wasn't until I revealed the pregnancy to my partner that I learned how my new identity became a shared, collective process. In telling my partner I was pregnant, he immediately acknowledged my new identity, affirmed it by gathering even more books, and collectively accepted and engaged my identity by reading baby books with me each night. This socializing process soon affirmed my feelings of excitement because it became real, shared, and acknowledged. That is, instead of the secrecy women may first feel upon "feeling" pregnant, it felt amazing to let out that secret and have people around me interact with me in ways that recognized my new identity. As I grew bigger and the nausea grew more intense, my life changed. Often times I was unable to cook dinner. Instead, I found myself napping in the afternoons just to survive the rest of the day. Although this was my newly emerging identity, it became a social practice when my partner had to make changes in his behavior to compensate for what I was no longer able to do: he cooked dinner, checked the kids' homework, and made sure I was well-hydrated before I went to nap. Essentially, my identity became a social phenomenon impacting others.

The day we told our twins we were expecting another child involved new socializing practices that affirmed my identity. In fact, immediately after we told the twins, they asked us to drive over to a baby store to shop for welcome gifts for their new baby brother or sister. Our twins soon became embedded in this new social practice. Each night my daughter made sure to kiss my belly or read stories to her little brother or sister. My son started helping out more around the house so I could rest. There was a point when the twins revealed to us that they were a bit frightened because as I grew bigger in the belly, they knew they would need to help out more in the house, a thought that gave them anxiety as to whether they could help out enough. Needless to say, the entire process of evolving my identity as a new mother once again became a socialization process that gave me understanding of my identity, my role, and ultimately who I was. Likewise, it gave my partner and the twins understandings of who they were in relation to me.

So one can understand why, after attending a routine exam, how distraught we all felt when the doctor said the baby was no longer growing and I would likely miscarry. It was as if the doctor had pulled the rug from right out of under my feet. *What was I to stand on if I no longer had the foundation which gave me sense of who I was?* I was in such disbelief of the thought of having a miscarriage that I found myself becoming defensive, refusing to believe the doctor, and ultimately hating her for delivering the bad news. Physically, I had not bled out and thus I emotionally rejected the idea that I perhaps would not be a new mother again. After a week of carrying around a baby inside me that was no longer viable, I felt cheated, angry, and deceived. As Thandeka (1999) so poignantly suggests, I was living a lie and dearly grasping onto an identity that was really not mine. Yet, I refused to let go partly because my body still physiologically responded as if it was pregnant and my heart still felt as if I were pregnant. Because the baby would not expunge itself, I had to undergo a sedated procedure to remove it. Life after this was not the same. Initially, I thought I was dead because it wasn't a normal grief as when one passes away and a community of people who recognize this passing share in the grief. Essentially, as my baby died, I died. Therefore, my mourning of what was once there but no longer there was an isolating experience. Though one of the twins had a difficult time sleeping through the night months after the miscarriage, and my partner had a hard time even acknowledging it happened, I was left with a weakened body, a twenty pound weight gain, and a broken heart, all of which served as symbolic reminders of my loss.

They also served as symbols of my dead identity. I couldn't just go back to running five miles a day or talking as if nothing happened. Oddly, I felt others did not know how to approach me. Instead of the welcoming arms I received on announcing I was pregnant, I was shunned, avoided, or misunderstood. People did not know how to react to my mourning because, after all, there wasn't a physical body to mourn.

Instead, I was the walking dead, spiritually murdered, a body emptied of the identity it once gave birth to. It was as if it were a phantom trauma, one where I experienced it, cried over it, and mourned it while not knowing whether it was ever really there. Essentially, my miscarriage was tantamount to a death because the person who died was not only my baby, but also who I thought I was becoming.

Despite the trauma of it all, the experience was instructive because it taught me the ways in which one experiences loss. Rather than quickly brush the loss aside in order to feign a false sense of strength, or relish in a depressed state of loss, I realized that my loss, grief, and mourning were and are a perpetual state of melancholia, one that need not reside solely in despair. Instead, it can also be a deep source of empowerment. Imagine the will, strength, and determination of people who have experienced loss and learned the preciousness and value of humanity from that loss. I am still traumatized by the entire experience. I still feel loss and have bouts of depression when I take the time to honor my trauma by acknowledging, not ignoring, it. Yet, by doing so I emerged anew. My loss became instructive to how I view myself now.

Although I admit it was in some way cathartic to write this out, I do not relay this personal story to narcissistically employ myself. In fact, I procrastinated writing this chapter for months because it was too painful to even recall; so painful that, to this day (and as I write now) I still cry over it, as if a perpetual state of melancholia forever shrouds my heart. Instead, I offer this story so that when I apply the sense of loss to the idea of whiteness one can truly feel what it is like. Though scholars like Thandeka (1999) have called the process of white racialization a "trauma" because of how painfully terrorizing it is for someone to develop a sense of self and community and then realize it was all a lie, it is not equitable to the racial trauma that people of Color experience under a racist system of racialization. With that said, I will delve into what leaving whiteness feels like.

APPLYING GRIEF, MELANCHOLIA, AND DEATH
WHEN LEAVING WHITENESS

Education proclaims itself to be about social justice. In fact, teacher education programs around the U.S. are redesigning their teacher preparation curricula, pedagogies, and instruction to adhere to socially-just principles. Sadly, often in those discussions of what constitutes social justice, the concepts of race, racism, white supremacy, and whiteness get silenced. Could it possibly be that the majority of U.S. teachers are White and thus never want to place a mirror before their own whiteness? As such, education needs to rethink social justice if they continue to overlook aspects of racial justice within it – especially during a time when misunderstandings of race leads to police brutalities of unarmed Black men, mass church shootings in Charleston, and conservative political campaigns that root themselves in racist ideology. Therefore, understanding race is of grave importance because if education continues to pontificate its commitment to social justice and social transformation, then in order for racial justice to materialize – by dematerializing whiteness as property (Harris, 1993) – education must take up the emotional deconstruction of whiteness. Even more important to remember is that a majority of U.S. teachers are White (NCES, 2012), and thus can perpetuate whiteness as a hidden curriculum (Gramsci, 1976) if their white fragility (DiAngelo, 2011) remains too unfettered to deconstruct their own emotional investment in whiteness.

So what is it like to lose something or someone you thought you were? Like my story above, engaging in a therapeutic process that decolonizes one's ideologies, behaviors, and emotionalities of whiteness will feel like grieving something you thought you had but never really did. Essentially, this is white grief. Jealous and Haskell (2013) captured interviews of White participants and how they experience a collective grief with regard to racism. The common themes that emerged were of guilt, shame, sameness, separation, and silence. Often connoting racism as "a spiritual abuse" that works to "harm everyone involved," Jealous and Haskell's book focuses on the cost Whites must pay in their complicity to racism (p. 73). Because the book heavily relies on documenting how Whites experience emotional grief under racism, readers may come away erroneously thinking that Whites' racial grief is the same as that of people of Color.

As Fanon (1967) so cogently argues, this is falsity. Though Whites and people of Color, generally speaking, do experience grief under a system of white supremacy, they do so from various points within the enterprise: one that is privileged, while the other is denigrated. One may be sensitive to the nature of trauma and how pain is felt, and thus acknowledge the many challenges, dangers, and losses felt by *race traitors*, defined by Ignatiev and Garvey (1996) as those who "struggle for human freedom" and "hope to take part, together with others, in the process of defining a new human community" (pp. 13–14). Yet, it is counterproductive to assume that such challenges and dangers are equitable to the life-threatening racism that people of Color, mainly Black Americans, experience. Therefore to explicate how Whites will undergo a process of grief, melancholia, and death, I first delve into the state of melancholy itself.

Cheng (2000) asserts that "dominant white identity in America operates melancholically – as an elaborate identificatory system based on psychical and social consumption and denial" (p. 11). This melancholy develops because Whites, though bearing witness to historic and current racial atrocities of people of Color, end up denying not only the reality of racism, but also the relationship they built on benefitting from such denial. Coined "white racial melancholia," Cheng argues that revealing this melancholia can itself "be damaging to say how damaging racism has been" (p. 14). Yet shoving melancholy under the rug, so to speak, will keep intact the hegemonic whiteness that supports a racist system.

White racial identity scholars like Janet Helms (1990) identify the various stages Whites must undergo to identify their racial identities. From early stages such as contact, to final stages like autonomy, each involves a plethora of emotionalities. For example, in the contact stage Whites experience fear of the Other, yet this fear is far less visceral than the fear people of Color hold when in contact with Whites because it carries a documented history of racial genocide, beatings, and whippings, and rape by Whites hands. However, in the automony stage Whites experience a sense of wholeness, welcoming, and freedom often associated when they release their racial biases of people of Color. Regardless to the stage, the emotionalities brought about by one's awareness to and involvement against racism is felt. Thus, when one develops a strong critical race consciousness that sheds light not only on how racism operates in society but how one's white identity may be complicit in that operation, she or he is at an utter loss. Additionally, since definitions of racism are inextricably bound to connotations of morality, one cannot help but rethink one's own moral stance. Am I bad person? Who am I?

This is the essence of this chapter. For when Whites engage in a process of abolishing their whiteness, as Allen (2002) suggests, they need to redefine who they thought they were even when they are in unchartered territory. Yet, Whites need to realize that this process of de-racialization is something people of Color do on a daily basis. In asking an Asian-looking person whether she speaks English, or commenting on how a Black person is "not like the rest of them," people of Color experience the existential moment of, *who am I then*?

Like my baby within me, whiteness is a like deeply-planted seed of the racist society. It does not self-conjure nor is it something humanly innate. Like my pregnancy made me a mother, a racist society impregnates Whites with whiteness. Through this impregnation, Whites then begin to develop their identity. They feel white. They see themselves as white. Similar to my evolving identity of becoming a new mother, the White individual assumes her or his new identity while trying to understand that it is an evolved understanding of the self: the original identity has not left the building, so to speak. Rather, because of this impregnation, one begins to acknowledge an evolving identity that builds on one's pre-existing identity. S/he may learn to feel comforted by this new identity. S/he may change behaviors, discourse patterns, or emotionalities to accommodate it. Instead of bearing witness to race, the new identity of whiteness teaches the individual that s/he is no longer to see race so must suppress this insight because it threatens the newly emerging identity.

But it is only when Whites socialize their identities to others that whiteness becomes more solidified. That is, when others either affirm or privilege white identity under a white supremacist system, the White individual is made to feel superior, to believe s/he is superior and thus worthy of privilege. A racist society then interacts with this identity, offering access and opportunities, assumed objectivity, and bequeathing unearned achievements. Be it as it may, the White individual, impregnated by whiteness, learns to interact with a white society that welcomes her or his new identity. Like my pregnancy, the social practices that surrounded my identity were similar to the social practices that surround Whites. Whites are taught to not see race, to be the Determiner of what does or does not constitute racism, and to master linguistic semantics to deter any trace of this racializing process. The individual is made to believe that her or his identity is completely of one's own doing and not consider how a pre-existing condition precipitated the evolution. This is how whiteness becomes as natural as a lion eats an antelope. Needless to say, this new identity makes meaning for the self and for the society that interacts with it. It is the basis of one's existence.

Because such a racialized identity becomes so enmeshed with the life of the individual, while also self-defining and affirming the lives of others who interact with the individual, one can understand the sentiment of loss when gaining critical race consciousness that counters the preexisting invisibility of whiteness. When one learns that everything on which s/he has based her/his identity, emotionality, behaviors, and speech is nothing but a lie, s/he feels cheated, angry, and depressed. Some will choose to defend it by any means necessary and thus express a level of defensiveness. You see this when those individuals who are attempting to defend their whiteness are resolute to claim "it's not about race." In fact, recently I went to an eye exam with a new optometrist and he relayed how his wife was a teacher at an elementary school in Denver that was receiving a lot of negative press lately. According to one of Denver's premier parent advocacy groups, Padres Unidos, a principal forced her Latino students to eat off the floor. The press surrounding this case included possible racial implications. However, when my optometrist brought it up to me he was quick to inform me that "it wasn't racist." He went on to explain how his wife also disliked the principal for her unruly ways, but ended his speech with "but she's not a racist." Four times during the exam, he felt compelled to remind me that the entire situation "had nothing to do with race." As a critical race motherscholar, I was tempted to ask, "How do you know it wasn't about race," but I needed my eye exam completed with no further microaggressions.

I share this story to illustrate how whiteness can be so resolute. It burrows itself into the fabric of one's identity so much so, that when it is challenged, people get defensive. To borrow from Collins's (1989) commentary that Black feminist are deemed "obstinate mules" in a racist and patriarchal society, those with whiteness ideology are also obstinate. And this obstinacy is so resolute. That is, Whites' refusal to see race and racism is in itself too overbearing to their identity that they structure all their beliefs, dialogue, and behaviors upon the lie that society is not racist without actually learning about how it might just be. Suffice it to say, when confronted with the lie of whiteness, those who embraced it as a part of their identity are at a loss.

I want to be careful here to not equate this to the loss people of Color endure under a racist system. Although the loss experienced by people of Color in a racist society is the loss of their humanity through subjugation, degradation, violence, and oppression, for Whites, generally speaking, their loss is tantamount to losing their "super saiyan[4] power"; one which was unfairly given in the first place. Frankly speaking, the super id is no longer super. Regardless, when losing something as dear as an identity, the mourning and grief become so overbearing it can leave a person in a perpetual state of melancholia. In fact, it can make a person feel resentful. Similar to how I was resentful for having the miscarriage, someone who loses their whiteness can also be resentful. They, like Helms (1990) suggests, can revert further back into whiteness because the reality of how oppressive whiteness really is challenges one's sense of moral being. Since Ignatiev and Garvey (1996) argue "treason to whiteness is loyalty to humanity" (p. 10), the converse is also true. That is, loyalty to whiteness is treason to humanity. Acknowledging this puts the person who opts back into whiteness in juxtaposition to humanity. Ostensibly, if one is against humanity, what moral ground can she or he claim? This internal dilemma eats at the soul, so much so that it becomes the death of a person. It is a death of who the person thought s/he was, especially with regard to a once-presumed ethical, moral stance. The internal turmoil moves from loss to death when one questions whether one could have ever been moral because that morality was based on an immoral foundation. S/he is forced to ask, *am I a good person*? Just as I pondered who I thought myself to be before and after I miscarried, Whites escaping whiteness ponder whether they were ever humane? Knowing that exertion of whiteness demoralizes people of Color, a White person realizing his/her own complicity in whiteness feels guilty, ashamed, and betrayed.

However, such a death is not only internal because, one's identity is socialized through the interactions received from and sent to society. As such, the "dead" persona becomes a socialized entity too when one realizes one's fictive identity set the basis for a fictive membership in a fictive community. The notion of the self, society, and where one resides in society become a farce. For example, when one recognizes that their identity and sense of self-worth is predicated on the denigration of another, as Baldwin (1963) suggests Whites do to Blacks, the notions of individualism, naturalism, and meritocracy crumble. S/he begins to question whether she *really* earned something, or was it earned through a preference for her skin color over another's? Furthermore, it questions her friendships, relationships, and/or social interactions. Are we friends because we are White? Because we opt to deny race? Because it makes all of us uncomfortable? The realization of whiteness and attempt to abolish it is indeed a death, complete with grief, mourning, resentment, shame, and guilt. And because of this, the process is melancholic, for the individual has no idea who to become except in terms of who s/he already was. Plainly, s/he is so consumed with her loss that she forever "feeds on it, as it were" (Cheng, 2000, p. 8).

Most interesting to note is that this entire process of grief, loss, death, and melancholia stems from an implantation of whiteness which is both there and not really there, just like the last days of my pregnancy. Thandeka (1999) calls whiteness a lie, but it is a lie that has real consequences. As such, the individual who attempts to abolish his whiteness undergoes a strange experience of losing what he never knew he had (or possibly suppressed the knowledge of having), but made him who he was.

Alas, the conundrum of whiteness: that which is so invisible it ceases to exist in the conscious mind but lives out in subconscious, repressed ways. Further, regardless of the attempts to abolish, lose, ditch, and/or push out whiteness, it will forever remain as an incriminating ink stain on white rug. Just as I cannot fully release my identity of having been pregnant again even if the baby is no longer there, it is

111

ultimately still there to haunt me like *la llorona's*[5] faint phantasmal cries. Hence, this is the melancholic state of existence that constantly mourns and grieves its own death yet, in actuality, never really dies; 'tis the ghost of a lost identity ever roaming the deepest nooks and crannies of one's heart. Just as a mother can never get over the loss of her child, neither can Whites ever fully let go of their whiteness or the sense of loss of whiteness. It becomes a perpetual state of being, one that becomes the shared burden for humanity.

CONCLUSION

The quandary over defining the self is a forever project. I paralleled the emotional grief of losing one's whiteness to that of a losing a child through miscarriage in order to best illustrate the intensity what it is like to truly self-investigate the inborn roots of whiteness. One must grieve over what was once there but is no longer, and yet it forever remains in one's mind – as well as the heart of humanity. Undergoing the emotional labor of racial justice is a necessary project Whites must engage with in order to share in the burden of race. Unless they do so, how can they bind their racial repression of whiteness to the racial liberation of people of Color?

NOTES

[1] The use of @ indicates a recognition of both Latinas and Latinos.
[2] Ms. R's performance eerily reminds me of the case of Rachel Dolezal, the White female director of an NAACP chapter who pretended to be Black (although that deserves a whole other analysis).
[3] Terms that refer to those individuals who serve as a translating medium for two different languages or cultures.
[4] In reference to the cartoon "Dragon Ball Z" whose characters can transform into a super powerful race. See http://dragonball.wikia.com/wiki/Super_Saiyan
[5] A Latin America folklore that describes a ghost of a weeping woman who mourns the loss of her children. See https://en.wikipedia.org/wiki/La_Llorona

REFERENCES

Allen, R. L. (2002). *Pedagogy of the oppressor: What was Freire's theory for transforming the privileged and powerful?* [Presentation]. Paper presented at American Educational Research Association, New Orleans, LA.
Allen, R. L. (2004). Whiteness and critical pedagogy. *Educational Philosophy and Theory, 36*(2), 121–136.
Ayers, W., Ladson-Billings, G., Michie, G., & Noguera, P. A. (2008). *City kids, city schools: More reports from the front row*. New York, NY: New Press.
Baldwin, J. (1963). A talk to teachers. In R. Simonson (Ed.), *The Graywolf annual five: Multicultural literacy* (1988). Saint Paul, MN: Graywolf.
Cheng, A. A. (2000). *The melancholy of race: Psychoanalysis, assimilation, and hidden grief*. London: Oxford University Press.
Clark, K. B., & Clark, M. K. (1939). The development of consciousness of self and the emergence of racial identification in Negro preschool children. *The Journal of Social Psychology, 10*, 591–599.
Collins, P. H. (1986). Learning from the outsider within: The sociological significance of black feminist thought. *Social Problems, 33*(6), S14–S32.

DiAngelo, R. (2011). White fragility. *The International Journal of Critical Pedagogy*, *3*(3).

DuBois, W. E. B. (2007). *The souls of Black folk*. Oxford & New York, NY: Oxford University Press.

Espiritu, Y. (2001). Ideological racism and cultural resistance: Constructing our own image. In M. Andersen & P. Collins (Eds.), *Race, class and gender: An anthology*. Belmont, CA: Wadsworth/ Thomas Learning.

Fanon, F. (1967). *Black skin, White masks*. New York, NY: Grove Press.

Gillborn, D. (2005). Education policy as an act of white supremacy: Whiteness, critical race theory and education reform. *Journal of Education Policy*, *20*(4), 485–505.

Gramsci, A. (1971). *Selections from prison notebooks* (Q. Hoare & G. Smith, Eds., & Trans.). New York, NY: International Publishers.

Harris, C. I. (1993). Whiteness as property. *Harvard Law Review*, 1707–1791.

Helms, J. E. (1990). *Black and White racial identity: Theory, research, and practice*. Westport, CT: Greenwood Press.

hooks, b. (1994). *Teaching to transgress*. New York, NY: Routledge.

Ignatiev, N., & Garvey, J. (Eds.). (1996). *Race traitor*. New York, NY: Psychology Press.

Jealous, A. T., & Haskell, C. T. (2013). *Combined destinies: Whites sharing grief about racism*. Sterling, VA: Potomac Books, Inc.

Ladson-Billings, G. (1998). From Soweto to the South Bronx: African Americans and colonial education in the United States. In C. Torres & T. Mitchell (Eds.), *Sociology of education: Emerging perspectives* (pp. 247–264). New York, NY: SUNY Press.

Leonardo, Z. (2009). *Race, whiteness, and education*. New York, NY: Routledge.

Lewis, A., & Manno, M. (2011). The best education for some: Race and schooling in the United States today. In M. Jung, J. Vargas, & E. Bonilla-Silva (Eds.), *State of White supremacy: Racism, governance and the United States* (pp. 93–109). Palo Alto, CA: Stanford University Press.

Matias, C. E. (2015). "Why do you make me hate myself?": Re-teaching whiteness, abuse, and love in urban teacher education. *Teaching Education*, 1–18.

Memmi, A. (1965). *The colonizer and the colonized*. Boston, MA: Beacon Press.

National Center for Education Statistics. (2012). *Fast facts: Teacher trends*. Institute of Educational Sciences, U.S. Department of Education. Retrieved from http://nces.ed.gov/fastfacts/display.asp?id=28

Sleeter, C. E. (2001). Preparing teachers for culturally diverse schools research and the overwhelming presence of whiteness. *Journal of Teacher Education*, *52*(2), 94–106.

Tatum, B. (1994). Teaching White students about racism: The search for White allies and the restoration of hope. *The Teachers College Record*, *95*(4), 462–476.

Tatum, B. (1997). *Why are all the Black kids sitting together in the cafeteria?* New York, NY: Basic Books.

Thandeka. (1999). *Learning to be White: Money, race, and god in America*. New York, NY: Continuum.

Yancy, G. (2008). *Black bodies, White gazes: The continuing significance of race*. Lantham, MD: Rowman & Littlefield.

CHAPTER 8

WHITENESS AS SURVEILLANCE

Policing Brown Bodies in Education

Consider: A Poem about Power

That which makes *you* feel

THREATENED

e-x-p-o-s-e-d

revealed

UNcovered

B A R E

naked

Discovered

UNfolded

disclosed

Unmasked

Unearthed

What will you do…
when you know you have the power to cover it up?

Though seemingly innocent, the poem above not only divulges what it feels like to be revealed, but also how power operates in such a way that it can, with all its might, stop the revealing. In essence, the power of whiteness is nothing more than a policing of what can and cannot be said, divulged, examined, and exposed due in part by white fragility (DiAngelo, 2011). So often in racial justice work, those who are "revealed" as having racist ideologies, behaviors, and/or discourses become so emotionally unfettered that they opt to further exert their power in whiteness by shutting down, silencing, and/or dismissing the revealer. In doing so, this dismissal becomes a sad and pitiful display because, if we as a society so commit to racial harmony, how can we even fathom its fruition if individually we are more concerned about a label than how we may, in fact, be acting racist. This chapter delves into how whiteness acts as a policing entity constantly surveilling its own white interests at the expense of dehumanizing us all.

THE LEGAL PRECEDENCE FOR WHITE SURVEILLANCE

The phenomenon of policing is not new to U.S. race relations. For one, the racist science, Eugenics, was used in the U.S. to justify the maltreatment of Black slaves, claiming Blacks were inferior beings through phrenology, muscular studies, etc., a delineation that made it right and just for their subjugation. Essentially, eugenics was a just way to police Black bodies in order to re-conceptualize who was a part of humanity and who was not; the delineation justified its enforcement of capitalistic racism. In fact, Coates (2015) describes the U.S. legacy of disembodying the Black person from humanity to a point at which the Black body is rendered nothing but property; such rendering has left a legacy of denigration to Black peoples in the U.S.

Second, laws throughout U.S. history were created to delineate the inhumanity of Black bodies so that legalization of slavery – or in modern day terms: high incarceration – was justified (Alexander, 2012). Sadly, this plays out too often in current U.S. contexts with the overzealous, racist shootings of unarmed Black men, women, and – in the case of Tamir Rice – children.

Additionally, Whites were given legal privileges through the use of colorblind racist laws (Haney López, 2006). Two such court cases stand out. In *Ozawa v. United States*, 260 U.S. 178 (1922), Takao Ozawa claimed he should be afforded citizenship via naturalization after his 20-year stay in the U.S. because his skin color was whiter than that of most Whites. His argument was based on the Naturalization Act of 1906 which dictated that only "free white persons" were eligible for citizenship via naturalization.[1] For the verdict, Justice George Sutherland wrote, "the words 'white person' were meant to indicate only a person of what is popularly known as the Caucasian race." Since Ozawa was of Japanese descent, he was then ruled ineligible for the label "free white person" and thus denied naturalization.

Later, Bhagat Thind challenged this ruling in *United States v. Bhagat Singh Thind*, 261 U.S. 204 (1923), claiming that although he was of northern Indian descent, his ancestry did hail from Aryan (read: Caucasian) blood lines so thus he met Sutherland's Caucasian requirement and, by virtue of this classification, be deemed a "free white person," afforded all the rights and privileges of naturalization. While Thind's initial naturalization petition was granted, federal attorneys filed suit and ultimately the Supreme Court again ruled that Thind was not "white" and thus not deserving of citizenship. Again, Justice Sutherland wrote the majority opinion and denied Thind's request, because through "common speech" and "common understanding," Thind could not be White. Sutherland's common understanding dismissed the reality: the 1920 *Encyclopedia Britannica* in fact claimed that Aryan invaders of the Hindu culture were considered White. Moreover, the Court masked the power structure that allowed certain "common" men to make the racial decisions about other "common" men. That is, although Ozawa and Thind were common men who obviously had legal grounds to challenge racist laws, they were, upon the verdict, rendered less than the common man. Instead, what was not said explicitly but implied was that the White, propertied man is the common man who is the sole police/Determiner of who is and who isn't White.

This same mentality can be said of Whites who claim to never see race but nevertheless proclaim themselves as the Determiner of what is and what isn't about race. How are they – or Sutherland – the subject matter experts of race if they cannot even see it? This is as absurd as proclaiming you are an oncologist by virtue of watching *Gray's Anatomy*[2] without ever having to experience the burden of medical school, residency, and hospital life. Therefore, between *Ozawa* and *Thind*, what is clearly apparent is that the common man does *not* include people of Color, just as the U.S. Declaration of Independence claims "all men are created equal" without allowing all men (or women, for that matter) such equality. Instead, Whites have legally perched themselves atop the U.S. racial hierarchy via laws, court cases, and policies so as to police racial categories, racial access, and racial discourse, while silencing or denying racial hypocrisies, racism, and race baiting. Needless to say, these court cases ignored *the* fundamental question: *why do only Whites get citizenship?* The answer, across time, is because whiteness upholds white supremacy which has the power through the policing, the gun of justice, and the English language itself, *to determine.*

The take away here is that there is a legacy of surveillance that polices "colored" bodies in a way that serves the interest of unearned benefits and privileges solely given to Whites. It is precisely this culture from which whiteness as surveillance maintains itself.

PANOPTICISM, SURVEILLANCE, AND THE ROLE OF WHITE SUPREMACY

The journal *Surveillance and Society* greatly relies on the works of Michel Foucault to undergird its purpose to "encourage policy and political debate about surveillance."[3] Wood (2002) corroborates Foucault's contribution to the field stating, "for Surveillance Studies, Foucault is a foundational thinker" (p. 235). I draw from Foucault's (1977) ruminations of the panopticism[4] to set the foundation of how whiteness's domination works in the same manner. Foucault (1977) begins his analysis of the "gaze" by describing the operations the city enforced during the Plague. Such a gaze is noteworthy because, as Yancy (2008) so argues, the (White) gaze "function(s) to objectify the Black body ... restrict Black bodies" (p. xvi).

For Foucault, everything was systematic: the ways in which people were identified as "diseased," the procedures of lock downs, purification processes, etc. In all these experiences, Foucault claims that such an operationalization of surveillance:

> ... [l]ays down for each individual his place, his body, his disease and his death, his well-being, by means of an omnipresent and omniscient power

117

that subdivides itself in a regular, uninterrupted way even to the ultimate determination of the individual, of what characterizes him, of what belongs to him, of what happens to him. (p. 197)

Essentially, such a mechanized discipline is about power and how it is used to control bodies and individuals, "controlling their relations, of separating out their dangerous mixtures" (p. 198). However, surveillance is also about rendering the power which controls individuals, their bodies, actions, and life or death, itself invisible. As Foucault states above, it becomes "regular" and "uninterrupted." This is of grave importance because popular notions of power clearly identify an abuser and the abused, power is quite easily recognized. Alas, this is not the case, according to Foucault. Instead, power operates in a hegemonic way that becomes insidious, as if happening but in absence of awareness.

Take, for example, a relationship between a parent and a child. No matter how many times a parent may include the child in decision-making, or ask the child what s/he wants as a form of middle-class egalitarianism (see Lareau, 2000), there still exists a power structure whereby the decisions, emotions, and ideas of the parent will always reign supreme over those of the child. Therefore, it becomes irresponsible for one to overlook that the power structure of "parent over child" does indeed exist inasmuch as it is irresponsible for one to assume society is vacant of its own power structures. If one assumes that the behaviors, discourses, and ideologies of men and women are equitable, then one is seduced by a false romance of gender equity; the same can be said about race.

In fact, recently in one of my doctoral classes a White male student was co-facilitating a discussion of whiteness in education via Leonardo's book, *Race, Whiteness, and Education* (2009). In his pedagogy, this student regularly cut off his female colleagues and "gave" permission for several other women to speak in class. He did this while allowing his male colleagues plenty of time to speak, question, and critique some of the ideas that were brought up during the dialogue. One particular female doctoral student of Color, a self-identified "indigenous tribal woman," was trying to enter the conversation many times, just as many of her female colleagues had been trying to do, but she was continually cut off by the White male co-facilitator. He did this by raising his voice over hers so that she would stop talking or, at times, he cut her off with questions, so as to control her discourse. Finally, the White male co-facilitator gestured his head and hand (almost dismissively) to the female doctoral student of Color and said, "Go ahead, talk." Upon this display of being "given" permission to speak, the female doctoral student of Color rebuffed him, claiming that whiteness and maleness was happening in this very dialogue because the women were being cut off and given permission to speak when the men were not. The class grew tense. Several men and women nodded in agreement. No one said a word for a while. This was its own Panopticon.

The students then provided the White male co-facilitator with pedagogical feedback. On his reflection of his evaluations, he commented on being called out on his sexist ways of handling the classroom dialogue. However, instead of recognizing the ways in which he normalized his power as a man to control the dialogue of women, or how he normalized his power as a White man to control the dialogue of women of Color, he emotionally projected onto his classmates, claiming they needed to stop "taking it so personally." This was so ironic because, despite his projections claiming that his female colleagues were taking it too personally, *he* was taking the evaluations of his pedagogy for improvement so personally that he refused to own up to his own behaviors. This is exactly how Foucault sees power, surveillance, and discipline. Like the parent-child relationship, the relationship between men and women in a patriarchal society cannot be assumed as equal, especially when one has the authority to control, dismiss, and give permission over the other in terms of how to behave, what they may say, or when they are allowed to say it.

The White male student, in this sense, became a transmitter of the Panopticon, the one who "induce[d] in the inmate [in this case, his female colleagues] a state of conscious and permanent visibility that assures the automatic functioning of power" (p. 201). Essentially, the White male co-facilitator was the police of patriarchy enforcing a discipline (controlled routine of power of patriarchy) and ensuring a punishment (silencing, cutting them off, etc.) for those who broke away from the controlled order. This discipline was so enforcing that most of the female colleagues complied, never saying anything at the moment of their own oppression. Instead, most of them spoke to me after class, in private, to agree with the one female doctoral student of Color who raised her voice against the power-holder. This is how the Panopticon becomes a "relation to the discipline" (Fanon, 1977, p. 208), too fearful of the surveillance or gaze such that discontent is expressed *incognito*. The female students feared punishment despite the fact that I, as a female, was also the professor of the course and thereby should have professorial power. Instead, they feared the discipline of control brought about by the power of patriarchy.

The surveillance within the Panopticon is of grave importance because this policing of undesired traits is what continues to enforce white supremacy via the sanctioning of racism, all while turning a blind eye to its own practices. Because of whiteness, the Black body "has been historically marked, disciplined" (Yancy, 2008, p. 1) and this produces what Yancy calls the *elevator effect* in that the white gaze is constantly alienating the Black body, subjecting it to its own racist interpretations and thus justifying its behaviors of maltreatment toward the Black body. One can say this is all "just interpretation," but these exact interpretations have real consequences.

These racist interpretations built within the white gaze surveil, discipline, and punish bodies of Color every day. It is seen in the U.S. through the constant denigration of women of Color, often stereotyped as "welfare queens" unworthy of humanly recognition and the institutional racial extermination of unarmed Black men. In fact, George Zimmerman, the man who shot and killed seventeen-year-old Trayvon Martin, invested his entire case on the suspicion and policing of young Black male bodies; that is, the wearing of a hoodie on Black skin in a White suburban community is akin to discipline and punishment under the surveillance of

119

the white gaze. Whiteness operates in society in a manner which produces a state of surveillance: "what is passed off as seeing, however, is really a form of *reading*" (Foucault, 1977, p. 22). The gaze is not benign; rather, the gaze, like the Panopticon, becomes a power structure that allows a state of surveillance that continually protects the interest of white supremacy, ensuring that anything that may disrupt it is quickly put in its place.

As much as we talk about equity, justice, diversity, and inclusion, the surveillance of students, faculty, and staff of Color – or White allied individuals – who promote racial justice are always targeted. In this white Panopticon, the discipline and punishments are rendered so discreetly, those faculty members who study racism, like me, live in perpetual fear, much like my female students during a sexist pedagogy. By exposing how whiteness operates, I bravely engage in how whiteness as surveillance has impacted my own career.

WHITENESS AS SURVEILLANCE IN THE ACADEMY: JUST ONE STORY

In the fall of 2015, I was asked to speak to faculty, administration, and staff at a university system-wide discussion on "Ethnicity and Minorities." I discussed what whiteness is and what it has to do with race to a lecture hall full of medical doctors, administrators, diversity officers, faculty members, graduate students, and community members. After my presentation, one audience member asked me what whiteness looked like in the academy, especially with respect to how it is institutionalized. I had had many experiences I could draw from to answer her question, and without reservation I honestly shared one such experience. During my relation, one audience members, a female faculty of Color, left the auditorium in tears because, as I later found out, my story was so overbearingly similar to her own battles. The story I relayed is a familiar one experienced by other faculty of Color, female faculty (especially female faculty of Color), faculty with critical dispositions, and faculty whose work directly addresses racism (see Berry & Mizelle, 2006; Gutierrez y Muhs, Niemann, Gonzales, & Harris, 2012; Stanley, 2006).

The story I relayed was this: one semester I received an odd email early on a Monday morning from an administrator I had never met. Supposedly this administrator was in charge of human subjects research. She claimed she needed to meet with me about some "questions" about the role of research in one of my doctoral courses and gave me the "option" to meet with her that Friday within a three-hour window and to which I would make a 45-minute drive. Curious as to what the questions were and who was raising them, I naturally responded with those inquiries in an email. The administrator then emailed back stating that she preferred I meet with her. As a junior faculty, nothing is more terrifying than getting an email about something you are not sure about or how to address when someone refuses to divulge the context. It became a dirty little secret, so to speak, one that was never told to me although it was about me. *Did I not have a right to know what questions arose? Did I not have a right to know who was raising them? Did I not have a right to due process?*

True to faculty mentorship of junior faculty, I sought advice from my many mentors on campus including my school faculty mentor, my school administrator mentor, and my Vice Chancellor of Diversity. Also, perturbed about the secrecy behind such a meeting, my school administrator mentor, an African American woman, also of the same administrative rank as the human subjects faculty, got involved and left a voicemail for her inquiring as to what questions were being raised about the course. The human subjects administrator returned with a voicemail of a very different tone than that of her emails to me which were shrouded with secrecy and very patronizing. In the voicemail she apologized to my mentor for having been "dragged" into the situation and, after mocking the pronunciation of my very Spanish last name, she claimed she wanted to know how I was running my class and had just a "quick question" to clarify things. Despite being an issue that could seemingly be answered by a casual, friendly phone call, she "instructed" that I *had* to meet with her. Knowing the dynamics of power, this was tantamount to enforcing a power structure whereby I, the untenured faculty member, was expected to submit to her, an administrator's, demands even when I was not given the courtesy of knowing the context.

Needless to say, we met the following Monday with my school administrator mentor present. There, the human subject administrator, a White female, laid out before me a file with my name on it. It included my course syllabus with colored tabs, an article I published four years prior, a copy of my pre-course survey for the course in question, and a list of all my IRB-approved projects for the past six years. Being that it was supposedly a meeting to answer a "quick question," it was obvious she had done her homework on me. Over the course of what turned out to be a lengthy conversation she pointed out something on my syllabus which I clarified was a mistake about which I had already notified my students and talked about in class. Here was The Secret exposed, revealed as corrected, not as it was perceived by her. However, the meeting was not finished – though held under the guise of it "being about my course," the meeting was really about something else…

After my clarification, the woman then pulled out a copy of my pre-course survey and one of my publications from four years ago. She asked me whether this was the same survey provided to the publication because she had read my article and knew a survey was used in its analysis. I explained that I had used another survey and turned to the page in the article that showed an exact replica of it, putting it next to the pre-course survey used for my course.

One would think that this settled everything and the meeting should have been over. Alas, it was not. Again, the secrecy and feigned concern were just a guise for something deeper. The human subjects administrator then pulled out the IRB sheet on all my prior projects for the past six years – I saw now that this meeting was not about a single course but my entire body of scholarship. After indicating that she had already cross-referenced everything to make sure all my publications – especially the one in question – were properly conducted, she pulled out another of my publications, revealing an even deeper agenda because it was not one assigned as reading for the course in question. When I asked her where she got the publication, she responded, "anonymous tips," first hinting that my students were the suppliers. I refuted this veiled accusation because my students and I had already talked in depth about the mistake I had made on the syllabus, not to mention that we had developed a very strong bond. She then switched tacks and alluded that colleagues and "other people in the public" who had read my publication were the tipsters, or tipster – it was never clear if it was one or more people. At this juncture the meeting went from disconcerting to threatening.

The human subjects administrator then suggested that I footnote all my publications with a disclaimer that this was an IRB-approved study. She added that I should do so to let "others know that I am professional." To this I replied, "Perhaps, 'others' should not assume that I am *not* professional. I am a professor with an earned doctoral degree." She acknowledged what I said and pressed further that it would be best practice for me to, in the future, make such a footnote. I complied.

Through all of these accusations, which placed the undue burden of professionalism onto me, never was there acknowledgement of: (1) the unprofessional nature of this inquisition and that it was an inquisition over my scholarship, not "questions about my course"; (2) a presumption of innocence before the trial of this "accuser" and her anonymous "tipsters"; nor, (3) my earned and substantiated professional position *ipso facto* and her assumption that it needed to be validated by others in order to exist.

During the meeting, my mentor pointed out that she did not want me (or my scholarship) to be targeted simply because I study racism in education (including higher education). At the mention of race, the human subjects administrator appeared flustered and quickly shuffled her words around, claiming that my research was "revealing" and a "bit critical." My mentor and I responded that shouldn't research indeed be revealing and critical? Though she agreed with us, she then said my research might "intimidate some people." To this, my administrator and I smiled: of course it is intimidating. It's intimidating to reveal sexism, homophobia, able-ism, and racism, especially to those who are sexist, homophobes, able-ists, and racists. But not to reveal it is to continue to threaten and or intimidate women, Queers, people with varied abilities, and people of Color. If we truly believe in diversity, equity, and inclusion, then shouldn't we refocus who needs to be intimidated? This entire inquisition into my work was a way to breach academic freedom and intimidate junior faculty, especially since I was going up for tenure that same year. If this entire conversation was truly about mutual relationships, or just "needing clarification," then why the secrecy, why the file of my work that did not pertain to the course in question, and why couldn't she have just called me?

No, whiteness works in the academy as a way of policing or, in the words of Foucault (1977) *surveillance*. The academy was surveilling my scholarship under its white gaze (Yancy, 2008), searching for ways to protect its own white interests without ever revealing itself as doing so. In fact, this entire experience – from the cryptic email to the secret questions and anonymous tipsters – was nothing but an exertion of how "disciplines have to bring into play the power relations, not above but inside the very texture of multiplicity, as discreetly as possible" (Foucault, 1977, p. 220). I call this "hush-hush" policing and through it, along with the imposition of discipline and punishment, the white gaze was scouting for anything that might disrupt the power structure that perches whiteness as normal, moral, and/or correct. It does so in unjust ways that infringe upon the humanity of its target. It does so knowing that it can do so precisely because the power structure of whiteness is such that it *can* discriminate, target, and marginalize faculty, students, and/or ideas that unfetter its sovereignty. All of this was about power and concession to that power through making people of Color – especially those who challenge the institutional normalization of whiteness – fearful.

After relaying this story, an audience member asked how an administrator should act under similar conditions. I responded that s/he should stand behind his/her faculty and assume professionalism, especially since we were hired for our subject matter expertise and our earned credentials. That because an administrator should assume good intent and have trust in his/her faculty, s/he should be transparent about concerns about your courses and present them in a way that is not accusatory. S/he should conduct due diligence to vet any "anonymous tipper," strongly advise that the accuser meet with the professor first to see if concerns can be answered, and provide the professor with due process if any merit is found in the accusations. Is that not what people in the professional world do? Or are we reduced to old-school bullying tactics whereby someone with power aligns with anonymous tippers as a way to instill fear to those with less institutional power? If one has an inquiry whereby we assume good intent, shouldn't we speak directly to the person instead of treating them as suspects already deemed guilty by accusation? And finally, s/he should acknowledge the power dynamics between the individuals involved. Who is of authority and who is not? How can this be perceived as an act of intimidation?

In revealing – as often research does – this personal altercation, I want to be clear that I share my story not to demonize this particular human subjects administrator, but because her behaviors represent common behaviors of many others. I say this because too often in race-related work the public assumes that racists are malicious, hateful, and immoral beings. Indeed, there are some who are; but others are socialized into behaving, discoursing, and thinking in racist ways, though not obviously hateful or malicious. This is seen in the example of a person talking about a family member or a friend who says or does racist things, but quickly interjects, "But he's not a bad person." By positioning racists as only ones who are hateful, malicious, immoral, or "plain bad," it relinquishes responsibility of those who may be acting in racist ways by virtue of distancing themselves from "those" hateful racists. Since whiteness is a process of socialization that still exerts itself in racially microaggressive ways, these "not bad persons" need to realize how they are exerting whiteness regardless, and recognize the impact it has on people of Color fostering the institutionalism of racism and whiteness.

In this case, the human subjects administrator, though not a demon, should recognize how her behaviors institutionalize whiteness in such a way as to intimate faculty of Color or faculty who study racism. If, however, she refuses to understand how her behaviors contribute to institutional racism, whether it is because of denial or fear of being exposed, she then reasserts her white racial privilege and affirms institutional whiteness as a policing body. Hopefully, she will truly listen, despite the discomfort of being revealed, to how her actions contribute to the dehumanizing policing of race scholarship and race scholars, a factor that will impact how faculty of Color or diverse faculty feel about their host institution.

Talks about diversity's inclusion in higher education too often focus on how diverse faculty, students, or staff must learn how to be collegial, humanizing, and collaborative with existing faculty, staff, or students, without focusing on the climate that existing faculty, staff, and students create to make diverse faculty, staff, and students feel unwelcomed. This is of grave importance because, if we are truly committed to diversifying our world, those who have benefited from that which initially created no diversity must start to learn of their biases. Regardless to one's intentions, the impact here of their biases maintains racism and whiteness in the academy. Furthermore, targeting diverse individuals (diverse in either identity or in critical perspective) becomes nothing more than a way to make them feel policed, uncomfortable, and threatened in a space that presumes, presents, and believes itself to be welcoming and diverse.

CONCLUSION

I often tell my students that, despite the fact that women occupy many positions in the field of education (however not often in the higher echelons such as deans, principals, and full professoriates), it does not negate patriarchy's presence there. In fact, I mock this concept in a class where most of my students are female. I pretend that patriarchy or sexism cannot exist in education because of the sheer number of female educators. I assert this to a point where my students get angry and argue with me, claiming that patriarchy does not stop by crossing the threshold of a college classroom. I smile. Then I posit, *why is it then that we assume whiteness can?*

To illustrate, we read John Dewey, Paulo Freire, and Henry Giroux, all amazing contributors to the field of education and society. I believe education would be remiss to not pay credence to their contributions to the field. However, Dewey, Freire, and Giroux are all White men; they share their views and theorizations of the world through a white male ocular. When my students begin to read bell hooks, Beverly Tatum, and W.E.B. DuBois, I often receive resistance saying that such pieces are written "differently" or are of "just one perspective" – a minimalist argument used to belittle the contributions of scholars of Color, especially female scholars of Color. I even had one doctoral student who claimed that DuBois's work is not scholarly because he did not cite literature nor gave a methodology for his observations. Alas, another surveilling act of whiteness via coding, what I call, "the methodological side step," and a qualification that was never asked of Freire or

Dewey. Despite that DuBois is one of the grandfathers of the research method of sociological ethnography, a White student feels empowered enough to discredit him on a merit she did not apply to the White scholars we discussed: this is a common maneuver to police research on whiteness in the academy. But I digress, saving that argument for another day.

Returning to the point here is that if we normalize white male perspectives such that any other perspective is considered biased, then it is important we acknowledge that we are also complicit in promoting a power structure of white male supremacy in education. bell hooks (1994) claims the same phenomenon happens in the academy when syllabi readings only reflect white male perspectives. Therefore, to avoid being complicit in the act of white surveillance, we educators must actively seek out ways to expose and reveal the dominant power structures in place to silence and intimidate those with different perspectives. In fact, it is not only about people simply having different perspectives as it is about those of dominant perspectives continually attempting to threaten, intimidate, and silence those with marginalized perspectives. As such, the purveyance of whiteness is not simply about differing perspectives, but rather about how a power structure places one perspective in a role that polices all others.

As much as the academy and all its institutions of higher education promote and proclaim their love and yearning for diversity, inclusion, and equity, how can it truly be equitable if any scholar of a differing perspective is policed, surveilled, and threatened for exposing such dominant paradigms such as whiteness? Can we, as ones committed to humanity, look beyond our own self-interests to realize a greater humanity, one that recognizes the courage it takes to stand up to that which oppresses? In this lofty endeavor, we, as faculty of Color, female faculty (and of Color), and/or faculty with critical dispositions finally get reprieve from being unfairly targeted for our commitment and dedication to a more racially-just humane society regardless of the discomfort it brings to those in power. The responsibility is left on the shoulders of those who enforce whiteness. Can you – and I speak directly to those who are enforcers of whiteness and constantly surveilling white interests – be humble enough as to let go of your white privilege by laying down the academic policing gun you've held to our targeted backs, and instead open yourself to examine your whiteness and thus support diverse faculties?

NOTES

[1] *Naturalization* is the process by which U.S. citizenship is granted to a foreign citizen or foreign national after s/he fulfills the requirements established by Congress in the Immigration and Nationality Act. See https://www.uscis.gov/us-citizenship/citizenship-through-naturalization

[2] An American television show that depicts life in a Seattle hospital.

[3] See http://library.queensu.ca/ojs/index.php/surveillance-and-society/about/editorialPolicies#focusAndScope

[4] A panopticon is a circular prison designed to facilitate more effective surveillance from the center; in Foucault's sense, this metaphor describes social power exerted by whiteness.

REFERENCES

Alexander, M. (2012). *The new Jim Crow: Mass incarceration in the age of colorblindness*. New York, NY: The New Press.

Berry, T., & Mizelle, N. (Eds.). (2006). *From oppression to grace: Women of color and their dilemmas in the academy*. Sterling, VA: Stylus Publishing.

Coates, T. (2015). *Between the world and me*. New York, NY: Spiegel & Grau.

DiAngelo, R. (2011). White fragility. *The International Journal of Critical Pedagogy*, *3*(3).

Foucault, M. (1977). *Discipline and punish: The birth of the prison* (A. Sheridan, Trans.) New York, NY: Vintage.

Gutiérrez y Muhs, G., Niemann, Y. F., Gonzalez, C. G., & Harris, A. P. (2012). *Presumed incompetent: The intersections of race and class for women in academia*. Salt Lake City, UT: Utah University Press.

Haney López, I. (2006). *White by law: The legal construction of race*. New York, NY: New York University Press.

hooks, b. (2014). *Teaching to transgress*. New York, NY: Routledge.

Lareau, A. (2000). *Home advantage: Social class and parental intervention in elementary education*. New York, NY: Rowman & Littlefield.

Stanley, C. (Ed.). (2006). *Faculty of color: Teaching in predominantly White colleges and universities* (Vol. 69). San Francisco, CA: Jossey-Bass.

Wood, D. (2002). Foucault and panopticism revisited. *Surveillance & Society*, *1*(3), 234–239.

TEARS WORTH TELLING

Urban Teaching and the Possibilities of Racial Justice

As a critical race teacher educator of Color, I constantly reflect on my K-12 classroom experience (both as an urban student and teacher) so that the essence of what I teach and research remains grounded in the struggles of my Black and Brown students. After years of teaching in both the Los Angeles Unified School District and the New York City Department of Education, forever burned in my heart were the tears of my urban students of Color. There was a specific teaching moment when I openly shared my own counterstories of pain and realized that my students were crying too. Riddled with guilt, I asked my students, *why the tears?* The closed mouths belied an unspoken knowledge of shared experiences. Shaking her head, one student echoed my pain by saying, "It's just racist. It's just so racist." This chapter is a counterstory of the tears of urban students of Color and how I, as their teacher, acknowledge and invest in them in order to find a way to wipe those tears away.

In bearing witness to their tears, I never once felt I must "save" my students of Color like the dominant narrative of missionaries or saviors in poor communities so popularized by mainstream films such as *Dangerous Minds, Freedom Writers, The Blind Side,* etc. (see Matias, 2013b; Vera & Gordon, 2003). Rather, I have to support them because, in their anguish, I see myself: these are familiar tears of my own racialized past. I felt the pain when I heard one of my students say, "What's the point? I'm Black." Embedded in that seemingly simple question is the painful result of a "colorblind" educational system that renders the double consciousness of colored beings as "false" when, in fact, it is the conscious reality of people of Color (DuBois, 2007; Solórzano & Yosso, 2002).

Although I intimately understood the cries of my students, I admittedly received my teacher training from White teacher educators whose focus on celebrations of multiculturalism, cultural pluralism, and cultural responsivity were nonetheless filtered by the ocular of whiteness (Leonardo, 2009; Matias, 2013a; Yoon, 2012). This inadvertently trained me to teach like a White missionary teacher, meaning that, although my White teacher educators trained me with theories conceptualized by scholars of Color, they filtered out the salient aspects of *why* these theories came to be – namely, they were policies born of racism and white supremacy in education (Gillborn, 2006; Ladson-Billings, 1998). The permanence of these manifestations were hushed by the white noise appropriated as the "correct" filter for training urban teachers in studies of diversity and multiculturalism. Ironically, this was the same training of *my* K-12 urban White teachers, whose colorblind racism – a process of claiming not to see race, yet acting out racist practices (Bonilla-Silva, 2010) – produced these same tears in me. Therefore, instead of submitting to this colorblind racism, bound by my principles in racial justice, I decided to become a new kind of critical race teacher and validate all these tears.

This chapter shares the uncertain path of putting race into daily classroom teaching since operating under the rigidity of the colorblind racism plaguing urban schools was too difficult. My counterstory as an urban teacher of Color amidst an overwhelming White teaching force exemplifies how a teacher can disrupt the normalcy of whiteness in education such that the tears of our students of Color are not shed in vain. I do not insist that it is *the* model for racial justice in urban classrooms, precisely because the most beautiful aspect of teaching – as teachers know – is that we always try amidst failure and hopelessness. Thus, I present my counterstory replete with the metacognitive emotional and spiritual struggles I underwent in attempting to resist the repressed violence that normalizes the silencing of race (see Leonardo & Porter, 2010). It would be disingenuous to not divulge that I am now responsible for training the next generation of urban teachers as a teacher educator; fortuitously, through this new role, I can look back at my own career with the critical lens needed to analyze the context of urban teaching.

MARRYING THEORY: CRITICAL SOCIAL THEORY, CRITICAL RACE THEORY, AND CRITICAL WHITENESS

My reflective counterstory draws from a plethora of critical race theories. In isolation, each was not enough for me to fully grasp the complexities of race; however, in concert I found a more complete understanding of why teachers and urban students of Color experience dehumanization in a white-dominated educational system. First, I draw from critical social theory of race because it "encourages the production and application of theory as a part of the overall search for transformative knowledge" (Leonardo, 2009, p. 13). For example, Leonardo and Porter's (2010) Fanonian application of repressed violence and false safety in race dialogues provides a context that, when applied to teaching, can best explain the conditions of urban teachers and students of Color. Just as symbolic violence and false safety in race dialogues ultimately uphold the narcissism of whiteness, the same applies to the entire context of teaching. Since the teaching force, curricula, policies, and teacher education pipeline are White-dominant, the context for repressed forms of violence is maintained. If disrupted, white performative recurrences of anger, avoidance, guilt, dismissal, and repression stifle race knowledge.

In order to survive this repressed white violence, students of Color are merely "playing along" to become "masters of deflection" (Leonardo & Porter, 2010, p. 151). They do this to maintain a sense of "safety in [these] violent circumstances" (p. 151). The emotional cost is exemplified through their tears.

Teachers must employ a humanizing violence that "shifts the standards of humanity by providing space for the free expression of people's thoughts and emotions that are not regulated by the discourse of safety" (Leonardo & Porter, 2010, p. 148). In training teacher candidates, I teach them the falsity of a benign *status quo* because *status quo* is replete with repressed violence. Teachers who maintained this repressed violence – whether intentional or not – left both my students and me in tears. This leads to the need for resistive humanistic violence, necessary for true race dialogue to begin.

I also employ critical race theory (CRT) because it acknowledges the endemic nature of race, racism, and white supremacy while validating counterstories (Delgado & Stefancic, 2001). Counterstories provide people of Color an understanding that the daily acts of racism they incur are not isolated acts of violence; rather, they are systemic acts of macroaggressions and macro-violence (Gildersleeve, Croom & Vasquez, 2011; Sue, Nadal, Capodilupo, Lin, Torino & Rivera, 2008). When they are spoken aloud, they disrupt dominant narratives and allow people of Color to feel supported, heard, and validated, which in turn contributes to *everyone's* understanding of a larger dynamics of race (Matias 2012; Solórzano & Yosso, 2002).

Applied to teaching, counterstories that reflect racial microaggressions, racial battle fatigue, and/or internalized racism are racially-educative because their articulation shows how race, racism, and white supremacy are enacted (Bernal, 2002; Dixson & Rousseau, 2005). However, this racially-rich knowledge is often silenced in the colorblind, racist, urban classroom (see Zamudio, Russell, Rios, & Bridgeman, 2011) precisely because:

1. the majority of urban teachers who are White are discomforted by discussions of race (Duncan, 2002);
2. Eurocentric curricula and standards do not explicitly address the advantages of creating a racial hierarchy which systematically shuts out dialogues of race (Ladson-Billings, 1998); and
3. although there has been pedagogical application of CRT in higher education (Jennings & Lynn, 2005; Lynn 1999), ways in which teachers can pedagogically enact CRT inside the K-12 classroom are lacking.

Managing dialogues of race inside the K-12 classroom becomes an arduous task despite the overwhelming possibilities it has for creating humanizing projects of race. Relating to my classroom teaching experiences, CRT reminds me that the permanence of race, racism, and white supremacy are so entrenched in the fabric of our educational society that they often render similar phenomena for those racially marginalized. Recognizing this helps me understand why I had such an intimate kinship to my urban students of Color; in them I see me.

Lastly, I utilize critical whiteness studies precisely because I needed to fully comprehend the complexity of why voices, stories, and identities of people of Color are marginalized in the first place. If racism is the symptom, then it is white supremacy and whiteness that are the disease. Critical whiteness studies go beyond the acknowledgement of white privilege (McIntosh, 2001) and stages of white racial identity (Helms, 1990), and into an interdisciplinary approach to how whiteness is materialized through political, economic, and emotional means (Allen, 2001; Massey & Denton 1993; Roediger, 1999).

For example, Thandeka (1999) explores the emotional well-being of Whites entrenched in whiteness by positing that their emotional investment stems from their shame of recognizing the reality of race. She articulates this as a form of psychological abuse because it teaches Whites to ignore to what they bear witness. Such a process thus produces a form of neurosis that forces Whites to believe in colorblindness despite its known falsity. Acknowledging this dynamic adds to how I understand Leonardo and Porter's (2010) violence. When white shame is revealed, it becomes too emotionally unbearable in the context of interracial dialogue. However, as CRT asserts, this type of racial humiliation happens to people of Color on a daily basis, thus its application helps balance views on whiteness. Such humiliation is necessary to open the possibility of true humanizing race dialogue (Leonardo & Porter, 2010).

Counterstories must be heard in a race dialogue in order for White teacher candidates to feel the pain of racism, quite a task when the professor is the only person of Color in the room and because White teacher candidates resist both the content of the course and me as the symbolic representation of their shame. Too often my largely White, middle-class, female teacher candidates are so entrenched in their whiteness, complete with colorblind racism, that they choose to ignore how that investment hurts people of Color (see Matias, 2013b; Bonilla-Silva & Embrick, 2006; de Jesús & Ma, 2004; Williams & Evans-Winter, 2005). They proclaim an overwhelming passion to teach urban students of Color without ever demonstrating emotion about the racial context that burdens their future students. How can one be genuinely passionate when s/he becomes emotionally frozen when discussing race, one of the most salient issues of urban schooling? With respect to CRT's tenet for social justice, how can urban teachers who are not emotionally, intellectually, and critically versed in race expect to engage in prolonged projects about racial justice if they themselves emotionally disinvest when it gets uncomfortable? Until teachers re-learn emotional investment, they will not engage in the emotional discomfort needed to *feel* racial justice. Below is my story of how I became emotionally invested through tears.

REFLECTIVE COUNTERSTORY

Instead of sitting inside the teachers' lounge early in my career, I often chose to eat alone. Inside that white space, White teachers performed an ongoing liberal discussion that pathologized students of Color and their parents as low achievers, at-risk, and in need of additional special education. Most disconcerting was how this racially-coded discourse entrenched itself in a false empathy (Duncan, 2002).

In so asserting the educational pitfalls of urban students of Color, my colleagues placed the blame on the student, rendering her/him a deficit. Beyond a mention of the cultural bias of standardized testing, as they were benignly taught to say, these White teachers never critically examined the larger systemic dynamics that continually keep urban students of Color at the periphery of success. They never acknowledged how the normativity of whiteness perches itself as the exemplar of educational success while turning a blind eye to the institutional advantages that support White students' academic success at the expense of others (Ladson-Billings, 1998; Lewis & Manno, 2011. Instead of listening to this disparaging rhetoric, I opened my classroom door and ate lunch with any student who walked in.

At first, I thought the dialogues that centered on friendships, family, and relationships with other teachers were nothing more than pre-adolescent complaints about society. Yet, when I employed CRT, I realized these complaints were counterstories, rich with intimate knowledge of how my students of Color struggle with power, marginality, and pain. These were intimate moments that allowed me to truly empathize, care, and reflect, such that it cultivated within me an *authentic care* (Valenzuela, 1999). In this revelation, I knew we *must* discuss race in the classroom. The continuous echo of "those teachers just don't get me" was as much about race as it was about mere misunderstandings. But how was I going to develop a critical dialogue of race inside a K-12 urban classroom while under the intellectual surveillance of a scripted curriculum? In order to answer this, I stripped teaching down to some basic core elements: curriculum and standards, objectives, and instructional/pedagogical strategies.

Racial Project #1: Curriculum & Standards

I knew I must incorporate a critically-raced curriculum that countered the hegemonic silencing of race in textbooks (Apple & Christian-Smith, 1991; Takaki 1993). If, as Gillborn (2006) articulates, race and racism leave an "imprint on virtually every aspect of life," then curriculum is also impacted by race and racism (pp. 324–325). It thus warrants the application of CRT and critical whiteness studies to unveil embedded racism in curriculum.

In CRT the permanence of race is a state of fact. In acknowledging the fact of race, CRT and critical whiteness studies assert that whiteness gets so normalized it becomes invisible inside educational policies (Gillborn, 2005). Just as an educational policy is not exempt from race, nor is the curriculum teachers employ. In fact, critical whiteness studies demonstrate how the literary canon is replete with exertions of normalized whiteness (Morrison, 1993). Because I have come to critically understand curriculum as a dehumanizing project that purports whiteness to normativity and colorfulness to biased subjectivity (Ladson-Billings, 1999), I needed to strategically insert race and a critical analysis of whiteness in each of my U.S. history lessons. Under a standards-based era, I needed to begin with the standards themselves.

For example, California History/Social Science Content Standard 11.4[1] indicates that students must trace the rise of the United States as a 20th century world power; it recommends that one way to do so is to describe the Spanish-American War and U.S. expansion into the South Pacific. Knowing history textbooks are wrought with political purpose (Symcox, 2002), I felt it essential to problematize the intentional one-sided account, or "master narrative," by interjecting multiple perspectives (Takaki, 1993; Zinn, 2005).

Thus, in preparing a lesson on how the Spanish-American War and U.S. expansion to the South Pacific contributed to the U.S. world power role, I had the students read Memmi's (1965) *The Colonizer and the Colonized* while they read the textbook's version this history. Additionally, I provided excerpts from Vicente Rafael's (1995) *Discrepant Histories* which chronicles the inaccurate documentation of U.S. annexation of the Philippines. We paid specific attention to purposes behind why the annexation benefitted the U.S. (which met the standard); yet we also focused on how Dean C. Worcester's depictions of Filipinos as indolent, lazy, and culturally-retarded served the widespread belief of white racial superiority, and how these racist sensibilities impacted the decision to colonize these people of Color (Sullivan, 1991) and present them in cages at the 1904 St. Louis World Fair.

Racial Project #2: Critical Race Lesson Objectives

Nieto and Bode (2008) warn that curricular insertions are not enough to address the pervasiveness of racism. As such, I drew from my teaching training in *backwards design* (Wiggins & McTigue, 2000), i.e., keeping the learning outcome in mind before proceeding further. I had to clearly explicate two lesson objectives lest I be responsible for reproducing the same normative discourse that renders race irrelevant. Content objectives are the articulation of how the goals of this lesson meet the standardized content standard. Critical race objectives strategically and directly link the content objective to an overarching CRT analysis of how oppressions of race, class, and gender are operating within that content itself. For example, if the content objective is that students will be able to describe the events, figures, and significance of the Spanish-American War, as well as the control of the South Pacific thereafter, in relation to the rising role of the U.S. as a world power, then the *critical race objective* which builds on it is that students will be able to critically dialogue how mechanisms of race, racism, and white supremacy, and other forms of oppression such as colonization, impacted the decision to annex the Philippines in order for the U.S. to become a world power.

Since clearly-stated lesson objectives are key to ensuring standards-based instruction, the explicit inclusion of critical race objectives provides a directive on how to implement race dialogues. Acknowledging that critical social theory of race is committed to the production of transformative knowledges, it then becomes *a priori* for teachers to test out new strategies not yet articulated in the Eurocentricity of standards-based curriculum. In fact, with respect to race dialogue, the strategic inclusion of critical race objectives produces the *humanizing violence* Leonardo and Porter (2010) encourage. Ergo, because curriculum violently silences race, it allows for the permanence of whiteness; however, including critical race objectives in the pedagogy attacks and disrupts the invisibility of whiteness in the curriculum, prompting racial justice and discourse.

Racial Project #3: Pedagogies and Instructional Strategies of Race

Curriculum and objectives only go so far in cultivating race dialogues in the classroom because society strategically silences discourse on race. This "speech impediment" needs a pedagogical strategy to let students unlock what was once forced to remain silent in their hearts. Like Leonardo and Porter's (2009) theory of humanizing violence via shared experiences of racism, I opted to use myself as a model in a strategy I call "critical race metacognition" (CRM).

Just as metacognitive think-alouds in literacy instruction increase reading comprehension (Zimmerman & Keen, 1997), CRM is a cognitive schema students can apply to better understand race. I began with having my students review newsreels, videos, commercials, political cartoons, and print articles. For example, I showed a video clip of 2004's *Crash* (2004) where Ludicris and Larenz Tate critically dialogue how Black men are treated in a racist society. I often stopped the clip and queried: *What is being said about Blackness and unsaid about the presumed innocence of Whites?* My students then applied this thought process to McKinley's "Benevolent Assimilation"[2] speech on the colonization of the Philippines. Through CRT, my students were better able to challenge the dominant racial ideology by applying it to their daily experiences of race. For example, a tearful Muslim American student described being pushed into a pool and taunted as a "terrorist"; she initially assumed it was not an act of racism because "racism stopped after the Civil Rights Movement." Her re-analysis of the event at the end of the semester drastically changed this view.

Racial Project #4: Vocabulary

As a content specialty teacher I know my students often struggle in understanding concepts when they do not have access to a helpful vocabulary, so I employed such terms as *racial battle fatigue*, *racial microaggression*, *white supremacy*, and *counterstorytelling* to arm them with a better articulation of their personal accounts with racism. Therefore, I knew I had to teach a new language to engage in race dialogues, which thus behooved me to synonymize critical race language acquisition to instructional strategies of language acquisition for multilingual learners.

Hill and Flynn (2006) state that "teachers need to explicitly teach those content-specific terms that bring meaning to the lesson" (p. 104). By explicitly teaching critical race vocabulary, students acquired new vocabulary to better achieve the goals set forth by the lesson's critical race objective. To ensure my students used vocabulary in meaningful ways, I had to provide ample opportunities to model, read, write, talk, and listen to each other using this newly-learned vocabulary.

IMPLICATIONS FOR URBAN TEACHING AND TEACHER EDUCATION

As hooks (1994) argues, teaching can be a healing praxis for both the educator and her students, a healing that has the possibility to stop the tears. Because teachers are not robotic extensions of a scripted curriculum, we acknowledge that teaching goes beyond a strict job description. We are cultivators of humanity and we recognize that those tears break the heart of our hope. This is an incredibly painful burden that no student should have to suppress.

It is essential to build an arsenal of pedagogical, curricular, and ideological tools so that teachers can always be a part of the humanizing project of racial justice, one where dialogues of race can take place free from the violence of colorblind racism. However, such projects must not strictly focus on urban students of Color since they are erroneously pathologized as deficit. Rather, articulations of how we can engage White suburban communities in critical race dialogue are vital precisely because that is where whiteness is produced, and in its permeation silences race throughout all communities.

Furthermore, we must consider how to engage in race-conscious teaching in systemic ways. For example, how can teachers systemically advocate for racial justice in faculty meetings, parent and community groups, and district-wide planning, initiatives, and new school development? Perhaps advocating for district representatives for racial justice will ensure that a racially-just agenda is enacted at both district and local levels; or, by increasing race understanding by enforcing continuous professional development on racism and whiteness in education; or, by incorporating racial justice in school missions and vision would break the silence. Until schools take an active stance to systematically and openly address race, race will continue to be silenced; in that silence, the tears of urban students of Color will once again be ignored.

Further, the recycling of white normative rhetoric (such as missionary/savior perspectives or strategic silencing of critical race knowledge) ostracizes the few teachers of Color who do matriculate into teacher education, while simultaneously creating disingenuous perspectives of urban students of Color. White teacher candidates must first be exposed to both critical whiteness studies and critical theories of race lest they inadvertently recycle white normativity. As Helms (1990) posits, one can only guide others in racial identity development if – and only if – they first take that journey themselves. As such, White teacher candidates must first learn about whiteness beyond mere recognition that they are White and therefore hold privilege. They must be able to articulate the socio-historical, political, economic, and emotional consciousness that led Whites to have privileged status to then "know themselves." Doing so will better prepare them for understanding their urban students of Color. Second, White teacher candidates must learn to re-learn their emotions. Instead resonating in guilt, ferociously denying the saliency of race or crying emotional angst, they must be re-directed to racially-just projects – i.e., it is okay to be angry, sad, and guilty – but then transform those feelings to projects of antiracism despite the discomfort to feel again.

CONCLUSION

Never swayed by the harsh realities of living a racialized life as an urban student of Color, urban teacher of Color, and now as an urban-focused teacher educator of Color, I realize that my students' tears are a continuance of mine, the result of the permanence of race. CRT, critical whiteness studies, and critical social theory of race reminded me that my tears are not only my own; rather, they are part of a larger cry so often ignored in education. This "sadness in perpetuity" are tears worth telling.

NOTES

[1] See http://www.cde.ca.gov/be/st/ss/documents/histsocscistnd.pdf
[2] See http://www.msc.edu.ph/centennial/benevolent.html

REFERENCES

Allen, R. L. (2001). The globalization of white supremacy: Toward a critical discourse on the racialization of the world. *Educational Theory, 51*(4), 467–485.
Apple, M. W., & Christian-Smith, L. K. (Eds.). (1991). *The politics of the textbook*. New York, NY: Routledge.
Bernal, D. D. (2002). Critical race theory, Latino critical theory, and critical raced-gendered epistemologies: Recognizing students of color as holders and creators of knowledge. *Qualitative Inquiry, 8*(1), 105–126.
Bonilla-Silva, E. (2010). *Racism without racists: Color-blind racism and the persistence of racial inequality in the United States*. Lanham, MD: Rowman & Littlefield.
Bonilla-Silva, E., & Embrick, D. G. (2006). Racism without racists: "Killing me softly" with color blindness. In C. A. Rossatto, R. L. Allen, & M. Pruyn (Eds.), *Re-inventing critical pedagogy: Widening the circle of anti-oppression education* (pp. 21–34). Lanham, MD: Rowman & Littlefield.
de Jesús, M. L., & Ma, S. M. (2004). R.A.W: "Raunchy Asian Women" and resistance to queer studies in the Asian Pacific American studies classroom. *The Radical Teacher, 70*, 26–31.
Delgado, R., & Stefancic, J. (2001). *Critical race theory: An introduction*. New York, NY: New York University Press.
Dixson, A. D., & Rousseau, C. K. (2005). And we are still not saved: Critical race theory in education ten years later. *Race Ethnicity and Education, 8*(1), 7–27.
DuBois, W. E. B. (2007). *The souls of Black folk*. Oxford & New York, NY: Oxford University Press.
Duncan, G. A. (2002). Critical race theory and method: Rendering race in urban ethnographic research. *Qualitative Inquiry, 8*(1), 85–104.
Gildersleeve, R. E., Croom, N. N., & Vasquez, P. L. (2011). "Am I going crazy?!": A critical race analysis of doctoral education. *Equity & Excellence in Education, 44*(1), 93–114.
Gillborn, D. (2005). Education policy as an act of white supremacy: Whiteness, critical race theory and education reform. *Journal of Education Policy, 20*(4), 485–505.
Gillborn, D. (2006). Rethinking white supremacy who counts in 'Whiteworld.' *Ethnicities, 6*(3), 318–340.

Haggis, P. (Director). (2004). *Crash* [film]. Santa Monica, CA: Lions Gate Entertainment.

Helms, J. E. (1990). *Black and White racial identity: Theory, research, and practice*. Westport, CT: Greenwood Press.

Hill, J., & Flynn, K. (2006). *Classroom instruction that works with English language learners*. Alexandria, VA: Association for Supervision and Curriculum Development.

hooks, B. (1994). *Teaching to transgress: Education as the practice of freedom*. New York, NY: Routledge.

Jennings, M. E., & Lynn, M. (2005). The house that race built: Critical pedagogy, African-American education, and the re-conceptualization of a critical race pedagogy. *Educational Foundations, 19*(3/4), 15.

Ladson-Billings, G. (1998). Just what is critical race theory and what's it doing in a nice field like education? *International Journal of Qualitative Studies in Education, 11*(1), 7–24.

Ladson-Billings, G. (1999). From Soweto to the South Bronx: African Americans and colonial education in the United States. In C. Torres & T. Mitchell (Eds.), *Sociology of education: Emerging perspectives* (pp. 247–264). New York, NY: SUNY Press.

Leonardo, Z. (2009). *Race, whiteness, and education*. New York, NY: Routledge.

Leonardo, Z., & Porter, R. K. (2010). Pedagogy of fear: Toward a Fanonian theory of 'safety' in race dialogue. *Race, Ethnicity and Education, 13*(2), 139–157.

Lewis, A., & Manno, M. (2011). The best education for some: Race and schooling in the United States today. In M. Jung, J. Vargas, & E. Bonilla-Silva (Eds.), *State of White supremacy: Racism, governance and the United States* (pp. 93–109). Palo Alto, CA: Stanford University Press.

Lynn, M. (1999). Toward a critical race pedagogy a research note. *Urban Education, 33*(5), 606–626.

Massey, D. S., & Denton, N. A. (1993). *American apartheid: Segregation and the making of the underclass*. Boston, MA: Harvard University Press.

Matias, C. E. (2012). Beginning with me: Accounting for a researcher of color's counterstories in socially just qualitative design. *Journal of Critical Thought and Praxis, 1*(1), 9.

Matias, C. E. (2013a). Who you callin' White?: A critical counterstory of colouring White racial identity. *Race, Ethnicity, and Education, 16*(3), 291–315.

Matias, C. E. (2013b). On the "Flip" side: A teacher educator of color unveiling the dangerous minds of white teacher candidates. *Teacher Education Quarterly, 40*(2), 53–73.

McIntosh, P. (2001). White privilege and male privilege: A personal account of coming to see correspondences through work in women's studies. In M. Andersen & P. Collins (Eds.), *Race, gender, and class: An anthology* (pp. 177–184). Belmont, CA: Wadsworth Publishing.

Memmi, A. (1965). *The colonizer and the colonized*. Boston, MA: Beacon Press.

Morrison, T. (1993). *Playing in the dark: Whiteness and the literary imagination*. New York, NY: Vintage.

Nieto, S., & Bode, P. (2008). *Affirming diversity: The sociopolitical context of multicultural education*. Boston, MA: Allyn & Bacon.

Rafael, V. (1995). *Discrepant histories: Translocal essays on Filipino cultures*. Philadelphia, PA: Temple University Press.

Roediger, D. R. (1999). *The wages of whiteness: Race and the making of the American working class*. New York, NY: Verso Books.

Solórzano, D. G., & Yosso, T. J. (2002). Critical race methodology: Counter-storytelling as an analytical framework for education research. *Qualitative Inquiry, 8*(1), 23–44.

Sue, D. W., Nadal, K. L., Capodilupo, C. M., Lin, A. I., Torino, G. C., & Rivera, D. P. (2008). Racial microaggressions against Black Americans: Implications for counseling. *Journal of Counseling & Development, 86*(3), 330–338.

Sullivan, R. J. (1991). *Exemplar of Americanism: The Philippine career of Dean C. Worcester*. Ann Arbor, MI: Center for South and Southeast Asian Studies, University of Michigan.

Symcox, L. (2002). *Whose history?: The struggle for national standards in American classrooms*. New York, NY: Teachers College Press.

Takaki, R. (1993). *A different mirror: A history of multicultural America*. Boston, MA: Little Brown and Company.

Thandeka. (1999). *Learning to be White: Money, race, and god in America*. New York, NY: Continuum.

Valenzuela, A. (1999). *Subtractive schooling: US-Mexican Uouth and the politics of caring*. New York, NY: SUNY Press.

Vera, H., & Gordon, A. M. (2003). The beautiful American: Sincere fictions of the white messiah in Hollywood movies. In A. Doane & E. Bonilla-Silva (Eds.), *White out: The continuing significance of racism* (pp. 113–128). New York, NY: Routledge.

Wiggins, G., & McTigue, J. (2000). *Understanding by design, standards-based instruction and assessment*. Alexandria, VA: Association for Supervision and Curriculum Development.

Williams, D. G., & Evans-Winters, V. (2005). The burden of teaching teachers: Memoirs of race discourse in teacher education. *The Urban Review, 37*(3), 201–219.

Yoon, I. H. (2012). The paradoxical nature of whiteness-at-work in the daily life of schools and teacher communities. *Race, Ethnicity and Education, 15*(5), 587–613.

Zamudio, M., Russell, C., Rios, F., & Bridgeman, J. (2011). *Critical race theory matters: Education and ideology*. New York, NY: Taylor & Francis.

Zimmerman, S., & Keene, E. (1997). *Mosaic of thought: The power of comprehension strategy instruction*. Portsmouth, NH: Heinemann.

Zinn, H. (2005). *A people's history of the United States*. New York, NY: Roman & Littlefield.

CHAPTER 10

"WHO YOU CALLIN' WHITE?!"

A Critical Counterstory on Coloring White Identity

Numerous articles examine the importance of *kuwentos* (Jocson, 2008) and counterstories (Delgado, 2001; Gillborn, 2009). Just as Renato Rosaldo (1989) argues that his analysis of a Filipino tribe's headhunting practice was remiss without applying the personal context of his wife's death, I argue research is remiss without the personal context that led to the design itself. I offer a counterstory of one racial microaggression[1] (Solórzano, Ceja, & Yosso, 2000) to illuminate the basis of this action research.

White Americans often ask me, "Where are you from?" When I answer "California," I observe the questioners' perplexity. For them, the expected answer is somewhere outside of the U.S. due to the pigmentation that racially categorizes me, a third generation Filipino American, as a "forever foreigner" (Suzuki, 1995). To reassert Whiteness, they counter with, "No, where are you *really* from?" Whether I choose to acquiesce and answer with what the racial microaggressor expects to hear ("Oh, I'm from [a country outside of the U.S.].") or transformationally resist by saying "Los Angeles," the discourse is imbued with hegemonic whiteness. Although this racial microaggression gives me racial battle fatigue, it also allows me to intimately understand the dynamics of race, racism, and White supremacy, as well as re-examine my racial identity amidst those operating mechanisms. Although racial microaggressions place the proprietary burden on people of Color, they also unveil a racially-aware praxis: a teachable moment in understanding race. How, then, do I re-appropriate this racial microaggression and deliberately redirect it toward Whites so that they better understand the dynamics of race, racism, and White supremacy, and examine their white racial identity to ultimately debunk white epistemology of ignorance (Mills, 2007)? To what extent can Whites share in this racial burden? Additionally, how does my racial identity as a brown-skinned Filipina impact the transmission of such a redirected microaggression? When asked "Who you callin' White?" this chapter screams: "I'm callin' *you* White, and you best recognize!"

THEORETICAL FRAME

Counterstories make the study of race so salient and dynamic because they unveil intricate racial nuances embedded in everyday life (Gillborn, 2010; Solórzano & Yosso, 2002). My counterstory of racial microaggression is, as Leonardo (2009) argues, a process of racial interpellation, as well as an opportunity for a counter-interpellation. That is, racial microaggressions are oppressive acts of subjugation yet, through these acts, I develop a nuanced understanding of how race, racism, and White supremacy operate while re-examining my racial identity. Therefore, racial microaggressions become both a site of oppression and a potential site of anti-oppression.

Despite my racial fatigue from the constant challenges of who I am expected to be, it is via these challenges that I understand who I am. As a critical race motherscholar of Color, I question how microaggressors understand who they are in juxtaposition to how I define myself, especially if I purposefully challenge their preconceived racial constructs. I propose racial identity is symbiotic in that people of Color are defined by our ontological opposite (that of whiteness) as much as Whites *can* be defined with respect to our "colorness" (Morrison, 1992). The question for critical race educators then becomes how. How do we, as educational researchers of Color, use the same indoctrination whiteness uses to define our racial identities via otherness (Memmi, 1965; Said, 1979) to reconceptualise and redefine a racially "awared" white identity (this time in juxtaposition to colored racial identities)? How do we "color" white racial identity? And, after understanding the deleterious effects possessive investment in white privilege entails, what becomes of white identity? Although such a task is the same burden people of Color have historically faced in "helping" Whites see their race, this chapter documents my counterstory on how I burdened myself to seek answers to these questions while identifying and critically analyzing the responses to such an undertaking.

ARRIVING AT IDENTITY

Chela Sandoval (2000) argues our repertoire of history greatly influences our understanding of meaning. For instance, if an individual draws from her/his understanding of history, then (reflexively) that individual will base her/his understanding of the self on that point of departure. Consider George Orwell's *1984* (1949) wherein the concept of "he who controls the past controls the future" is manifested in the protagonist, Winston Smith. Smith's understanding of self was presumed a natural extension of history. Only when Smith begins to challenge the validity of Big Brother's version of history does he undergo a new process of identity, one that is situated in new historical discourse.

Also, history is HIS-story in that the victors, the colonizers, and the dominant culture secure sole authorship of its reproduction (Francisco, 1976; Loewen, 1995; Memmi, 1965). Suffice it to say that this master narrative is in actuality a political battle of histories combatting for the stamp of single "truth-dom" (Symcox, 2002; Takaki, 1993). When applying this politicized history to identity, understanding which history reigns supreme becomes vital to understanding self-identity. Peter Berger and Thomas Luckman (1966) posit, "Societies have histories in the course of which specific identities emerge; these histories are, however, made by men with specific identities" (p. 173). Identities are extensions of history that are intrinsically subject to the identities from which they are wrought. Essentially, who informed the history from which I draw my identity? Acknowledging history as a "hegemonic control of meaning" (Leonardo, 2009) one must problematize its procurement.

To further exemplify, I employ Vicente Rafael's (1995) terminology: history is "discrepant" in that it is re-appropriated to serve political, economic, and social interests. History, then, is written for a purpose and becomes a metaphorical boxing ring that knocks out various historical perspectives in order to preserve a monolithic view history. Rafael contributes to how history is discrepant, on which I extend that we base our identity. However, I opt for different terminology to better describe history: *distorted*. If "distorted" means "perverting the truth of meaning," then nowhere is the word more applicable than to the subject of history. The nature of a master narrative history is hotly contested (Loewen, 1995; Takaki, 1993; Zinn, 1999). Yet the insistence not to use such forms of historical counternarratives in classrooms demonstrates a certain possessive investment in history (Lipsitz, 2006). Why hold onto a master narrative account? What is to gain?

Takaki (1993) cautions that history is raced and that this phenomenon leads to Whites' possessiveness of a historical master narrative. Just as Carl Grant (2011) argues that Black males are trapped on Devil's Island by the constraints of historical understanding, so then are Whites trapped by a raced history that depicts Whites in an elevated, almost savior-like status, a certain Hidalguismo or "son of" status (Rimonte, 1997). Such entrapment and refusal to escape entanglement demonstrate the possessive investment of race superiority. This distorted Eurocentric history delivers the message that, because of white historical glorification, Whites then have the proprietary claim to remain affixed at the apex of the racial structure. Similar to the reasoning of kings who rely on divine right, Whites rely on history as justification for their racial positioning. If Whites have conscious/subconscious possession of racial superiority via distorted history, then what does that reveal about white identity?

Herein lies the essence of my inquiry: *to what extent does distorted history influence the development of distorted identities?* The question about one's understanding of history, and thus identity formation based upon that historical understanding, allows us to analyze race in a different manner: considering the systemic effects of race on identity and how it is maintained through historical distortion.

The plausibility of historical distortion parallels the examinations of colonization. The racially colonized are expected to either accept a distorted history in which their identity was built by others, or resist it (Dubois, 2005; Fanon, 1967; Ladson-Billings, 1998; Memmi, 1965; Morrison, 1992). In the former scenario, the colonized internalizes the colonizer's socio-historical understanding through years of co-option, "benevolent" assimilation, or colonial education (Ladson-Billings, 1998; Freire, 1993; Necumopenco, 1981). Despite having Black skin, the colonized are historically forced to create, through co-optive measures, white masks (Fanon, 1967) in search of some "illusion of protection" (Lorde, 2001, p. 177). In the latter scenario, the colonized develops a double consciousness (Du Bois, 2005) whereby a constant state of resistance is methodically applied to counter the racial oppression enforced by the colonizer. On the one hand, involuntary acceptance leads to what Memmi (1965) describes as remaining in a "state of colonial being." On the other, constant resistance leads to what Lorde (2001) describes as "voluntary isolation." For the colonized, race then becomes a double-edged sword, one that cuts both ways: either accept a definition of self as determined by another or resist that definition and remain unaccepted. Meaning, as Fanon (1967) suggests, one can accept one's Blackness as defined by whiteness, or not. However, if one chooses to not accept that definition of Blackness, one will not be accepted in a world dominated by hegemonic whiteness.

And what of becomes of the colonizer in this process? In order to gain privileged status, the White colonizer must accept a distorted view of history (Brodkin, 1998; Roediger, 2005; Steinberg, 2001); indeed there is an implicit agreement to misinterpret the world through an "epistemology of ignorance" (Mills, 1997). The elevation of whiteness is masked behind the façade of a glorious Horatio Alger-esque[2] self-pulling of bootstraps (Brodkin, 1998). Such adherence to the myth of white ethnic strife to richness attempts to be a counternarrative to people of Color's counternarratives of systemic racial oppression. The whole notion that "we were discriminated against too, so get over it" is abandoned for a "me-tooism" which becomes widely adopted. Such an adoption masks the saliency of systemic injustice that positions certain groups of people with more access than others have, which is an operating mechanism of whiteness.

Ultimately, white adherence to the master narrative and resistance to counternarratives allows for an epistemology of ignorance (Sullivan & Tuana, 2007). By not learning counternarratives complete with raced history, Whites cultivate a *modus operandi* of not seeing race and, since race is out of mind, it becomes also out of sight. The constant claim of ignorance, as Sullivan and Tuana (2007) point out, is not an innocent by-product of limited access to knowledge. Rather, they argue, it is "actively produced for purposes of domination and exploitation" (p. 1). White loyalty to a distorted history accomplishes two things: (1) it develops a distorted identity, and (2) it makes viable an epistemology of ignorance. As such, my action research deliberately activates a history curriculum on the evolution of race and racism that centers the counterstories of people of Color and marginalizes Eurocentric normative history. Hence, the study was designed to debunk White epistemology of ignorance by redirecting the impact of racial microaggressions onto Whites instead of people of Color in hopes that Whites will share the burden of understanding their Whiteness and its role in race, racism, and white supremacy. Similar to Patricia Halagao's (2010) decolonizing curriculum for Filipino American students and how it emancipates the colonized minds of Filipino Americans, this raced curriculum seeks to decolonize the colonizer's mind.

TOWARD A METHODOLOGY AND DESIGN

Drawing from my years as a classroom teacher, I designed and piloted a history curriculum on the evolution of race and racism ("Raced Curriculum"). Expanding on previous work about racial identities, I implement pre- and post-racial attitude inventories and qualitatively conducted pre- and post-interviews. Additionally, students and I used journals as a two-way communication to: (1) record their responses to the explicitly raced curriculum, and (2) privately dialogue with me about their concerns. Set in a 40-student U.S. history honors course in an urban public high school, I conducted a three-phase action research: Pre-Intervention, Intervention, and Post-Intervention. Interestingly, this occurred while the U.S. was electing its first Black president. Hence, more than ever, race was presenting itself in mainstream society.

Leonardo (2009) states, "The possibility of ending race is the task of bringing back clarity to a situation that for so long has been clouded with the miseducation of racialized humans. This is the challenge of post-race thinking" (p. 69). My study accepted this challenge by drawing from Critical Social Theory (CST) and CRT to inform my methods. Like CRT, CST is an interdisciplinary approach that focuses on coalescing theory and application. Unlike CRT, however, CST's theory-building focuses on critiquing oppression as a whole. Henceforth, CST not only becomes a basis for theoretical analysis and practical applications, it also becomes a *mode of methodology* for race-related research. Since CST demands to dismantle whiteness, it leads us to inquire just how to do so. I begin where Leonardo (2009) left off: the creation of a critical social methodology of whiteness. The development of any apparatus that addresses this challenge with respect to CST also utilizes the theory to inform the mode of inquiry to which it is applied.

To be clear, my IRB-approved study's purpose was to begin a process of re-educating Whites via raced curriculum, from which they could begin a renewed process of identity development. Therefore, similar to the process of *Nigrescence* in Cross's (1971) Black racial identity, I posit a potential *colorscence* of white racial identity (Hardiman, 2001; Helms, 1990) that is predicated on learning raced history and re-centering the once marginalized counterstories of students of Color as part of canonical curriculum (Delgado, 2001; hooks, 1994). Colorscence is similar to Ruth Frankenberg's (1993) *race cognizance* in that White participants develop an understanding of race, racism, and whiteness. However, it falls short of capturing the development of racial identity so clearly described in Cross's (1971) conceptualization of Black racial identity. Because my project was deliberately implemented in a racially diverse classroom (Asian Pacific Americans, Latinos/ Chicanos, African Americans/Blacks, and Whites), the term "colorscence" better captures the symbiotic development of racial identities. Essentially, how are identities of racially diverse students co-constructed? How do we better understand our racial identities by collectively understanding each other? Simply put, *what happens to*

*our racial identities when we, as a multiracial society, begin to understand where
we are **really** coming from?*

For the purpose of this chapter, I focus on two high school students who I also
name, Hayley and Thurston, whose identity developments represent some of the
identity processes White students undergo in response to my raced curriculum. I
showcase these particular students because, although they have contrasting responses
to the curriculum, both ultimately demonstrate achievement in debunking white
epistemology of ignorance. That is, despite their different responses, I debunk their
epistemology of ignorance by using raced curriculum as a racial microaggression to:
(1) develop an understanding of race, racism, and white supremacy; and, (2) force
them to examine their emerging "colored" white identity. This chapter focuses on
their two distinct processes: *symbiotic transformation* versus *active resistance*.

MY COUNTERSTORY OF HAYLEY'S SYMBIOTIC TRANSFORMATION

During the pre-intervention interview, Hayley described herself as "White"
instead of "Caucasian." In fact, she went so far as to say she "never used the word
'Caucasian.'" Quickly identifying herself as White revealed Hayley's obvious
recognition of race as a social relation based on color. Insofar as she recognized
her identity as White, she also recognized the manifestation of race and racism in
modern society in the opening lines of our pre-intervention interview.

> Hayley: I think racism is still present in our society and I think it's unfortunate,
> but I do think that race does dictate some of the opportunities that
> you get and it can work for you or against you but, um, yeah. That's
> pretty much it.

Here, Haley has a rudimentary understanding of the dynamics of race as a system of
oppression via unequal opportunities. I take great interest in this articulation because
it sharply contrasts with the oft-invoked Algeresque philosophy of everyone having
the same opportunities but merely needing to pull themselves up by their bootstraps
(Brodkin, 1998). Interested in her recognition of race and its effect on the distribution
of opportunities, I asked her to elaborate.

> Hayley: Well, not only just race but, like, if you're immigrating to the country
> then you will not be as wealthy as someone who was already here.
> There are wealthy immigrants but often times you see immigrants
> trying to get through and wealth does, in some cases, determine your
> opportunities in life. But I think if everyone just strives to achieve,
> like, you need motivation and you have to want to do it, and race
> won't determine any of that. When it comes down to it, if you're
> motivated you can achieve what you want.

Contrary to Hayley's initial claim that race *does* in fact determine one's opportunities,
she then reneges that claim and draws from nativist and classist perspectives to

articulate the *real* determiner of unequal opportunities. Furthermore, she ends her analysis with an adherence to an Alger philosophy, although she starts with an open statement of how race "dictates" some opportunities. Overall, Hayley is blinded by her possessive investment in whiteness in terms of just exactly how race does dictate, because she cannot see beyond her own privilege; she ultimately retracts her previous claim and opts for the "you-just-have-to-be-motivated" approach.

However, Hayley indicates she "wants to learn" in her journal. Lesson #3's objective was "to gain an introductory understanding of how race and racism were historically developed in the United States and make connections to how it affects Americans." After a 20-minute lecture on various race-related court cases (*Ozawa v. United States,* 260 U.S. 178 [1922]; *United States v. Thind,* 261 U.S. 204 [1923],[3] etc.), historical raced events, and descriptions of a multitude of racist ideologies such as Eugenics, I began a conversation on the "divide and conquer" strategy and how it applies to race and racism. I drew from an example of the coalition between Japanese Americans and African Americans in the formation of the Black Panther Party[4] and its eventual dismantling upon the arrival of the Model Minority[5] thesis.

When I mentioned the Black Panther Party, I noticed several blank stares from my students. So I asked whether the students knew about the Black Panthers; most White students did not, and this seemingly shocked those African American students in the class who took on the task of providing an historical description of the Black Panther movement. A critical discussion ensued about why this important portion of history had been left out of textbooks. Hayley felt so compelled by this newfound knowledge that she documented her sentiments in her journal:

Journal Entry 2, 10/8/08: I have learned today about a group called the Black Panthers that my classmates basically described as a "Black militant group." I'm not exactly sure why but I have never heard of this organization before and when my classmates learned this they were shocked. I found it somewhat strange that something that was considered common knowledge was never taught to me.

Embedded in Hayley's entry is a seed of critical dissension. Her innocent explanation of why she had never learned about the Blank Panthers reveals her critique of what passes as "common knowledge." Specifically, she outlines her social critique when she writes about why this "was never taught." Yet, she is dismissive about her own responsibility in not knowing about the Black Panthers: her claim of ignorance is merely an effect of subscribing to the white epistemology of ignorance. Now that this option was so deliberately taken from her, what could she do, how could she have acted, and how could she resist the comforts of her privileged racial identity?

After teaching raced vocabulary, Hayley gained some *lingua franca* with which she could better articulate the manifestations of race and racism. This was seen in her analysis of the historical emergence of race and racism:

Journal Entry 2, 10/8/08: Slavery was a terrible institution that existed too long and taught intolerance. Slavery also influenced White supremacy and with that the feeling of inferiority of other races. Today in class, it was described as a "disease" and I think that has a lot of truth. On top of that the court cases were backing up this insane racial hierarchy with segregation, laws, etc. (emphasis added)

Here Hayley directly draws upon the information presented in Lesson 2 to formulate her reflection and analysis of the history of race and racism. Namely, by using terminology such as "White supremacy," "inferiority," and "racial hierarchy," she is better able to articulate race and racism. Rather than a collection of negative attitudes, white supremacy emerges as a structural relation. Haley even draws from a story I relayed during my lecture on how white supremacy is the disease and the symptoms are enactments of racism, such as segregation.[6] Hayley corroborates that lecture by writing, "I think that has a lot of truth." By using terms and becoming aware of various historical developments such as court cases and laws, Hayley begins a metacognitive counternarrative that sharply contrasts with the white master narrative. That is to say, the race blindness so needed to maintain whiteness begins to crumble when Hayley actively invokes her newly-learnt knowledge about a raced history and critical race vocabulary. Essentially, she draws from my modelling of critical race metacognition to apply these factors to her own critical race analysis. Not only does she gain a critical race perspective, she incorporates that knowledge into her sense of understanding and identity. Although I acknowledge critical race vocabulary can be appropriated by Whites to refute the very ideals it stands for, Hayley's sincerity to learn overcomes this. In fact, after the study finished, students invited me to participate in a student-generated critical race dialogue at which Hayley articulated counterstories of racism she had witnessed.

Sensing the hesitation to talk openly about race in Lesson 3, I opted for a new approach. After a discussion on racial slurs, I offered an example of one I heard growing up: that Filipinos eat dog. It was not until I researched the manifestations of this stereotype in my undergraduate senior thesis that I realized how much racism permeates U.S. history.[7] Although most students merely copied the list I wrote on the board, Hayley's notes summarized the importance of my example.

Critical Lesson on Race and Racism 3 Notes, 10/15/08: You need to think about the origins of racial stereotypes and derogatory words. The pain behind the words and how it hurts certain people.

Hayley's need to write down how to apply critical and historical race analysis to racial stereotypes indicates her struggle to transform her state of colonizer-being into a "colonizer who refuses" (Memmi, 1965). In a Foucauldian sense, Hayley refuses to be a vehicle of power whose blindness to a state of oppression inherently reproduces its power. In this critical lesson, she writes a "how to" guide for becoming more critically racially aware.

Since the raced curriculum forces Hayley to face the evolution of race and racism, she can no longer resist, refute, nor continue to ignore issues of race. Rather, she uses it to transform the lens she previously used to analyze a presumed raceless society. She articulated this newfound consciousness later:

Journal Entry 5, 10/29/08: The oppressors beat the ideas of inferiority into the oppressed until they actually believe them too which only reinforces the oppressors' feelings of superiority. Oppression and colonization is just a vicious cycle that only gets worse as it continues. We justify war with racism by saying we're really just protecting you. You're too uncivilized to do it yourself. (emphasis added)

Embedded in this entry is a multitude of dynamics. For one, Hayley's exposure to the curriculum forces her to use new *lingua franca* with which she better analyzes her newly-acquired raced reality. She uses terminology taken directly from Lesson 5, such as "inferiority," "oppressor," "colonization," "justify," and "superiority" to better articulate her thoughts on race. Linguistic scholars cogently argue the existence of embedded racism in the English language (Hopson, 2003, Moore, 2006). Scholar Donald Macedo and his colleagues (2003) assert how linguoracism is situated in the spread of English and thus there exists a need for new discourses. As such, Hayley's acquisition of critical race language gives her a new discourse with which she analyzed a raced society. Instead of adhering to her previous claims that it is not about race but about class and immigration, she now directly talks about the mechanisms of racism.

The second realization for Hayley is the saliency of race. Her comment "[w]e justify war with racism" indicates awareness about the effects of racism. Last and most interestingly, Hayley's writing style changes from expository to narrative when she states, "We justify war with racism by saying we're really just protecting you. You're too uncivilized to do it yourself." Using the term "we" connotes alignment with the subject of the sentence; that is, Hayley's purposeful use of the word "we" indicates her understandings of how her whiteness aligns her with racial oppressors. Therefore, exposure to the curriculum hastens Hayley's ability to see beyond the blindness of her white privilege. Further, instead of adhering to colorblind practices (Ladson-Billings, 1998, Schofield, 1986) that the "racial contract" (Mills, 1999) often stipulates, Hayley actively uses the knowledge she gained from the curriculum to practice race analysis of society in general:

Journal Entry #5: Racism is still used today to justify political social actions. There is still racism in America but it's not as blatant as it used to be. I feel like colonization might be occurring today in Iraq. However, like I said, racism today is not blatant but rather racial microaggression is seen more often than not. You definitely see racism in politics. I've heard people say America is not ready for a Black president. What would make America "ready"? Why aren't we ready now? Barack Obama is just as qualified as any other White, Latino, or Asian man and has just as much right to run for President.

Here Hayley translates her newly-acquired knowledge into a critical race analysis. First, she openly employs the term "racism" and, instead of obscuring its saliency with theories on class and immigration, she clearly outlines its connection to "political social actions." She also invokes newly-learnt language and concepts from the curriculum to articulate her thought process, seen when she asserts that "there is still racism in America but it's not as blatant as it used to be." Hayley goes as far as to associate colonization of the Philippines with what is "occurring today in Iraq."[8] Her newly-learnt knowledge becomes transformative as she applies it to a current socio-political condition. Her usage of the term "racial microaggression" allows her to better encapsulate her thoughts on the evolution of racism, from blatant to subtle.

Finally, Hayley applies her newly-learnt knowledge of race, colonization, oppression, and racial microaggressions to a raced analysis of the Obama presidential campaign. She questions the social normalcy of whether the U.S. is "ready" for a Black president with a counter-hegemonic line of inquiry; specifically, she questions, "What would make America 'ready'?" and "Why aren't we ready now?" to highlight the hegemonic operation of race silence.

Yet Hayley's race consciousness is not the only thing that changed; the curriculum also altered her sense of racial identity. In the beginning, Hayley simply stated that she is White and that the problem of race and racism falls squarely on the shoulders of people of Color, thus demonstrating her lack of awareness regarding how her positionality as a White person affects this dynamic. Specifically, she talked about how schools in the "ghetto" were not as "good" and noticed how students of Color come from "an hour or two hours away on the bus to come to this school." She also noted that many scholarships are "specifically aimed at certain races." In other words, whiteness is not part of the equation and remains invisible. In all her discussions about race and racism, she focused her attention on people of Color rather than looking at the other side of the raced coin: whiteness. Ignoring whiteness suggests that Hayley saw race and racism as an issue affecting communities of Color and did not understand the role that racial structures, including her white identity, play in that experience.

However, this orientation changed after exposure to dialogue, assignments and projects that the new curriculum demands. In her Mid-Project Journal Entry 6, Hayley wrote about this newfound awareness:

Journal Entry #6, 11/5/08: My views on race are definitely altered. Hearing my classmates' experiences and realizing the adversities that I, as a White female, yes, me, face... I have learned a lot in this class about how people have been discriminated against, my classmates. I didn't have the same experiences as they did and probably would have never heard about them of it wasn't for this class... I feel like I understand my race and other races better. It is really emotional to talk about race and racism [but] I feel it takes down a lot of barriers for me.

Interestingly, Hayley engages her white identity in the context of race by acknowledging that because of her race she "didn't have the same experiences and probably would have never heard about them." Hence, Hayley begins to understand her role as a White person by understanding the racial effects such positionality imposes on her peers of Color.

For Hayley, understanding the self became symbiotic in that learning about the history of race and racism mutually benefitted the identities of both racially dominant and nondominant groups. Hayley *gained* by accepting her loss of whiteness. By undergoing a colorscence of her white racial identity, Hayley debunked her epistemology of ignorance. Doing so crumbled whiteness on the basis of destroying the operating tenet of not seeing race. Hayley's emerging colorscence lifted the veil, thus her subscription to "I don't see race" because "I just don't know about race" couldn't be used. Ultimately, she was forced to see race and redefine her white identity within a new context, which altered how whiteness operated within her.

And this happened because I implemented the raced curriculum in a racially-diverse classroom so that we could all hear, feel, and internalize counterstories. Hayley became aware that her whiteness prevented her from seeing race and racism when she invoked her identity as a "White female" and subsequently wrote about how she would have never known about discrimination because of the inherent blindness in whiteness. The curriculum forced her to see the historical formation of systemic racism and was illuminated by the personal counterstories of her classmates of Color, all of which Hayley listened to, learned from, and was transformed by, as she documented throughout her journal and interviews. Therefore, despite having previously centered the issues of race and racism on "them," she realized it is also about her as "a White female." She wrote about this realization in the project evaluation:

Project evaluation, 12/: [The curriculum] influenced my views of myself because I feel like I'm missing something. I feel like I have no culture or traditions, like something is absent. I feel like being White makes you this blank slate and everyone around me is so colorful and has history and tradition. I don't really know who I am more than ever before. This class helped me immensely open my eyes more to race, something I didn't think too much. I feel like I understand my classmates better but not really myself. I'm left wondering more about my race and what it really means to be White. I feel like a divide between White and everyone else… I feel like my classmates understand me even better too… Even though this exercise makes me more confused about who I am, that's not necessarily a bad thing. I will continue to search and analyze myself and try to understand.

Ultimately, the project went beyond multicultural content integration (Banks, 2001) in that Hayley realized learning about race and racism was not only about learning the stories of the nondominant races but, reflexively, learning about herself as a self-proclaimed White female. Without a doubt, Hayley learned the colorful history of nondominant groups, but she moved away from the superficiality of just knowing others when she applied this lesson to her sense of self. In other words, it was not about others as objects of white study, but intimately about whiteness itself.

Although she drew upon the "having no culture" argument that many White Studies scholars point out (Nieto & Bode, 2008, Tanaka, 2009), the interesting and transformative aspect of the critical race lesson was Hayley's ability to identify the emergence of a white racial identity and realize that it is "not a bad thing" to feel a bit "confused about who [she is]." In fact, Nieto & Bode (2008) describes monocultural education as "incomplete education" and, if one bases one's understanding of the world on a monocultural and incomplete education, one is in fact "miseducated" (p. 50). Conversely, those who receive explicit lessons on race and racism have the ability to lift their "cultural blindness" (p. 50) and see anew.

It was Hayley's ability to see a more racially-explicit reality that sparked my interest in her. Instead of shying away from learning race and racism because it pulled the rug of identity out from under her white feet, she welcomed it and challenged herself to gain a better understanding of her whiteness by writing, "I will continue to search and analyze my self and try to understand." This is the essence of transformative praxis.

In no way do I assert that Hayley was "saved" from the insidiousness of a racially blind façade. Rather, I do assert that a seed was planted in her disposition, one that is beginning to take root. In her post-intervention interview she expressed how much this project was transformative for her. In all her responses she discussed what she had learned and how "it was definitely enlightening." She also claims she has "a better understanding of where [people] are coming from." Therefore, for Hayley, the raced curriculum was liberating and affirming in that she learned to listen to the once-silenced voices, experiences, and counterstories of her peers to better understand a marginalized perspective. It is her application of such knowledge to her sense of self as a White female that fractures the epistemology of ignorance that so defines white privilege. This is a process often dismissed by dominant groups.

Because the study was done in one school year, it is beyond my scope to document the lasting effects of such a raced curriculum. However, within the scope of the study, Hayley's new racial understanding altered her racial identity. Knowing that one's understanding of one's identity is a salient factor in how one interacts with the world, it is intriguing to recognize that Hayley's changed identity has the potential to transform more of society. Hopefully Hayley's changed belief system, sense of identity, and newfound understanding will act like tossed pebbles making waves throughout a lake. As an educator, what I find important and exciting in Hayley's example is that her understandings of the self, others, and society, combined with active search for more answers, is *the* hallmark of transformative education.

MY COUNTERSTORY OF THURSTON'S WHITE ACTIVE RESISTANCE

Critical whiteness literature often documents transformative racial awareness among Whites (Frankenberg, 1993; Howard, 1999; Schick, 2010). However, excluding documentation of white resistance renders critical whiteness studies overly indulgent, even romanticizing white racial epiphany. As such, I offer a counterstory of white resistance to remind critical race researchers that we will continue to experience resistance, and such resistance is a response worth analyzing. Essentially, *how can we learn from white resistance to make critical race work more effective in debunking whiteness?*

Active resistance to acquiring racial awareness is the other response to my racially microaggressive raced curriculum. However, such resistance is not oppositional as it was for "the Lads" in Paul Willis's *Learning to Labour* (1977) which documents the counter culture of the poor working class – even if the resistance is at times self-defeating. Nor does it relate to how students of Color transformationally resist in a hegemonic educational system that renders their histories and identities mute (Solórzano & Delgado-Bernal, 2001). Critical resistance theories articulate how resistance is a form of empowerment for the oppressed and, as such, are necessary for critical education (Giroux, 2001; Shannon, 1995; Villenas & Deyhle, 1999). Yet empirical data that examines the depth of white resistance to researchers of Color is lacking. In fact, in Carol Schick's (2010) study in which she interviews White pre-service teachers learning anti-racist pedagogies, she argues that she cannot separate herself from her White students because of being White herself. She further articulates the importance of recognizing student trauma and dissonance, yet does not offer empirical data to shed light on the "messy contingencies" of learning such anti-racist pedagogies (p. 100). In fact, Schick ends her discussion with a call for members of dominant groups to garner "responsible disillusionment" so that narratives of dominant selves do not reign supreme. Therefore, the response of white active resistance in my study to my racialized body, as a brown-skinned Filipina motherscholar of Color is important in that it depicts the trauma of a researcher of Color who undertakes such anti-racist pedagogy.

Schick's (2010) response is embodied in Thurston, a self-identified White male who, like Hayley, increasingly engaged as the curriculum unfolded. Unlike Hayley, however, Thurston's engagement with the curriculum was of active resistance instead of symbiotic transformation. Understanding various resistive strategies better informs how to effectively engage in critical race research. Consider, for example, the need in CRT to center the marginalized experience of people of Color in order to re-examine society. Then too should there be an exploration of white resistance in order to re-examine how to more effectively employ critical race research seeking to debunk white epistemology of ignorance.

In this section I draw from my counterstory to highlight the various strategies Thurston employed to resist the raced curriculum. Ultimately I argue that, although

151

such resistance may appear counterproductive, it is, in fact, a productive stage within the development of coloring white racial identity.

Throughout the project Thurston resisted, from his refusal to partake in the initial group interview to his insistence on participating in the post-intervention group interview to reiterating how he "didn't learn anything." Thurston's reaction to the curriculum was that of active resistance. One of the strategies he employed to resist the curriculum was the use of "false victimhood" by asserting that Whites are, in fact, the true victims of race and racism. The concept of false victimhood is well-used by White males to substantiate anti-affirmative action platforms (Cabrera, 2009). As such, critical race scholars need to revisit the concept in order to analyze how it is manifested and articulated.

In Thurston's case, this sentiment of false victimhood was manifested in one of his first journal entries after Lesson 1. This lesson was designed to utilize the racially-lived experiences of students to collaboratively define race and racism. Thurston journaled, "I personally have no problem with talking about race; it's just that it can be interpreted as racist since I'm White and Jewish." Here, Thurston ideologically supported the claim that Whites are themselves the true victims of racism because they are "labeled" racist by virtue of being White. He also engages his Jewish ethnicity. Although it is evident that Jews have undergone generations of proto-racism in the form of anti-Semitism and have historically been racially oppressed by other White people, Thurston's need to align "White" and "Jewish" as one concept entices some form of synonymy. Thurston's need to fuse his White racial identity with his Jewish ethnic identity illustrates his racial and ethnic confusion toward whiteness. Unlike Brodkin (1998), Thurston positions his newly-fused white identity as a victim rather than a beneficiary of a system of race.

He further articulated, "One must also know that depending on who you're talking to, race-wise, it can be interpreted as offensive." Although Thurston claims he does not want to be mislabeled as a racist, he adheres to white racist ideology by claiming such a misinterpretation ultimately depends on the race of the *other* person. By doing so, he invokes a "them versus us" ethos in that the racial mislabeling of Whites is dependent on races other than Whites.

Another resistive strategy Thurston employed was personally engaging me as an embodiment of the raced curriculum. Race scholar Carla Goar (2008) asserts that research is imbued with hegemonic white methodologies by examining the contradiction to objectivity in white methodologies that problematize the claim that the researcher's race is irrelevant. Goar warns that "by failing to seriously consider race, current experimental methodology reifies the interest of the prevailing culture by reflecting colour-blind racism" (p. 162). Thus, my race as a brown-skinned Filipina American is an important factor in how Thurston actively resists, and thus has huge implications for other researchers of Color embarking on similar studies. Instead of writing about what he learned from the day's session, as directed in the prompt, he wrote a personalized response to a counterstory that embodied the dynamics of white privilege and whiteness when the antagonist, Mrs. Watson, parcels out who can and cannot be American by virtue of skin color:

Journal Entry 1, 10/1/08: Very fluffy, Amateurish. Seems a bit racist in tone, a bit angry. I've been through the same thing, but I didn't take it as seriously as you did. (emphasis added)

Interestingly, Thurston's need to personalize and explicitly direct the comment to me by consciously using the word "you" demonstrates his need to actively engage me as a personified symbol for his dissent. In order for critical race dialogue to safely ensue, it becomes imperative to silence white discourse in order to create a racial microaggression for Whites (Leonardo & Porter, 2009). Thus, I responded to Thurston:

I'd feel more comfortable if you didn't personalize this using "you"; maybe use the name of the main character.

Not only did this comment point out my awareness of Thurston's need to engage my personal identity, I also offered an alternative way to engage in an effective critical race dialogue. By asking him to remove the directed engagement of me and make reference to the main character of the counterstory, I denied the operating mechanism of whiteness via white discourse. He responded to my comment as follows:

Journal Entry 1, 10/1/08: The definition stated by YOU and my classmates of racism completely differs from my own. I think race has nothing to do with skin color, but where you're from, genealogically speaking... I didn't really learn much today.

Thurston's decision to capitalize the word "YOU" clearly indicates his need to assert his personal opposition to the study and to me.

In Lesson 1, the students worked in groups to devise their own definitions of race and racism by writing them on a poster paper. Once these definitions were written down, students shared them with the entire class. Strategically, I did not offer my own definition of what constitutes race and racism because culturally-responsive curriculum must speak to the students' experiences and not be biased with one's own. In the face of this strategy, Thurston drew upon his privilege in whiteness to racialize me in alignment with the students of Color. Further, despite his insistence that he "didn't really learn much" that day, the internal dialogue expressed in his journal in response to the class activities and discussions demonstrated that he was, in fact, learning, albeit while simultaneously resisting.

Thurston again used false victimhood and the engagement of me to resist the curriculum. In his Journal Entry 2, he attacked my personal character and, once again, posited the notion that he was the victim by constantly being misjudged as a racist merely because he was White.

Journal Entry 2, 10/8/08: In discussing race, one must realize that anything he says may be interpreted as "racist" by others but I do not care; I say what needs to be said (seeing how you'll go through and write "in Love" about my words, "what" exactly needs to be said depends on the conversation). One must also know that depending on who you're talking to, race-wise, it could be interpreted as offensive.

Here Thurston writes about how he "does not care" if people interpret him as a racist and that he will "say what needs to be said," yet no one in the class identified him as a racist or alluded to him being racist. Hence, Thurston's focus on *being seen* as a racist, despite never having been called one during the course, invokes an "us versus them" argument. Either consciously or subconsciously, Thurston's words reveal his internal battle with his own white identity, one that compelled him to articulate that he is racially separate from the class because he is White.

Additionally, Thurston utilized personal engagement by deliberately attacking and mocking me as a person in several of his journal entries. Referencing how I refused to use combative strategies in response to his own combative strategies, Thurston wrote, "seeing how you'll go through and write 'in Love' about my words…" After years of classroom teaching, my pedagogy encompasses an authentic care (Valenzuela, 1999) and includes love for my students regardless of their dispositions. At the beginning of the project I explained how it was built on a social commitment to love, humanity, and a better society. Therefore, Thurston's deliberate mocking of my use of love directly engaged my character.

After Lesson 8, Thurston got so perturbed by the curriculum that he again engaged my personal self by writing "you" in another of his entries:

Journal Entry 8, 11/19/08: Directedness is the key to explanation; this being said, if I want to refer to someone in writing, I say their name or if I'm referring to you, I say "you."

Here Thurston clearly explains that he will engage me regardless of my instructions to refer to the exact author/theory with which he disagrees. The ultimate resistance for Thurston becomes not only the project itself but the fact that he associates my mere presence with the raced curriculum by personally engaging me as a natural extension of the raced curriculum. However, more important to note is that Thurston's harsh engagement of me stems from his personal resistance to debunking Whiteness. Schick (2010) analyzes this contradiction in her "technologies of Whiteness" (p. 92) and asserts that pre-service White Canadian teachers, though aware and committed to social and racial equity, still "call upon the investment in their whiteness as their underlying defence" (p. 92). However, Schick self-identifies as White; therefore, as Goar (2008) so argues, her racial identity within a hegemonic white methodology is considered objective and natural. Yet, in my case, it was phenotypically obvious I was *not* White, and it was this factor that played a role in the complexity of this study. Thurston's resistance to the curriculum on race and racism became personalized because he felt I attacked his belief system and his security in his white identity simply because of my skin color. His journal entries and notes were the medium wherein he engaged me in his internal battle to defend his whiteness.

Thurston also enacted his whiteness to decipher who held power. Throughout his entries, he not only challenged the lectures, examples, and counterstories, he challenged all scholars, theories, and articles with a critical race perspective. Instead of listening to and learning from the marginalized experiences of people of Color (Moule, 2009), Thurston discredited them. During Lesson 4, students engaged in critical race dialogue on whether it was racist for one to appropriate vernaculars used by particular racial groups. The class went back and forth, offering personal counterstories to illustrate their assertions. At one point Hayley asked, "Then why do Black comedians use racial stereotypes?" The class discussed Dave Chappelle,[9] and during this dialogue Thurston interjected, "I thought he just went crazy and went to South Africa." Thurston's remark about Chappelle's mental state enacted his power by determining who can deem whom worthy and/or sane.

Thurston also exerted his power to discredit and dismiss the racially lived experiences of an African American male; after talking about Cornel West's[10] theoretical contributions to race literature, Thurston said, "Oh yeah. Cornel West. He's that guy who has crazy hair and is all crazy when he talks." In this comment, Thurston uses his whiteness to not only dismiss West's body of work, but to judge his "craziness"; Thurston's whiteness ascribes him the power to decide who has merit or not.

Thurston also drew from his whiteness to demonstrate his power to deem what is fact and what is fiction. In Journal Entry 2, he wrote in response to a comment made during our discussion on racial profiling:

Journal Entry 2, 10/8/08: Look, racial profiling[11] is right if the ratios are correct. If someone of one race has such a larger chance of doing something than someone else then yes they should occur. *Usually* (let me emphasize on *Usually*) a White male is less-inclined to strap a bomb to himself and blow himself up in a grocery store than a Muslim middle-eastern [sic] male of the same age. It's just a fact.

Certainly, Thurston has a right to his opinion; however, his utilization of whiteness gives him power over what is and is not fact, a discourse inherently challenged by the design of this project. By ending his opinions with "it's just a fact," he ultimately cuts off the debate. As such, Thurston not only becomes the bearer of truth and knowledge, he also asserts his power to deem what is and is not fact.

Embedded in Thurston's project evaluation are enactments of his whiteness. He asserted that the only thing he learned is that other people are confused in their definition of racism. By stating so, he assumed that his definition of what constitutes racism is the correct definition. He then does not recommend the project on the basis that it changed people's "thought process" to see race and racism (which was ultimately one of the major purposes of the project and thus, should definitely be implemented elsewhere). By stating such revelation, Thurston could no longer subscribe to an epistemology of ignorance because he was now *seeing* race and racism. Adhering to a colorblind perspective to ultimately protect his power in whiteness, Thurston believed that we should not see racism and that a project that forces one to see the racism in our society is brainwashing. Ultimately, Thurston enacted his whiteness by accusing me of abusing my power as the principal investigator, yet never accounted for his own power.

In the end, Thurston clearly indicated that he is *not* changed by this study; however, unbeknownst to Thurston, he *did* change by becoming more aggressive and combative after each session. He resisted and, at times, even wrote how he "lost [his] train of thought" or was "too tired" to argue against topics discussed in class, a racially fatiguing feeling that people of Color experience every day to negotiate their racialized identities. In fact, Thurston's mere utterance of fatigue indicates how the proprietary burden of race, racism, and white supremacy is shared (Leonardo, 2009). What he did not realize is that he did in fact change because, instead of existing in a pseudo-reality where his beliefs ran supreme and uncontested, he was finally confronted with a different reality, one in which he felt he must resist. This is precisely the change I saw within him. He actively resisted against something. This is a process of racial identity development that must be further analyzed in terms of white racial identity. Although Thurston may not have been fully aware of his whiteness and the power it holds, he then realized he must resist against something that differed from his belief on all levels.

For so long, curriculum and pedagogical practices were designed to meet the needs of students. But we need to question *which* students. For Thurston, standardized Eurocentric curriculum and colorblind pedagogical strategies employed by schools and teachers inherently supported whiteness in his white identity. It was not until I implemented the raced curriculum that Thurston became decentralized, to which he responded with never-ending acts of resistance. Only until he trades active resistance for symbiotic transformation can Thurston, who perches himself at the apex of the racial pyramid and at the center of the curriculum, finally realize that he is no longer in Kansas.[12]

AN ENDING TO A BEGINNING OF CHANGE

This piece uses counterstories of how one teacher designed and implemented a standards-based history curriculum on race and racism to replace Eurocentric standardized history curriculum on which white students unconsciously or consciously base their identities. The findings are clear. On one hand, for students who had epiphanic transformations, so characterized by the counterstory of Hayley, the raced curriculum provides the means to realize their white privilege and thus inherently debunk epistemology of ignorance. Though the journey was rough for these students, they nonetheless needed to experience it. They must experience it precisely because it is a process which characterizes the daily-lived racial experiences of students of Color. These are the kinds of daily racial microaggressive acts, so detailed in my personal counterstory, that inherently force us to examine who we are in relation to society. Such a realization of societal positioning is needed for White students. Essentially, where do they stand in the context of race and how did they accumulate that racial standing? Herein lies the self-realization that Whites so need. Since people of Color have intimate knowledge of how race operates, their counterstories are essential in revealing to Whites how they (Whites) achieved their racial standing and how that standing, whether conscious or not, operates in a racially oppressive manner. For Hayley, the raced curriculum allowed her to see how Whites are elevated in society. By doing so, she could no longer ignore the once invisible privileges so embedded in her skin color. Hayley needed to experience racial dissonance in order to realize the color behind her racial identity. Despite her discomfort with dissonance, she learned to accept it within a process of re-coloring her white identity. Therefore, her gain is accepting her loss of whiteness.

On the other hand, for students who resist, like Thurston, the raced curriculum has the same effect of creating a realization of white privilege and inherently debunking white epistemology of ignorance. The difference resides in how these students respond. Instead of acknowledging the dissonance, these students choose to resist it. Although those with such responses miss an opportunity to learn from their dissonance, they do learn that they no longer live in blissful ignorance. Furthermore, the employment of such resistant strategies demonstrates the need to actively engage in resistance. It is this active engagement that allows Whites to share in the proprietary burden of race so forcibly placed upon people of Color. To exemplify, I am not the only one fatigued when asked, "Where am I *really* from?" when a racial microaggressor has to actively engage in resistance. Therefore, students like Thurston realize they incur a loss of ignorance. Yet such a loss is itself a gain in that losing one's blindness to white privilege is ultimately a gain in the war against racism. Essentially, instead of "Who you callin' White?", the gain and loss is in realizing, "Oh, it's me."

In the end, this project was emotionally, physically, and racially exhausting. Yet among these sentiments I found healing, a type of healing that combines the personal with the educational. hooks (1994) describes this as "self-actualizing the liberatory praxis" because it gives my students and me a shared language, theory, and historical understanding of race and racism. It is precisely this accumulated knowledge of language, history, and theory that helps us truly understand where we *really* come from.

NOTES

[1] Racial microaggressions are "everyday exchanges that send denigrating messages to people of Color because they belong to a racial minority group. These exchanges are so pervasive and automatic in daily interactions that they are often dismissed and glossed over as being innocuous" (Sue, Bucceri, Lin, Nadal, & Torino, 2007, p. 72).

²   Alger was a prolific 19th Century American writer who was known for his "rags to riches" stories about lower-class boys reaching the upper echelons of society through hard work, determination, and – invariably – luck.

³   See Chapter 8.

⁴   A 1960s American-based Black militant group that resisted racial, economic, and social oppression "by any means necessary," to quote Malcolm X, a notable Black activist of the time.

⁵   A term used in many disciplines; however, in CRT, it is a concept used to understand the racial positioning of Asian Americans during the post-1965 U.S. Immigration Act which selectively filtered "highly-skilled" Asian Americans into the U.S. typically from countries already colonized by the U.S. This produced a highly-skilled Asian American immigrant population which U.S. magazines argued were "model minorities" because they "overcame" racial barriers that many Blacks, Latinos, and Native Americans faced in the U.S.

⁶   A concept derived from a lecture made by critical race theorist, Danny Solórzano.

⁷   In Chapter 2 I discuss the St. Louis World's Fair and how Filipinos were displayed as caged animals in their "natural habitat," often starved and served dog meat to heighten the spectators' perceptions of Filipinos as savages. The U.S. annexation of the Philippines was so important that the Philippine exhibit in St. Louis comprised roughly one-fourth of the entire 1904 World's Fair. Such a dynamic played right into the political justifications of the U.S. colonization of the Philippines (Matias, 2005).

⁸   The U.S. invasion of Iraq and use of military to eradicate Iraqi "insurgents."

⁹   A famous Black comedian known for critically using Black stereotypes in his HBO series *The Dave Chappelle Show*. Chappelle's intent was to show the absurdity of Black racial stereotypes. Unfortunately, because his White audiences used his skits to reinforce their already racist mindsets instead of seeing the absurdity, Chappelle quit the show and wrote a public letter decrying the racial bigotry.

¹⁰   A prominent Black professor who is the author of *Race Matters* (1994) and lectures on how race and racism operate in the U.S.

¹¹   A U.S. practice used by police departments to stop and/or detain individuals simply on the basis of race.

¹²   A popular American phrase derived from the film *Wizard of Oz*. It is used to reference feeling estranged from one's surroundings.

REFERENCES

Adams, M. (2001). Core processes of racial identity development. In C. Wijeyesinghe & B. Jackson (Eds.), *New perspectives on racial identity development*. New York, NY: New York University Press.

Banks, J. A. (2001). Approaches to multicultural curriculum reform. *Multicultural Education: Issues and Perspectives*, *4*, 225–246.

Berger, P., & Luckmann, T. (1966). *The social construction of reality*. New York, NY: Anchor Books, Doubleday Publishing Group.

Brodkin, K. (2000). *How did Jews become White?* New Brunswick, NJ: Rutgers University Press.

Cabrera, N. (2009). *Invisible racism: Male hegemonic whiteness in higher education* (Unpublished Dissertation). University of California, Los Angeles, CA.

Cross, Jr., W. (1971). The Negro to Black conversion experience. *Black World, 20*(9), 13–27.

Cross, W. (1992). *Shades of Black*. Philadelphia, PA: Temple University Press.

Delgado, R., & Stefancic, J. (2001). *Critical race theory*. New York, NY: New York University Press.

Dubois, W. (2005). *Souls of Black folk*. Stilwell, KS: Digireads.com Publishing.

Fanon, F. (1967). *Black skin, White masks*. New York, NY: Grove Press.

Foucault, M. (1980). *Power/Knowledge* (C. Gordon Ed.). New York, NY: Vintage Books.

Francisco, L. (1976). The Philippine-American war. In J. Quinsaat (Ed.), *Letters in exile*. Los Angeles, CA: UCLA Asian American Studies Center.

Frankenberg, R. (1993). *The social construction of whiteness: White women, race matters*. Minneapolis, MN: University of Minnesota Press.

Freire, P. (1970 & 1993). *Pedagogy of the oppressed.* New York, NY: Continuum.
Freire, P. (2000). *Pedagogy of oppressed* (30th Anniversary Ed.). New York, NY: Continuum.
Freire, P. (1992, 1994, 1998, 2004). *Pedagogy of hope.* New York, NY: Continuum.
Freire, P., & Macedo, D. (1987, 2001). *Literacy: Reading the world and the word.* London: Routledge.
Grant, C. (2011). Escaping Devil's Island: Confronting racism, learning history. *Race, Ethnicity, and Education, 14*(1), 33–49.
Gillborn, D. (2010). The colour of numbers: Surveys, statistics and deficit-thinking about race and class. *Journal of Education Policy, 25*(2), 253–276.
Giroux, H. (2001). *Theory and resistance in education.* Westport, CT: Bergin & Garvey.
Goar, C. (2008). Experiments in Black and White: Power and privilege in experimental methodology. In T. Zuberi & E. Bonilla-Silva (Eds.), *White logic, White methods: Racism and methodology.* Lantham, MD: Rowman & Littlefield Publishers.
Halagao, P. (2010). Liberating Filipino American through decolonizing education. *Race, Ethnicity, and Education, 13*(4), 495–512.
Hardiman, R. (2001). Reflections on White identity development theory. In C. Wijeyesinghe & B. Jackson (Eds.), *New perspectives on racial identity development.* New York, NY: New York University Press.
Harding, S. (2001, 2003). *The feminist standpoint theory and reader.* New York, NY: Routledge.
Helms, J. (1990). *Black and White racial identity.* Westport, CT: Praeger Publishers.
hooks, b. (1994). *Teaching to transgress.* New York, NY: Routledge.
Hopson, R. (2003). The problem of the language line: Cultural and social reproduction of hegemonic linguistic structures for learners of African descent in the USA. *Race, Ethnicity, and Education, 6*(3), 227–243.
Housee, S. (2008). Should ethnicity matter when teaching race and racism in the classroom? *Race, Ethnicity and Education, 11*(4), 415–428.
Howard, G. (1999). *You can't teach what you don't know: White teachers, multiracial schools.* New York, NY: Teachers College Press.
Jocson, K. (2008). Kuwento as a multicultural pedagogy in high school ethnic studies. *Pedagogies: An International Journal, 3*(4), 241–253.
Ladson-Billings, G. (1998). From Soweto to the South Bronx: African Americans and colonial education in the United States. In C. Torres & T. Mitchell (Eds.), *Sociology of education: Emerging perspectives* (pp. 247–264). New York, NY: SUNY Press.
Leonardo, Z. (2009). *Race, whiteness, and education.* New York, NY: Routledge.
Leonardo, Z., & Porter, R. K. (2010). Pedagogy of fear: Toward a Fanonian theory of "safety" in race dialogue. *Race Ethnicity and Education, 13*(2), 139–157.
Lipsitz, G. (1998). *Possessive investment in whiteness.* Philadelphia, PA: Temple University Press.
Lipsitz, G. (2006). *The possessive investment in whiteness: How White people profit in identity politics.* Philadelphia, PA: Temple University Press.
Loewen, J. (1995). *Lies my teacher told me.* New York, NY: Touchstone Simon and Schuster.
Lorde, A. (2001). Age, race, class and sex: Women redefining difference. In M. Andersen & P. Collins (Eds.), *Race, class and gender: An anthology.* Belmont, CA: Wadsworth/ Thomas Learning.
Macedo, D. P., Dendrinos, B., & Gounari, P. (2003). *The hegemony of English.* Boulder, CO: Paradigm.
Matias, C. E. (2005). *The development of the colonized Filipino – With a Capital F* (Unpublished master's thesis). California State University, Long Beach, CA.
Matias, C. E. (2010). *Where are you REALLY from? Raced curriculum, racial identity, and a project for a fuller humanity* (Unpublished dissertation). University of California, Los Angeles, CA.
Matias, C. E. (2010). *Who I am is who you is? Racial symbiosis and the colorscence of White racial identity via critical race dialogue* (Paper presentation). American Educational Research Association, Denver, CO.
Memmi, A. (1965). *The colonizer and the colonized.* Boston, MA: Beacon Press.
Mills, C. (1997). *The racial contract.* Ithaca, NY: Cornell University Press.
Mills, C. (2007). White ignorance. In S. Sullivan & N. Tuana (Eds.), *Race and epistemologies of ignorance.* Albany, NY: State University of New York Press.

159

Moore, R. (2006). Racism in the English language. In J. O'Brien (Ed.), *The production of reality* (pp. 199–126). Newbury Park, CA: Pine Forge Press.

Morrison, T. (1993). *Playing in the dark: Whiteness and the literary imagination*. New York, NY: Vintage Books.

Moule, J. (2009). Understanding unconscious bias and unintentional racism. *Phi Delta Kappan.*

Nepomuceno, J. G. (1981). A theory of the development of the Filipino colonized consciousness (unpublished dissertation). University of Michigan , Ann Arbor, MI.

Nieto, S., & Bode, P. (2008). *Affirming diversity: The sociopolitical context of multicultural education.* Boston, MA: Allyn & Bacon.

Orwell, G. (1949). *1984*. London & New York, NY: Penguin Group.

Pollock, M. (2004). *Colormute*. New Jersey, NJ: Princeton University Press.

Rafael, V. (1995). *Discrepant histories: Translocal essays on Filipino cultures*. Philadelphia, PA: Temple University Press.

Rimonte, N. (1997). Colonialism's legacy: The inferiorizing of the Filipino. In M. Root (Ed.), *Filipino Americans* (pp. 39–61). Thousand Oaks, CA: Sage.

Roediger, D. (2005). *Working toward whiteness: How American's immigrants became White*. New York, NY: Basic Books.

Rosaldo, R. (1993). *Culture and truth: The remaking of social analysis*. Boston, MA: Beacon Press.

Said, E. (1979). *Orientalism*. New York, NY: Vintage Books.

Sandoval, C. (2000). *Methodology of the oppressed*. Minneapolis, MN: University of Minnesota.

Schick, C. (2010). By virtue of being White: Resistance in anti-racist pedagogy. *Race, Ethnicity, and Education, 3*(1), 83–101.

Schofield, J. (1986). The colorblind perspective in school: Causes and consequences. In J. Dovidio (Ed.), *Prejudice, discrimination, and racis* (pp. 231–253). Cambridge, MA: Academic Press Company.

Shannon, S. M. (1995). The hegemony of English: A case study of one bilingual classroom as a site of resistance. *Linguistics and Education, 7*(3), 175–200.

Smith, W., Yosso, T., & Solórzano, D. (2007). Racial primes and Black misandry on historically White campuses: Toward critical race accountability in educational administration. *Educational Administration Quarterly, 43*(5), 559–585

Solórzano, D., Ceja, M., & Yosso, T. (2000). Critical race theory, racial microaggressions, and campus racial climate: The experiences of African American college students. *The Journal of Negro Education, 69*(1/2), 60–73.

Solórzano, D. G., & Bernal, D. D. (2001). Examining transformational resistance through a critical race and LatCrit theory framework Chicana and Chicano students in an urban context. *Urban Education, 36*(3), 308–342.

Solórzano, D., & Yosso, T. (2002). A critical race counterstory of race, racism, and affirmative action. *Equity & Excellence in Education, 35*(2), 155.

Steinberg, S. (2001). *The ethnic myth: Race, ethnicity, and class in America*. Boston, MA: Beacon Press.

Sue, D., Bucceri, J., Lin, A., Nadal, K., & Torino, G. (2007). Racial microaggressions and the Asian American experience. *Cultural Diversity and Ethnic Minority Psychology, 13*(1), 72–81.

Sullivan, S., & Tuana, N. (2007). *Race and epistemology of ignorance*. Albany, NY: State University of New York Press.

Suzuki, B. (1995). Education and the socialization of Asian Americans: A revisionist analysis of the "Model Minority" thesis. In D. Nakanishi (Ed.), *The Asian American educational experience.* New York, NY: Routledge.

Symcox, L. (2002). *Whose history?* New York, NY: Teachers College Press.

Takaki, R. (1993). *A different mirror: A history of multicultural America*. Boston, MA: Little Brown and Company.

Tanaka, G. (2009). The elephant in the living room that no one wants to talk about: Why U.S. anthropologists are unable to acknowledge the end of culture. *Anthropology & Education Quarterly, 40*(1), 82–95.

Valenzuela, A. (1999). *Subtractive schooling*. Albany, NY: State University of New York Press.

Villenas, S., & Deyhle, D. (1999). Critical race theory and ethnographies challenging the stereotypes: Latino families, schooling, resilience and resistance. *Curriculum Inquiry*, *29*(4), 413–445.

Vygotsky, L. (1978). *Mind in society*. Boston, MA: Harvard University Press.

Willis, P. (1977). *Learning to labor*. New York, NY: Columbia University Press.

Zimmerman, S., & Keene, E. (1997). *Mosaic of thought*. Portsmouth, NH: Heinemann.

Zinn, H. (1999). *A people's history*. New York, NY: Harper Perennial Modern Classic.

DECOLONIZING THE COLONIAL WHITE MIND

*Forever trapped in an illogical lie, the racial colonizer believes he is the rightful, etiolated king of a land he unjustly usurped. In his delusional elation, he prances around, changing the kingdom so that its history, language, and beliefs reflect his desires. In doing so, he is never confronted with its converse, especially since he has, for too long, subjugated all the racially colonized. He has done this by robbing their history, denigrating their languages, silencing their beliefs, and rendering anything that reveals their unfair conditions as nothing more than mere whines made by a lackluster group who, according to the king, refuses to put in the effort, an effort the king, himself, has not put in. Alas, because he is king of a robbed land, he creates and enforces rules and laws that contribute to the subjugated conditions of the racially colonized. He denies them any rights to housing by turning a blind eye to loan discrimination, redlining practices, and racial covenants. He denies them access to well-paying jobs by ignoring racially discriminatory practices in employment or by instituting mandatory credentials which the racially colonized are denied access to achieving. He makes a legal system that acknowledges his wrong doings like racism only if one can prove that the wrong doing was done with malicious intent, yet, ironically, he institutes degrees of intent with regard to crimes like murder or rape. He sanctifies his beliefs in racial purity and superiority by drafting anti-miscegenation laws and denying citizenship to those who violate his law. He re-creates history, glorifying his conquests and silencing the atrocities against the racially colonized incurred during those conquests. But worst of all, he comes into the racially colonized communities, befriending their children, convincing them he cares for them only so **he** can live a more etiolated life – they need only follow his lead and trust in him. And to this the king joyfully walks around his kingdom, feeling as if his immoral usurpation is atoned by his seemingly benevolent, altruistic moral token to "give back" to the racially colonized. Outside the dungeons of his kingdom, wherein most violators are the racially colonized, the king stands, perched on his throne, feeling accomplished for having brought onto people a life he is accustomed to having. This is, after all, the land of the free.*

White supremacy, enacted through individual and institutionalized racism, is like colonization in that it has an overarching oppressive state of coloniality that impacts the relationships and social positions of racial colonizers and the racially colonized. In the story above, the king swears he is the rightful king despite "the lovelessness that lies at the heart of [his] violence … even when clothed in false generosity" (Freire, 2003, p. 45). Admittedly, the proverbial quandary of "who made him king" is noteworthy here. His kingdom, like that of the U.S., is mainly about who has the power in the colonial enterprise and what that person will do within it for his sole security. Therefore, the positionality of those who usurped colonial power is worthy of interrogation because the manner to which he achieved that power and how he maintains is the essence of how racial colonization manifests itself.

Whether I am preoccupied with romancing the portraiture of the racial colonizer because his unique mentality undergirds his loveless quest for power or with the ceaseless idealistic hope for racial justice, I cannot escape the thought that my hopeful ruminations, by understanding the colonizer more deeply, will one day foresee a better future. Call me romantic – for I am in deep love with a more racially harmonious society and will forever flirt with such an idea.

Beyond my selfish desires to understand more clearly, comprehending the racial colonizer is of grave importance because, although Freire (1993) suggests that those in the oppressor position "cannot find in this power the strength to liberate either the oppressed or themselves" (p. 44), the onus of liberation cannot be placed solely on the backs of the oppressed. This is tantamount to assuming that patriarchy will become dismantled by virtue of women's participation against sexism without men ever challenging their own male privilege in the patriarchal enterprise. By claiming that the fight is among the oppressed and not of the oppressors, those oppressors who detest oppression, much like Memmi's (1965) colonists who refuse a state of colonization, are deemed as useless as a pierced condom. Obviously I do not subscribe to such a thought despite that closet racists, or those who are resolute in their whiteness ideology, will erroneously assume that studying whiteness is "white bashing." Such an assumption is as ridiculous as claiming that someone who studies women's studies hates women, or someone who studies ethnic studies hates people of Color. Indeed, I study whiteness because I know all too well that there is a role that colonizers must assume in order to do their part in dismantling the dehumanizing state of racial colonization. As such, this chapter looks into the processes by which a colonizer must decolonize his/her own mind in order to free it from the colonizing state of racism and white supremacy.

THE STATE OF COLONIZATION

Much has been written about decolonizing the minds of colonized peoples (Smith, 1999). These writers argue that such a process is necessary because the state of coloniality becomes so oppressive that, as Memmi (1965) reminds us, it is a "diseased society" (p. 98). In such a society, the colonized are forced to "bow to the language of his masters" (p. 107), an assimilation process which ultimately "destroys himself" (p. 122). As such, educators, political activists, and socially-just minded individuals come together to reclaim what was once robbed from colonized people, namely their histories, language, and – yet less identified – their humanity. Although the state of colonization, as framed by Memmi, is "above all, economic and political exploitation" (p. 149), it is also a spiritual, emotional, and humanistic exploitation. That is, colonization demoralizes, dehumanizes, and wreaks havoc in the hearts, minds, and souls of the colonized and the generations thereafter.

Because of this systematic degeneration of those most colonized, some institutions and individuals have responded by creating multicultural curricula (Nieto, 1992) or culturally relevant pedagogies (Ladson-Billings, 1995), engaging in critical race analyses of laws that have racist implications, positing civil rights laws (Bell, 1992; Crenshaw, 1995), highlighting movements like Blacklivesmatter,[1] and creating films and television shows that are counternarratives of those media that portray whiteness as normal (e.g., Shonda Rhimes).[2] Needless to say, those most racially colonized are fighting back, especially in the context of the racial colonization of the United States.

The U.S. has a unique colonial history. Indeed, it has conventional imperialistic ventures that forced militarized colonization on places like Puerto Rico, the Philippines, and Guam. It also has contested colonization in the annexation of its entire southwestern states from Mexico, as well as the displacement of *Mexicanos*. But unique to the U.S. is the colonization of Native Americans and African Americans. Plainly, American Indians were colonized in their own home, whereas African Americans were kidnapped, bound, and sold into a country that colonized them. All of these colonizing projects wreak havoc on colonized people and are committed while dominant U.S. history refuses to acknowledge its colonial supremacy (Zinn, 2014), points its finger toward other country's bigotry, and continues to self-promote as the "Land of the Free." The hypocrisy of it all becomes one of colonial education whereby, as Ladson-Billings (1989) so suggests, it is nothing different than Soweto, South Africa, the axis of Apartheid. Plainly stated, amidst the land of the free and the home of the brave there exists a colonial power structure that forces colonized people to beg to be heard, recognized, and respected.

This is the psychological, emotional, and material trauma one endures when an entire people are dismissed by colonial education. In fact, Fanon (1967) argues that such colonial racism has left the Black man to internalize a sense of inferiority stemming from his dependency complicit to his white masters. Needless to say, the state of colonization and the need to decolonize the minds of those most colonized become a forever racially just project; people of Color have, for too long, been made to believe that they are savages, indolent, and in need of "benevolent assimilation" to use U.S. President McKinley's[3] phrasing. Yet, inasmuch as this is a forever racially-just project to reaffirm the identities, cultures, languages, and experiences of the colonized people of Color, something must be done to decolonize the colonizer's mind; for, if we leave such a mindset intact, we risk recycling the state of colonial racism all over again.

THE COLONIAL WHITE MIND

In Chapter 6 I speak much about the racial colonizer. I discuss his portraiture, sense of narcissism and entitlement, and how his racialization process – one marked by dehumanization – has led to avenues by which he forever seeks atonement. In this section I speak specifically to how the white colonial mind feels and emotionally protects itself. Much like the story above, the way the racial colonizer asserts his importance leaves me in awe because, although it is resolute in finding ways to forever protect its entitlement through the dehumanization of Otherized peoples, the process by which he does fascinates me. Let me be clear: it is fascinating to see how he self-defines himself as king when the process by which he does so makes him look like a desperate pauper.

I relate the situation to the childhood story of the Emperor's New Clothes. In the story, charlatans come into town and, playing on the Emperor's narcissism, convince him that they can create a whole new wardrobe with a special cloth that can only be seen by the best people of society. Of course the Emperor, assuming his superiority, pretends to see the invisible cloth and subsequently commissions a new wardrobe. Once the wardrobe is completed and the charlatans hightail it out of town, the Emporer proudly wears his new clothes around his kingdom. Although onlookers see him in nothing but his "chonies,"[4] no one dares speak up because they know the Emperor has a power structure in place that can punish them if they speak. All but one child, who has yet to be conditioned to the colonizer's view of the world, speaks out to the Emperor's nakedness. The Emperor, embarrassed by his blinded narcissism, runs back to the castle, duped, naked, and revealed.

I relay this story for a particular purpose. My awe is with how the white colonial mind works because, like the Emperor with his new clothes, the white colonizer believes himself to be supreme and, in this blinded narcissism, prances around town fully exposed yet refusing to admit exposure. Despite its revealing character, the power structure of racial colonization has left the white colonial mind perched atop others and, by doing so, never has to realize its own exposure. That is, the white privilege embedded in whiteness never has to realize itself because it has operationally created an infrastructure that coddles its false reality.

Emotionally speaking, the white colonial mind feels constantly embraced in a land of its own imagination. It constructs a reality whereby its sense of safety is predicated upon the violence toward and lack of safety for others. Like the Emperor with his new clothes, the villagers are made to feel unsafe and understand there will be impending violence if they so dare to speak the truth, a process that forces their complicity in comforting the Emperor's mindset. Therefore, this notion of safety, much like the notion of freedom of speech so essential to the American identity, is mainly about the protection of comforts of the white colonial mind instead of promoting that which (e.g., free speech) combats oppressive ideals (see Leonardo & Porter, 2010).

As a female professor of Color, I often witness this dynamic play out in class, and as an instructor I have two choices: (1) silence those who have already been systemically silenced in order to once again placate and comfort the discomfort felt in white colonial minds – and it is important to note that such a comfort is predicated on the discomfort of those most marginalized; or, (2) change the power dynamics of the white colonial mindset by facilitating a discussion that exposes the truth behind white comfort. Recently, during a discussion on whiteness and racism per the course's weekly readings, this exact phenomenon played out in class. Students were engaged in discussing what whiteness is and how it impacts people of Color. This often racially-diverse class focuses on processes by which Whites can engage in decolonizing their colonial mindsets using literature on whiteness, scholarly definitions of whiteness, and articles that conceptualized whiteness. Some of my White students applied the literature to their own emerging racialized identities, while students of Color shared in and discussed how such application is necessary to dismantle racial microaggressions and institutionalized white supremacy. Each student was engaged in the conversation, applying the literature found in the field of critical whiteness studies to their understandings of whiteness in general – well, all but one.

This particular White female student sat in the circle with her arms crossed, occasionally rolling her eyes and letting out sighs of disapproval. She finally cut into the conversation about whiteness as narcissism that stemmed from one of the course readings. She began by not focusing on the articles or the relevancy of race; instead, she claimed that the narcissism so found in whiteness is not because of whiteness but rather because of a person's age, claiming that "millennials" (those born in the 1990s) are narcissistic because they were raised in a narcissistic, social media-ridden society. Though such an observation makes sense and could possibly be substantiated, it was an obtuse contribution to what was being discussed. We, as a class, were not discussing millennials or ruminating over our emotional reactions to the readings. Instead we were focused on what we could learn from the week's readings and how it could apply to education, society, and race-relations. This student had such an emotional reaction to the readings that she emotionally refused to engage in it at all. In fact, she was letting her own discomfort dictate what everyone else should talk about – based on her outside knowledge of literature not used or known in the class, she single-handedly comforted her white colonial mind by refuting the entirety of the discussion at hand and positing something else to talk about, thus silencing everyone else around her.

She then went on to claim that Whites cannot engage in race until they feel "safe." These "safe spaces," according to Leonardo and Porter (2010) should not exist in interracial race dialogues precisely because whiteness will continue to operate by silencing people of Color. Then she started to get emotionally flustered. Her voice quivered, as if about to cry; her face turned red and she began quickly wiping away tears that never fell. What was most odd was how she semantically changed the topic away from whiteness and racism to something she was more comfortable talking about (e.g., safety and millenials), then began a dialogue about *her* need to feel safe though everyone else was feeling that safety. By doing this, she perched her sense of comfort over that of the others in the class. Her white colonial mind was so unfettered by the topic at hand – whiteness – that her white fragility (DiAngelo, 2011) was shattered. As such, she began to assert her white privilege, embedded in whiteness, in order to control the discourse yet again so as to feel comfort for herself at the expense of all others'. She did this by starting to cry, though no tears were actually shed. The class went silent. The student facilitators for that week quickly sensed the tension in the room and were about to pose a new question to the group in order to avoid the emotional drama brought by this one person. I stopped them, asserting my professorial standing, and asked the rest of the students to respond.

As a professor I often "take up"[5] for students. I am their teacher and am therefore responsible for their learning. This learning, however, need not always look rosy and cheerful. Learning can be rough at times, especially when one moves beyond the comforts of one's zone of proximal development (per Vygotsky, 1978). In fact, in the field of education we – practitioners and researchers alike – often claim that we need a level of cognitive dissonance to push through what we find most difficult to learn. As a social scientist, I admit that learning another science, like astrophysics, would be very difficult; however, if I wanted to one day be an astrophysicist and speak, research, and teach on behalf of that field, I would need to garner a level of cognitive dissonance to emotionally withstand the difficulty of learning such a topic. Clearly, I would need to "stick it out," get over my emotional resistance to the material, and dive right into learning what I found most difficult to learn. Hence, learning is not always about sunshine and rainbows; the downpour of rainy days will one day produce a clearer sky.

Additionally, as a professor I am responsible for the learning of *all* my students and therefore need to look at the larger picture, beyond one person's discomfort – especially when that discomfort is brought about by reactional sentiments to ideas that challenge a dominant discourse and attempts to regain comfort by enacting the very dominant discourse we, as a class, are learning to challenge. As a socially-just professor, I must ensure that normalized systems of power, whether through white supremacy or patriarchy, do not once again settle themselves in my classroom. Allowing such systems to embed themselves in my course is, at the very least, antithetical to socially-just teaching. Thus, I see this particular student struggling with her own sense of entitlement yet I cannot, in good faith, allow her sense of entitlement to destruct the content of the course, both in the context of my responsibility as a teacher and in debunkning whiteness. Amidst it all, I can, however, be there for her by listening to her, continuing to challenge her preconceived ideologies, and helping her identify the emotionalities she needs to work herself out of her entitlement.

I return to what happened after I stopped the student facilitators – the classroom was silent for a bit. It was tense and awkward to say the least, but I was not going to let it go. I often tell my students that, if people are truly committed to each other, they never leave the table when discussing something so dear. In fact, I tell my students what happens when a person decides to leave the table because it is too much to bear – they often respond with how much the trust is broken. In this instance, I refused to have us break our trust by glossing over the tension. Instead, I forced the students to deal with it. One indigenous student, the only tribal American Indian enrolled in any of my university's School of Education Ph.D. programs – broke the silence. She talked at length about how things are never safe for her and, as an early childhood specialist, that she understood the need to take risks to learn something new. She relayed a story about one of the babies in her early childhood program. The infant was nine-months-old and was delayed in his gross motor skills to stand. To support him, she helped him take risks with standing by himself. He fell many times but eventually began to stand on his own. The point of her story was a direct comment to the particular White female student who had issues taking risk and learning something new. While saying this, the tribal student was holding back tears – real ones – tears that reflected years of silencing, discrimination, and being told not to expose the white colonial mind for its nakedness.

One of my African American female students talked about how whiteness enacts in ways wherein she is never safe. She explained that she is instead expected to be subservient or risk losing her job. Following her, another White female student spoke about her experiences of learning whiteness. She relayed stories about her upbringing during desegregation and bussing, and revealed how she came to awareness of how, despite her hardships, she was never treated with the same disrespect as bussed students of Color. A few others chimed in, trying to relate the situation to the readings. I then stopped them again. I said whiteness works in ways that we placate the white colonial mind and, in doing so, we veered from the topic of learning about whiteness and race, and began focusing on how to make one person feel better. Then I left them with two questions: *Did our discussion right now just prove Leonardo and Porter's (2011) point that whiteness continues to manifest in interracial race dialogues such that we had to stop the learning to placate it? What have you learned about whiteness and what does it feel like?* Like I do with my readers here, I left these questions floating with unspoken answers already felt in the heart of my students.

DECOLONIZATION OF THE COLONIAL WHITE MINDS

Often times I relay personal stories of my experiences to a point where others feel unsettled. Instead of focusing on what they can learn from these experiences, naysayers focus on their feelings of being threatened, exposed, or revealed, much like the naked Emperor. In doing so, they miss the point. Instead, they are focused on being exposed as a racist instead of realizing how their actions, ideologies, and discourses might, in fact, be racist. As Bonilla-Silva (2006) so suggests, how then can racism exist when no one wants to own up to being racist? Without identifying these acts of racism and white supremacy, regardless of intentionality, these folks will continue to reign supreme while rendering the power whiteness uses to perch itself atop the invisible hierarchy. Let me be clear: this is not about shaming a person who may have repressed consciousness of holding onto her/his whiteness, more so than revealing why s/he is ashamed in the first place. Shaming has a lot to do with self-realization, perhaps a realization that is so repressed in the white colonial mind that, once it is exposed, it feels ashamed. And it is precisely this feeling of being ashamed that the white colonial mind will go to great lengths to mask and further repress. Be it immoral and unethical, the white colonial mind works in ways to defend its existence, even if such existence is predicated on the usurpation of power. What I find most tragic is that instead of digging deeply into what makes one so ashamed when realizing something about oneself, some emotionally project their angst onto the one who is doing the revealing, i.e., the person who is indeed bringing to the surface the latent and repressed emotions of shame. Needless to say, such misplaced angst is nothing more than killing the messenger or, in the case of the Emperor and his new clothes, killing the villagers who dare reveal the truth of his nakedness. And, there is another route down which the white colonial mind can meander. When such white colonial minds take onus of their shame, by not deflecting the shame onto someone else, they are, in essence, beginning a process of decolonizing the white mind.

To exemplify this, I look again at my resistant student who, perhaps, is only beginning to realize her nakedness. As another White female student once posited in that same class, individuals who subscribed to whiteness ideology may digress and resort further into whiteness to comfort their sensibilities. In doing so, the resistant student became cognizant of not wanting to leave her comfort zone and therefore could not deny the dynamics which delineate "discomfort" from "safe," meaning, if one finds racial justice discomforting and thus refuses to partake in it, s/he must admit they are doing the *opposite of racial justice* precisely because it comforts them. In fact, one *chooses* to be racist and exert white privilege when elevating one's own discomfort and sensibilities above the systematic denigration of people of Color.

As said before, whiteness is resolute and will find ways to use its power to affirm itself while burrowing deeply into the truth of such power usage. Although such situations are present in U.S. society, I now talk directly to my readers about what it takes to decolonize the white mind; therefore, I will write the word "you," assuming that "you" (the reader) are either a facilitator or someone who is doing the much needed self-work to decolonize your own white colonial mind. However, I do so cautiously because I do not want to assume that I am providing a roadmap or blueprint. Instead, I offer some theoretical and pedagogical applications that can be applied to situations which can aid in the decolonization of the white colonial mind. In presenting these strategies, I am aware that race, as Leonardo (2013) asserts, is so complicated that it is deserving of complex answers that may or may not be relevant in a given situation.

For the Facilitator

First, if you are facilitating race dialogues, teaching about racism, or researching whiteness, know where you stand. I often remind myself that, despite the vehemence I receive in doing this work from neo-Nazis and well-intentioned White liberals alike, I still stand for the prospect of a greater humanity. As such, the focus should always remain on improving humanity despite the discomfort one feels in doing the work of racial justice. The discomfort is a small price one can pay to realize racial justice. Although many racially-just individuals acknowledge they are doing the work for a greater humanity, it is nevertheless important to reiterate this. Too often in this work, racially-just individuals get attacked from hate groups, racists, and other individuals who are, whether conscious or not, inoculated with whiteness ideology. In their vehemence, they pervert the topic of race and call racially-just individuals "racists" for merely discussing racial oppression. They denigrate the racially-just individual by attacking the person her/himself, claiming their degrees are unworthy, they are unpatriotic, or, in a place like the U.S. whereby Christianity reigns supreme, are like to Lucifer himself. This is taxing on the hearts and souls of racially-just individuals because, as they seek a greater humanity, they do so in the face of those who continue to dehumanize them. Therefore it is vital to always remember, despite the critiques, that the work of racial justice and decolonizing white colonial minds is, and will forever be, a project of humanity.

Another aspect the facilitator must acknowledge is that of power: you must recognize the power structures that exist both inside and outside of the classroom. I like to remind my students that racism, patriarchy, capitalism, and heterosexism do not stop upon crossing the threshold of a classroom. Indeed, such aspects find a way to creep back into the discourse. Thus, it would be erroneous of us to assume that such power structures are not at play, even when we are discussing revolutionary ideas. Certainly, such power structures will manifest themselves in the classroom through the ideological underpinnings of classroom conversation. This is seen when dominant rhetoric tries to structure the conversation – much like the example of my resistive student attempting to disrupt those engaged in the deep conversation about whiteness and racial justice in education – by redirecting it to placate her needs. However, I do not subscribe to the notion of power that is in totality unidirectional, meaning that the big, bad, rich man beats up the poor, little, innocent man. Instead, like Foucault (1980), I acknowledge power is also hegemonic and that those who are oppressed may, perhaps, facilitate and recycle the same power structure that marginalizes them.

Applied to the situation above, I cannot place the onus directly on the shoulders of the one student whose emotionality in whiteness was unfettered. However, this is not to relinquish the power she did exert to reframe the entire discussion around her emotionality in whiteness. Instead, I also acknowledge that whiteness works in a way such that everyone in the class placated the emotionality of whiteness and turned away from the deep work of racial justice. As such, I remind facilitators that if they stand on the side of humanity, they cannot, in good faith, allow such power structures inside their classrooms to re-infect the mindsets. In fact, in one of my articles, "Who You Callin' White?" (2013), I discuss at great length the critical race praxis behind racial microaggressions. I am aware that racial microaggressions denigrate people of Color, but they also teach them two things: (1) the existence of a racial structure, and (2) where people of Color are located in that racial structure. In this chapter I discuss how we must be racially microaggressive to Whites in order for them to acknowledge a racial structure and realize how they are using their privilege to oppress others. This is nothing different than Leonardo and Porter's (2010) postulation that there is always a latent, repressed violence when dialoguing about race in an interracial setting. In fact, I show how this repressed violence operates to my students. I ask my female students if they would feel "safe" in a feminist course taught by a man with mostly male students; many agree they would not. I then ask how they expect the few students of Color in our graduate course to feel safety in a space dominated by White students, many of whom will have whiteness ideology in their white colonial minds. Therefore, to stand on the side of humanity, one must be a soldier, so to speak – brave enough to combat power structures that try to take hold of the learning.

For the White Colonial Mind

I have discussed the burden of Whites asking people of Color to give them some sort of checklist in order to become racially-just and to better acquaint themselves with people of Color. I discuss how this places the burden of racial justice back on the shoulders of people of Color, whereby Whites get an easy "to-do" list in becoming an ally. Instead, I have asked Whites to do the emotional work to stop racial microaggressions, dismantle their white privilege, and, by doing so, promote a more humanistic relationship with society. The person must first look at her/himself *before* assuming the role of white ally.

First you must, as Helms's (1990) theory of white racial identity model suggests, place yourself in contact – continuous contact – with people of Color who are racially aware. Too often Whites rely on that one "Black best friend" as a means to justify their "I'm not a racist" stance. Or, they have friends of Color who also inhabit whiteness ideology and use such a relationship to promote whiteness ideology even further – precisely because the relationship serves as a co-signing of whiteness ideology. Those types of friends are often labeled "Uncle Toms," "ding dongs," "coconuts," or "bananas" (color on the outside, but white in the inside) to communities of Color and White allies who are racially aware. Often times, Whites who befriend these individuals use their friends' racial identity as a symbolic representation of their own ideologies.

You can see this in social media; for example, Facebook circulated several Youtube videos of a White woman, Lauren Southern, decrying feminism,[6] and actor

Morgan Freeman, a Black male, decrying race.[7] Although Freeman's response was truncated, only exposing his ideas about getting rid of racism by not talking about race, he actually talked at length about how he would stop seeing the "white" in White men only when White men can stop seeing the "Black" in Black men. Despite his deeper analysis of race relations, most circulated was the clip of Freeman saying to stop talking about race. Southern's anti-feminist clip was circulated mainly by males, whereas the Freeman clip was circulated mainly by Whites. If one stopped to really consider why Whites would recycle Freeman's words and why men would recycle Southern's words, one could then see the mechanisms of power so used in historical usage of Black minstrels – those Whites who recycled Freeman's clip did so knowing that race is, in fact relevant, but, instead of acknowledging it publically, they manipulated it by using "Black face" to convince others it was not real. The same can be said for the antifeminist clip, meaning that men used a woman to project their own ideas and, by circulating the clip, are using her as a female-faced token to state their case.

Let me be absolutely clear: whiteness can inhabit the minds of people of Color just as internalized sexism can inhabit the minds of women (albeit for different processes of survival). However, what is most noteworthy here is that the colonized are used as puppets by the colonizers to justify a colonizing agenda. As such, Whites must build relationships with people of Color and White allies who do *not* inhabit whiteness mindsets.

Second, take an inventory of your own emotionalities. In my workshops, I often ask attendees, many of whom are White, to trifold a piece of paper. I then ask them to write down three column headings: (1) My feelings, (2) What caused them, and (3) Where do these feeling come from? As I go through a lecture on race, racism, whiteness, and white supremacy, they are to begin the work of identifying their own emotionalities which, left unchecked, can hinder the progress of racial discussions. I ask them to be precise. In the second column I ask them to write down exactly what I had said or what concept was being explained that elicited the particular emotion written in their first columns. I then ask them be self-critical in thinking from where these emotions stem. In closing, we "share it out" and I present a psychoanalysis of whiteness to help them frame some possible root causes of the emotions.

Third, stop emotionally projecting your angst onto people of Color or White allies. If you feel discomforted, flustered, and/or defensive, you must first think about *why* you are feeling these emotions instead of emotionally reacting. I relate this to simple schoolyard dynamics. If a child points out that another has mismatched shoes, an emotional projection would look like this: instead of recognizing that he indeed has mismatched shoes and thanking the child who let him know, the emotional projector will immediately emotionally react toward the messenger. He may say, "Well you're clothes are ugly" or he may punch the other child. Either way both emotional reactions do not get at the root of what has just been revealed. Instead, he deflects the fact that he has mismatched shoes and makes the messenger feel badly for pointing it out.

Applied to adult relationships, this can be seen in partnerships. Take for example a heterosexual couple in which the woman in the relationship just revealed she is upset that her partner lied to her. The man in the relationship has several ways to emotionally respond to this. He can realize that this is his partner, one who loves him, is telling him about what makes her hurt, and does so because she, knowing they are in a partnership, so entrusts him and wants him to stop lying to her. The man, in turn, could see how his actions have hurt someone he proclaims to love, care, and respect. Not feeling threatened, he acknowledges his behavior and how it hurt the one he loves, and commits to not hurting her further. On the other hand, he could emotionally project to deflect his actions of lying to her in the first place. In this case he may call her "overly sensitive," "jealous," and/or focus on something she has done wrong in the past. In doing so, he does not take onus of his actions and behaviors. Instead, he ruins the relationship between them by dumping his emotional insecurities and baggage onto the wife, thus never getting to the crux of the issue of lying. In all these applications, the problem here is that of emotionally projecting; instead, perhaps, you can take on a more responsible response to your own emotions.

Fourth, racial progress gets nowhere if you emotionally stonewall while others are being emotionally vulnerable, and there is nothing useful by not engaging whole-heartedly in the conversation. Take for example, a relationship between two committed partners. If one partner becomes emotionally devoid by erecting a wall that her partner cannot scale, then what good is it for the relationship? How can one expect to feel a union with another if he/she is unwilling to be present? In my courses I relate this concept to personal relationships. I ask my students whether they have ever experienced a huge argument with someone they truly love, be that person a friend or family member. I ask them if, when they confronted the individual with the conflict, it was tense or uncomfortable? I also ask if, despite these feelings, did they care so much about the relationship that they were willing to stick it out? My students often realize they have had such an experience. They relay how hard it was and how both of them "duked it out" by talking about the conflict to a point of exhaustion. I then ask them, how did your relationship feel after that arduous talk? Many say that, although it was tough, the conversation made them even closer. I ask them to speculate about what would happen in the other person emotionally walled up. Many claimed that when this did happen, it severed the relationship.

I relay this personal application because the same can be said for dialogues of race. If one claims to be antiracist, racially-just, a White ally, and/or someone who is committed to humanity, then shouldn't one be willing enough to duke it out without emotionally leaving the conversation? The white colonial mind operates in ways that shut down when emotionally overloaded, and so shuts out the possibility of racial justice. By forcing oneself to be emotionally vulnerable, the potential for decolonizing the white colonial mind becomes ever more real. For, in the end, one can only ask to be emotionally present and, in that mutual presence, commit to each other.

Finally, take it upon yourself to read more about whiteness. Often in my talks, my audience members, with bewildered eyes, are surprised on hearing the words "whiteness," "white privilege," and "white supremacy." Once, a senior colleague attended one of my conference panels at which I talked about the emotionality of whiteness. He claimed that I needed to "stop making up words like whiteness." Although I wish I could take such credit, I was not the coiner of the term – whiteness has been around for a long time, and if just hearing the word elicits wonder, shock, and/or unfamiliarity, then perhaps – in the essence of being direct – you need to "get with the program." Start reading about whiteness:

- economic and housing considerations (Allen, 2009; Massey & Denton, 1993; Oliver & Shapiro, 2006),
- legal groundings (Delgado & Stefancic, 1997; Harris, 1993; Haney López, 2006)
- court cases (e.g., *Ozawa v. United States,* 260 U.S. 178 [1922]; *United States v. Thind*, 261 U.S. 204 [1923]),
- political identity (Lipsitz, 2006; Rothenberg, 2008),
- history and class (Brodkin, 2006; Roediger, 2006),
- the invisibility of whiteness in all factions of society from literature to film (Morrison, 1992; Sullivan, 2006; Vera & Gordon, 2003; Yancy, 2008),
- racialization (Frankenberg, 1993; Hill, 1997; Helms, 1990; Thandeka, 1999),
- education (Allen, 2004; Leonardo, 2009; Sleeter, 2015),
- discourse (Bonilla-Silva, 2006), and
- operations (Doane & Bonilla-Silva, 2003; Ignatiev & Garvey, 1996; Jung, Vargas & Bonilla-Silva, 2011).

Although not an exhaustive list, I share a few of these works because, if one wants to truly engage in racial justice, from a colonizer's standing one must first understand who one is in relation to the state of colonization in order to support the humanity of those colonized. Begin with you.

CONCLUSION

Although the state of colonization is a very real construct that allows a king or emperor to walk around as if he has the divine order of conquest over his kingdom, it is not without rebellion. However, the rebellion we so seek to dismantle a patronizing state of colonization cannot be placed solely onto the shoulders of the racially colonized. To do so would relinquish the responsibilities colonizers must assume in order to readdress the unjust state of colonization. If a colonizer so seeks to undo the unjust state of colonization, then it is also a burden s/he must endure; but, he should never assume that his mere discomfort brought about by assuming such burden equates to that of the colonized. Just as Memmi (1965) argues, once the state of colonization is finally uprooted, the identity and the role of the colonizer will cease to exist; so too will the role of the white colonial mind. Put another way, as a racial justice educator, my role in racial justice will be rendered obsolete the day racial justice is finally realized. And although I would be out of a job, one that defines my role and identity upon the fruition of racial justice, that day would as rapper Ice Cube wrote, still "be a good day."

NOTES

1   See Twitter, Deray McKesson.
2   Shonda Rhimes is an influential African American TV producer, writer, and director. She is the creator and executive producer of the current American shows *Grey's Anatomy*, *Private Practice*, and *Scandal*, all of which cast African American women in lead roles.
3   See http://www.msc.edu.ph/centennial/benevolent.html for the full text of McKinley's "Benevolent Assimilation Proclamation of 1898."
4   American slang for under garments.
5   American slang for protection and support.
6   See https://www.youtube.com/watch?v=vNErQFmOwq0
7   See https://www.youtube.com/watch?v=GeixtYS-P3s

REFERENCES

Allen, R. L. (2004). Whiteness and critical pedagogy. *Educational Philosophy and Theory*, *36*(2), 121–136.
Allen, R. L. (2009). What about poor White people. W. Ayers, T. Quinn, & D. Stovall (Eds.), *Handbook of social justice in education* (pp. 209–230). New York, NY: Routledge.
Bell, D. A. (1992). *Faces at the bottom of the well: The permanence of racism*. New York, NY: Basic Books.
Bonilla-Silva, E. (2006). *Racism without racists: Color-blind racism and the persistence of racial inequality in the United States*. New York, NY: Rowman & Littlefield.
Brodkin, K. (2006). *How Jews became White folks and what that says about race in America*. New Brunswick, NJ: Rutgers University Press.
Crenshaw, K. (1995). *Critical race theory: The key writings that formed the movement*. New York, NY: The New Press.
Delgado, R., & Stefancic, J. (1997). *Critical White studies: Looking behind the mirror*. Philadelphia, PA: Temple University Press.
DiAngelo, R. (2011). White fragility. *The International Journal of Critical Pedagogy*, *3*(3).
Doane, A. W., & Bonilla-Silva, E. (2003). *White out: The continuing significance of racism*. East Sussex, UK: Psychology Press.
Fanon, F. (1967). *Black skin, White masks* [1952] (C. L. Markmann, Ed.). London: Pluto Books.
Foucault, M. (1980). *Power/Knowledge: Selected interviews and other writings, 1972–1977*. New York, NY: Pantheon.
Freire, P. (2003). *Pedagogy of the oppressed*. New York, NY: Continuum.
Frankenberg, R. (1993). *White women, race matters*. Minneapolis, MN: University of Minnesota Press.
Haney López, I. (2006). *White by law: The legal construction of race*. New York, NY: New York University Press.
Harris, C. I. (1993). Whiteness as property. *Harvard Law Review, 106*, 1707–1791.
Helms, J. E. (1990). *Black and White racial identity: Theory, research, and practice*. Westport, CT: Greenwood Press.
Hill, M. (1997). *Whiteness: A critical reader*. New York, NY: New York University Press.
Ignatiev, N., & Garvey, J. (Eds.). (1996). *Race traitor*. East Sussex, UK: Psychology Press.
Jung, M. K., Vargas, J. C., & Bonilla-Silva, E. (2011). *State of White supremacy: Racism, governance, and the United States*. Stanford, CA: Stanford University Press.

Ladson-Billings, G. (1998). From Soweto to the South Bronx: African Americans and colonial education in the United States. In C. Torres & T. Mitchell (Eds.), *Sociology of education: Emerging perspectives* (pp. 247–264). New York, NY: SUNY Press.

Ladson-Billings, G. (1995). Toward a theory of culturally relevant pedagogy. *American Educational Research Journal, 32*(3), 465–491.

Leonardo, Z. (2013). *Race frameworks: A multidimensional theory of racism and education.* New York, NY: Teachers College Press.

Leonardo, Z. (2009). *Race, whiteness, and education.* New York, NY: Routledge.

Leonardo, Z., & Porter, R. K. (2010). Pedagogy of fear: Toward a Fanonian theory of 'safety' in race dialogue. *Race, Ethnicity and Education, 13*(2), 139–157.

Lipsitz, G. (2006). *The possessive investment in whiteness: How White people profit from identity politics.* Philadelphia, PA: Temple University Press.

Massey, D. S., & Denton, N. A. (1993). *American apartheid: Segregation and the making of the underclass.* Cambridge, MA: Harvard University Press.

Matias, C. E. (2013). Who you callin 'White?! A critical counter-story on colouring White identity. *Race, Ethnicity and Education, 16*(3), 291–315.

Memmi, A. (1965). *The colonizer and the colonized.* Boston, MA: Beacon Press.

Morrison, T. (1992). *Playing in the dark.* New York, NY: Vintage.

Nieto, S. (1992). *Affirming diversity: The sociopolitical context of multicultural education.* Boston, MA: Allyn & Bacon.

Oliver, M. L., & Shapiro, T. M. (2006). *Black wealth/White wealth: A new perspective on racial inequality.* New York, NY: Routledge/Taylor & Francis.

Roediger, D. R. (2006). *Working toward whiteness: How America's immigrants became White: The strange journey from Ellis Island to the suburbs.* New York, NY: Basic Books.

Rothenberg, P. S. (2004). *White privilege: Essential readings on the other side of racism* (2nd ed.). Boston, MA: Macmillan Learning.

Sleeter, C. (2015). *White bread: Weaving cultural past into the present.* Rotterdam, The Netherlands: Sense Publishers.

Smith, L. T. (1999). *Decolonizing methodologies: Research and indigenous peoples.* London: Zed Books.

Sullivan, S. (2006). *Revealing whiteness: The unconscious habits of racial privilege.* Bloomington, IN: Indiana University Press.

Thandeka. (1999). *Learning to be White: Money, race, and god in America.* New York, NY: Continuum.

Vera, H., & Gordon, A. M. (2003). *Screen saviors: Hollywood fictions of whiteness.* New York, NY: Rowman & Littlefield.

Vygotsky, L. (1978). *Mind in society.* Boston, MA: Harvard University Press.

Zinn, H. (2014). *A people's history of the United States.* New York, NY: Roman & Littlefield.

CHAPTER 12

CONCLUSIONS FOR FEELING AGAIN

Pending

Have we, as a society, become so feelings-phobic that we pretend to live life, much like the walking dead, without ever feeling humanity? Since we all have experienced some sort of trauma and fear its repetition, do we resort to amassing an impenetrable emotional wall, hoping it will protect us from ever hurting again, feeling again, and truly living again? And in this state of deadness, are we necrophilically pretending to love, engaging in emotionalities that are often rendered mere sentimentalities or saccharin expressions of what we truly feel, as if false niceness is enough? Beyond the fakeness, are we that scared to know how much we truly love each other, and how much it hurts to witness others be denigrated, dehumanized, and killed? Putting up the emotional wall and performing false pleasantries for fear of feeling any traumatic pain is "punking out" on humanity. A critical race teacher educator (and good friend) once told me that unless we are willing to be reciprocally vulnerable, teachers will never be effective. The same holds true for humanity. Unless we have the emotional ovaries to confront that which we fear most and allow ourselves the latitude to explore deeper into our feelings, we are nothing but zombies, devoid of true heart and connection.

In the spirit of vulnerability, I have shared with you, the reader, a bit of my life in this book: the joys and struggles of learning and teaching, the trials and tribulations of being a female scholar of Color in the vast whiteness of academia (see Preston, 2013), the pains of my personal life, and the genuine critical hope I have for us all (see Duncan-Andrade, 2009). Some may take this and interpret it negatively because the message of understanding the emotionalities of whiteness it too much to bear. Others, hopefully, see this as a cry for humanity. As such, I hope you see me, in all my bareness, and realize that I am sincerely, vehemently, and vigilantly angry and sad at racist power structures that divide us and how we, as people, submit to them via our actions, ideologies, emotions, and discourses.

What pains me the most is that we have for too long perverted our own emotionalities such that we often feel unsure of what it is we are truly feeling. We can say "I am angry with you" but never realize that deep down it is not about anger and hatred. Instead, when we dig deep into our hearts, we begin to realize the emotions we are expressing are just mere reactions to the deeper emotions we truly feel, be they betrayal, disrespect, or humiliation. If we stay at the surface level of expressed emotionalities, we become as fake as the sexual predator who pretends to love someone as a means to selfishly satisfy his own lustful intentions. Yes; I said it. To live by surface-level emotionalities is to be an emotional predator, unwilling to understand how our subscription to surface-level emotions might perpetuate a loveless society, yet always under the guise of rainbows and sunshine.

One can say I am preoccupied with emotions, that I am romancing them too much. To that, I say, "Yes, I am!" I love dancing with emotions, a steady four-beat count in an old Bachata dance. I embrace them as if they remind me of my own humanity, even if, at times, I am aware it will hurt. I study them diligently, processing every passing sensation. And I hope for the sake of humanity that others do too, lest we be forever ensnared in fakeness, too far removed from understanding our true selves. Therefore, I give credence to our emotions because too often they are easily and readily discredited. Sexists, for one, work hard to devalue the centrality of our emotions, claiming they are nothing but the whims and gripes of women. In fact, they would probably claim that I was "on my period" while writing this book! Alas, the mechanisms of patriarchy and how they silence women are too commonplace, and I will not submit to them, particularly with this book. So, instead of masculinizing emotions by relabeling them as "affects" so that the academy will finally deem it worthy of study, I have opted to use emotional words as a feminist stance to reclaim that which we, as women, have been historically chastised for having.

EMOTIONALITY OF WHITENESS IN TEACHER EDUCATION

It was not until my experiences in teaching teacher education that I realized emotions are racialized with whiteness, especially among the sea of White teachers and teacher educators who self-proclaim to be "serving" the needs of "underprivileged" communities. I always found it interesting that these White professors were easily emotionally accepted as subject matter experts in Latino education, culturally responsive teaching for urban students of Color and/or African American student pipelines, while I, a professor of Color who studies the emotionality of whiteness, was shunned and considered suspect by virtue of my subject matter expertise. For these professors, it was not possible that a scholar of Color could ever be an expert on the education of Whites, especially since they had already deemed themselves as the only ones with valued knowledge, and most especially because the normalization of whiteness renders the education of Whites invisible – moreover, nonexistent.

This is how the emotionality of whiteness operates, and in its operation, it shuts down any possibility of the deeper discussion required in a field that claims to be about social justice, educational equity, and diversity. In fact, I captured this in a co-authored paper, "Cockblocking[1] Critical Race Theory: How the Emotionality of Whiteness Cockblocks CRT in Teacher Education," with my doctoral students at the 2013 Critical Studies of Race in Education Association. Though the title of our paper was too salacious for publication, the idea was straight to the point, pun intended. That is, although research has proven that incorporating CRT inside teacher education is both beneficial to White teachers and the students of Color they will soon teach, it gets cockblocked by white emotionalities, meaning that white fragility becomes too unfettered when engaging in CRT's ruminations over race, racism, and white supremacy, that the ideas are blocked on site. Therefore, the potency of CRT's commitment to social justice − moreover racial justice − gets blocked because the emotionalities of whiteness refuse to fully digest it. And this brings us back to square one.

Although U.S. teacher education programs do attempt to incorporate social justice in their curricula, many urban education, multicultural education, and/or cultural responsive/relevant pedagogies are watered down. These curricula take out the reasons behind why these educational strategies and theories were left out in the first place: the context of white supremacy in education and how it is upheld by individuals' and institutions' reification of whiteness. In fact, Sonia Nieto (1992), a founding scholar of multicultural education, claims that multicultural education itself is antiracist education. Yet, when multicultural education is applied to teacher education programs that are intoxicated by whiteness, the focus on antiracism becomes diluted amidst savior mentalities, cultural competence checklists, and false professions of being antiracist, without ever understanding the context of white supremacy that calls for the need for antiracist approaches. It is like teaching people to label themselves "doctors" for putting a Band-Aid on a skin lesion without ever having to understand the context of the cancer that produced the lesion. Alas, these self-proclaimed "doctors" eventually become the diversity trainers and/or subject matter experts on diversity throughout the entire field of education. This is how far the tentacles of whiteness so stretch.

I recall a time when I was in the audience at a University of Colorado Boulder teacher education panel and these subject matter experts could not even detect their own whiteness. As expected, the panel was mainly comprised of White female teacher educators but with one Black male math teacher educator. After each of the panelists delivered her/his talk about her/his subject matter expertise (cultural responsive teaching, social justice education, etc.), I asked them all a question: *In a field whereby most of the educators are White and are serving the needs of students of Color, how do you model the deconstruction of whiteness to White teacher candidates?* To this, the Black male professor smiled and looked down. He was the new professor on the block, just hired that fall and, as a junior faculty then myself, I understood too well why he would refrain from speaking up. He lifted his head and casually mentioned how it is an "ever-going project," yet did not mention race.

The White female professors, however, talked about their White teacher candidates' racial identity development. They relayed stories about how White students came to understand they are white. I pressed further and clarified the question with *"How do you model your own deconstruction of whiteness to White teacher candidates?"* To this, both White female professors started to talk about their husbands, both of whom were of Color. They talked about the experiences their husbands of Color had in marrying White women. They talked about their mixed race children.

Yet, in all of their responses, *they never talked about their own whiteness*. It was almost as if whiteness developed a cognitive speech impediment whereby they became so frozen they could not even imagine addressing the question. On the urging of a mentor present in the room, herself is a senior Latina scholar, I pressed on and clarified, "I'm asking about you specifically, as a White female teacher educator, 'How do you deconstruct your own whiteness so that your White teacher candidates/students can do so themselves'?" One of the professors claimed she had not deconstructed her whiteness; in fact, she said "I can't" because she did not understand her own White race. How then is someone to be a subject matter expert in the racial identity development of students of Color if one does not even understand one's own racial identity? White racial identity scholar, Helms (1990), argues that only upon understanding the self can one expect to help others. It is like the airplane oxygen mask idea: put it on yourself first before helping others do it.

This is why the emotionality of whiteness must be explored. If we succumb to the fear of exposing or revealing that which is too scary, we risk never getting at the real issue. I often joke with my students, claiming it is like having a lover's spat with your partner: s/he does not even know why you are bothered and thus emotionally projects your discontent back onto you and your insecurities:

> *Partner: I really didn't like the way you interacted with Stacy tonight. I felt it was a bit inappropriate.*
>
> *You: What?! You are just jealous!*

You react because emotional projections are a way to deflect emotional culpability and are based on assumptions while attacking your character.

> *Partner: That's ridiculous! I'm not jealous. You're being an ass.*

Moments later, you both are in a full-fledged argument without ever talking about the initial issue that bothered you in the first place:

> *You: Not jealous?! Please. You are so jealous ever since I've started working out.*
>
> *Partner: Working out? What does this have to do with anything?!*
>
> *You: Have you ever thought maybe you should work out?*
>
> *Partner: Are you saying I'm fat?!*

When this happens, even if you both find some solace in the cascade of arguments that follow the initial issue, you have really never solved anything.

Although this does not specifically address race or whiteness, I provide this scenario in detail because it clearly shows how white emotionalities, like these between partners, never get fully understood because they are too often emotionally projected and emotionally deflected. For example, claiming that one has "never owned slaves" is an emotional projection of guilt that deflects emotional culpability; in doing so, the expresser never fully understands how s/he may, perhaps, be truly guilty of her/his complicity in the whiteness that led to justification for slavery.

This operates in teacher education among those who resist whiteness because they emotionally:

1. refuse to engage in such a topic so they, collectively, ignore it;
2. project by ostracizing faculty who broach the topic by repositioning them outside of the teacher education program, claiming discussions of race are too foundational and have no place in the core of teacher education;
3. deflect by making the topic as an elective only, one students will never take because teacher education programs rarely have elective choices and often do not let electives count toward degrees;
4. remove their commitment to urban education and social justice, not realizing that without addressing larger issues of power they are doing nothing but giving Band-Aid education; and,
5. re-allocate faculty who broach topics on race to social studies education, thereby confining the ideas to a single subject.

The emotionality of whiteness has grave power in silencing the very message of racial justice that critical race scholars so hope to get across. In this silencing, we, as humanity, are remiss if we do not give credence to the power education has to transform these existing inequities.

WHAT DOES THIS MEAN TO ME?

Often in my work I am asked, "Well, what does this have to do with people of Color? Is not focusing on whiteness centering whiteness yet again?" First, I remind my questioners that unlike many whiteness scholars in education, I am not White. I am a critical race, brown-skinned Pinay motherscholar of Color and my angle will always remain true to that positionality, one which Collins (1989) reminds us is both an insider and outside perspective and essential in discussing larger issues of power.

Second, although some whiteness scholarship over-heralds the racial epiphanies of Whites as a monumental marker of change, my work is dedicated to sustained racial awareness and racial activism, meaning it is one thing to become aware that one is white and acknowledge the privileges afforded to such a racial marker, but it is another thing to understand the self so intimately as to realize one's own complicity in whiteness and why one needs to reject whiteness in order to fully participate in racial justice, and to continually engage in that discomfort. When these individuals see their own dehumanization in whiteness, they can finally be a part of a joint effort for humanity and not one of patronizing missionary support. In fact, critical race legal scholar Derrick Bell (1992) labels interest convergence a dilemma not a theory. Although some have positioned this dilemma as a theory, it is still an issue involved in racial justice. When applied to how Whites must engage in deconstructing their own white emotionalities for re-humanization, interest convergence is evident: Whites will only engage in racial justice if they see their own stake in the matter. In this case, Whites need to re-humanize by understanding how whiteness has dehumanized them in the first place. Only through this work can they find a way, as educational scholar David Stovall once told me, "bind their liberation to our liberation." In fact, as I stated before, a joint effort in racial justice is more like binding Whites' racial repression of whiteness to the racial liberation of people of Color, for Whites cannot engage in such binding if they do not understand the context of their own actions, emotions, and discourses that pained – and pains – people of Color.

Third, and most importantly, racism hurts. According to the documentary series, *Unnatural Causes*,[2] racism also shortens the life expectancy of African American males. Therefore, emotionally, spiritually, and biologically, racism kills us all. So much great work has been done to unveil how racial microaggressions (Sue, 2010) impact people of Color. Black feminist author bell hooks (1994) describes how racism and white supremacy in education has made her "lose her love of school." Founding critical race legal scholar, Derrick Bell (1992), wrote a parable, "Space Traders," that emotionally captures the continuous maltreatment and degradation of African Americans. *New York Times* best-selling author Ta'Nehisi Coates (2015) describes the painful processes by which the Black body is disembodied from its humanity. Yosso & Garcia (2007) write about the various cultures of wealth Latino communities have precisely because they are often stereotyped in deficit ways. Valenzuela (1999) demands that teachers, many of whom are White, have an authentic care for their students so as to stop the "subtractive schooling" felt by Mexican and Mexican American students. Crenshaw (2009) describes how women of Color are so denigrated by race, class, and gender that "experience of violence by minority women is ignored" (p. 222). Cho (2003) corroborates this by revealing how Asian American female faculty are targets of racism and sexism because they are stereotyped as submissive and passive. Fanon (1965) describes how Black bodies have become the "wretched of the earth" due to colonial racism. And the list goes on.

Let me be clear: that Whites must dismantle their own whiteness relates to people of Color because it is our lives at stake. And although people of Color understand the contexts of racial microaggressions, racial battle fatigue, and the need to always counterstory our lives so that whiteness never swallows up our identities, we need to make it stop. In my role as a professor, I cannot get it to stop by only coaching the victims of racism: instead, like stopping domestic abuse, I needed to also address the abusers.

ADDRESSING WHITE RACIAL ABUSERS

When teaching about whiteness as applied to how people of Color experience race, I often put on the whiteboard the following diagram:

Variable X → racial microaggressions → hurt people of Color

I then ask my students, "What is X? What precipitates racial microaggressions? What makes one feel one can racially microaggress others?" Some students argue it is about entitlement. Some same it is about privilege. Still others argued it is about ignorance. These are all elements of whiteness. The variable X is whiteness in *all* its elements. This is vital because it is whiteness *and* all its individual and group enactments that uphold institutional white supremacy.

Most racially-just individuals will acknowledge that race, racism, and white supremacy are systemic and institutionalized. However, by looking too abstractly at the dynamics of race, one never realizes one's own individual culpability in maintaining institutionalized racism and white supremacy. In fact, Bonilla-Silva (2006) attacked this quandary with the question of *how can racism exist without racists*? As such, I offer the following diagram to better explain:

Operations of Power in Institutionalized White Supremacy *not an exhaustive list*

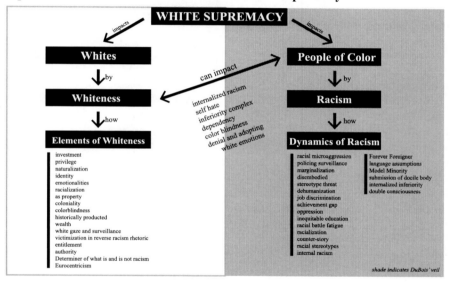

In this diagram white supremacy is the disease that impacts us all, albeit differently. For Whites, they experience white supremacy as a benefit through a process of whiteness, meaning that whiteness is the socializing process that upholds a systemic white supremacist structure and can enact it in many individual ways. Those described here (normalizations and naturalization of whiteness, white racial identity, colorblind racism, whiteness as property, White by laws, etc.) are just a few elements of whiteness that impact how Whites experience a white supremacist world. There are many others.

To exemplify this, I draw from one element of whiteness that can be applied to U.S. history: the belief of racial superiority and inherent white purity. This belief inhabited the minds of some White individuals and was socialized into a group belief when White parents dissuaded their White children from intermarrying

185

with people of Color. In fact, whole communities practiced this in U.S. history by conjuring up racial covenants that kicked people of Color out of their White communities. Those who decided to marry the Other were socially shunned and denied the privileges of whiteness. However, the shunning became institutionalized when U.S. anti-miscegenation laws, red-lining, home loan discrimination practices, and reneging citizenship were enforced, thus upholding these very individual and group beliefs in legal and systemic ways. All of a sudden beliefs became systemic, institutionalized, and legal ways to subjugate others. Clearly, white beliefs are not benign; indeed they are dangerous because the power structure of white supremacy affixes those beliefs atop others, rendering policies, laws, and judicial verdicts suspect. Seen in this way, white supremacy is not too abstract. There are clear players in its maintenance and, despite one's professed intentions, the actions nevertheless have lasting racist effects. Hence, we study whiteness because a more nuanced approach to understanding why my abuser is abusing me is needed in order to take the onus and responsibility of race off my Brown shoulders and onto the backs of those who abuse.

On the other hand, people of Color experience white supremacy through racism. Some elements of how racism is enacted are felt through racial microaggressions, racial battle fatigue, counterstorytelling, etc. Therefore, the expressions of whiteness, like the ability to perpetrate racial microaggressions, are what impact people of Color.

In the chart I also indicate how whiteness (e.g., ideologies, emotionalities, etc.) can also be indoctrinated inside the mindsets of people of Color. This is indicated with an arrow that connects whiteness with people of Color. Some argue these individuals are coconuts, dings dongs, bananas (color on the outside, but white on the inside). Others call them Uncle Toms, Stacy Dashes, and/or Don Lemons. Regardless to how they are labeled they are living proof of the malleability and insidiousness of how whiteness impacts us all. I must be clear, however, in that when whiteness impacts people of Color it does so through a different process than Whites. Instead of bequeathing privileges in an invisible manner as it does with Whites, adopting whiteness as a person of Color feigns protection against whiteness. Meaning, people of Color who adopt whiteness do so for many reasons. One, they may erroneously believe they have some protection of whiteness by promoting whiteness in "blackface." We often know this to be false later on when whiteness needs a scapegoat to pins its denigrating acts. For example, the first U.S. police officer to be convicted for unarmed shootings/killings of Black men was an Asian American New York Police Department (NYPD) officer. Also, the only officer to be held responsible for Eric Garner's (an African American male who was choked to death by NYPD) choking death was a Black police officer. Two, they may believe that in adopting whiteness they are seen as honorary whites, and in being seen this way, may have access to white privileges. Three, they may adopt whiteness as a means of self–survival in a white supremacist world. This is nothing different than women who have to deepen their voice to finally be heard and taken seriously in an all-male business meeting or a Queer person who stays in the closet in a homo-antagonistic world. Four, they may have internalize racism for so long that they believe themselves to be inferior. This is the internalized racism so often captured in the work of several critical race theorists. In fact, I wrote an article that garnered some national attention because I dared to posit how whiteness in teacher education, left unchecked, can produce a teaching force that teaches students of Color to "hate themselves." The title of that article is "Why do you make me hate myself?" Re-teaching Whiteness, Abuse, and Love in Urban Teacher Education. In the end understanding the mechanisms of whiteness is so complex, but as Leonardo once suggested to me, since race is so complex, we must not assume there exists a simple answer to it.

Sadly, this all interconnects. If I am to commit myself to racial justice, shouldn't I give it an honest deconstruction of where the racial injustice begins? Or should I solely focus on its impacts? Both are necessary for racial justice; however, in my role as a teacher educator, educating others about racial justice in field dominant with Whites, is to teach Whites first. For, they can never possibly understand the context in which I live until they realize that their behaviors, ideologies, and emotions impact my context.

TO FEEL AGAIN

Doth my heart protest too much? Perhaps it does. But never can I shy away from what makes us real and human: emotions. The very emotions we feel have a story to tell and we needn't ignore them any longer; if we do, we deny the complexities of our heart. Whether innate or socially or politically situated, emotions become a roadmap of humanly existence. Why do we learn to hate? Why do we so love? All of these are just markers of our emotionalities, situated within a context wrought with race, gender, and class, but also *enriched* by race, gender, and class. I guess one would call it the "dialectics of our emotions." But I will save that for another book.

One summer I wrote a chapter talking about the white tundra and how it becomes the emotional frozenness of whiteness. I described how Whites often get so emotionally overwhelmed with discussions of race that they, as described earlier, clam up and erect the emotional walls. Racial identity scholar Beverly Tatum (2009) described this phenomenon as becoming "emotionally frozen." In this emotional frozenness, nothing is more aggravating than pouring your heart out to a person who refuses to accept it. Some say people remain emotionally frozen because they cannot handle the realness put in front of them. In this sense emotional frozenness becomes a socialized process, one that happens too often in education. Although educators are expected to love, care, and have empathy for their students, they often refrain from expressing or receiving emotions in the classroom themselves precisely because it is too much to bear. That love can also remind us of pain, too traumatic to rehash for others.

This happened when I presented the chapter, "On the Flip Side" at the American Educational Research Association years ago. Before presenting, I knew the piece was so painfully raw to my own experiences that it might conjure up the feelings of trauma once again. I feared that I would be exposed, tears and all. Even writing the piece so elicited that same trauma that I did not go a day without reliving it again. And true to human emotions, I cried on the day I stood amidst a panel of all male teacher educators of Color and poured my heart out on the podium. As I did, the male teacher educators of Color stood still, as if holding in a breath they could not release.

One of the speakers after me could not focus on his delivery and went on to tell the audience how "pissed" he was that experiences like mine happen to his *sistas*. Alas, such a response is a common one that men divert to, responding to the socialized behavior of needing to protect women. However, true to the experiences of men and women of Color under a racist system that renders men of Color emasculated, he felt he could not protect me and so got angry. He shared his frustrations with the emotionally frozen audience. I honored his emotions, knowing that they stemmed from a deep historical context of racism. The crowd grew tense.

While I was presenting, the chair of panel, a renowned Black feminist female scholar stood up and put her arms around me as if to console my heart. She whispered I did not have to continue if I was not up to it. I looked up at her and felt assured because I knew I was staring straight into familiar eyes. She knew, all too well, what I felt in my heart, precisely because she went through it too. That gave me strength. So I looked straight at the audience, close to 100 people in attendance, and said into the microphone, "No, my tears are my strength and you all will bear witness to it even if it makes you uncomfortable."

If education is about love, care, and empathy I am sure an audience full of educators is ready to know what that feels like. That is my hope for this book. In its rawness, directness, and revelation, I hope you, my reader, feel again. Because what is at stake is an emotional apocalypse that can be the eternal sunset of our humanity. So regardless to whether or not you have ever owned slaves, begin to understand how these emotions are just a part of the complex dynamics of race, too often hiding behind the shadows of a large rock and a very hard place. Hopefully, within that dark place, you will see the light of day once again.

NOTES

[1] According to *Urban Dictionary*: "To hinder, by whatever means, the chances of another male from having a sexual encounter with a female."
[2] http://www.pbs.org/unnaturalcauses/

REFERENCES

Bell, D. (1992). *Faces at the bottom of the well: The permanence of racism.* New York, NY: Basic Books.

Bonilla-Silva, E. (2006). *Racism without racists: Color-blind racism and the persistence of racial inequality in the United States.* Lanham, MD: Rowman & Littlefield.

Cho, S. K. (1997). Converging stereotypes in racialized sexual harassment: Where the model minority meets Suzie Wong. *Journal of Gender, Race & Justice, 1,* 177.

Coates, T. (2015). *Between the world and me.* New York, NY: Spiegel & Grau.

Collins, P. (1989). The social construction of Black feminist thought. *Signs, 14*(4), 745–773.

Crenshaw, K. (2009). Mapping the margins: Intersectionality, identity politics, and violence against women of color. In E. Taylor, D. Gillborn, & G. Ladson-Billings (Eds.), *Foundations of critical race theory in education.* New York, NY: Routledge.

Duncan-Andrade, J. M. (2009). Note to educators: Hope required when growing roses in concrete. *Harvard Educational Review, 79*(2), 181–194.

Fanon, F. (1965). *The wretched of the Earth* (Vol. 390). New York, NY: Grove Press.

Helms, J. (1990). *Black and White racial identity: Theory, research, and practice.* Westport, CT: Praeger.

hooks, b. (1994). *Teaching to transgress.* New York, NY: Routledge.

Matias, C. E. M. (2014). *Cockblocking CRT: How the emotionality of whiteness blocks the potency of CRT in urban teacher education.* [Paper] Presented at Critical Race Studies in Education Association Conference, Nashville, TN.

Nieto, S. (1992). *Affirming diversity: The sociopolitical context of multicultural education.* Boston, MA: Allyn & Bacon.

Preston, J. (2013). *Whiteness in academia: Counter-stories of betrayal and resistance.* Newcastle-upon-Tyne, UK: Cambridge Scholars Publishing.

Sue, D. W. (2010). *Microaggressions in everyday life: Race, gender, and sexual orientation.* Sommerville, MA: John Wiley & Sons.

Tatum, B. (2009). Teaching White students about racism: The search for White allies and the restoration of hope. In E. Taylor, D. Gillborn, & G. Ladson-Billings (Eds.), *Foundations of critical race theory in education.* New York, NY: Routledge.

Valenzuela, A. (1999). *Subtractive schooling.* Albany, NY: State University of New York Press.

Yosso, T., & Garcia, D. (2007). "This is no slum!" A critical race theory analysis of community cultural wealth in culture clash's Chavez ravine. *Journal of Chicano Studies, 32*(1), 145–154.

Made in United States
North Haven, CT
27 June 2023

38288096R00115